INTEGRATIVE STRESS COUN

Titles in the *Stress Counselling* Series

Ellis, Gordon, Neenan and Palmer, *Stress Counselling: A Rational Emotive Behaviour Approach*
Milner and Palmer, *Integrative Stress Counselling: A Humanistic Problem-focused Approach*
Palmer and Dryden (eds), *Stress Management and Counselling: Theory, Practice, Research and Methodology*

STRESS COUNSELLING SERIES

INTEGRATIVE STRESS COUNSELLING

A HUMANISTIC PROBLEM-FOCUSED APPROACH

Pat Milner and Stephen Palmer

CASSELL

Cassell

Wellington House	370 Lexington Avenue
125 Strand	New York
London WC2R 0BB	NY 10017-6550

First published 1998

British Library Cataloguing-in-Publication Data
A catalogue record for this book is available from the British Library.

Library of Congress Cataloging-in-Publication Data
A catalogue record for this book is available from the Library of Congress.

ISBN 0–304–33491–X (hardback)
0–304–33492–8 (paperback)

Typeset by SetSystems, Saffron Walden
Printed and bound in Great Britain by
Redwood Books, Trowbridge, Wiltshire

To those clients, supervisees and colleagues who have taught me that the stress counselling perspective is seen best through bifocal lenses. (P.M.)

To Mum, Dad, Thersa, Jayne and Sara. And to my colleagues, supervisors, clients and students from whom I have learnt so much about stress management. (S.P.)

Contents

Note on Authors

Pat Milner is an experienced integrative counsellor and supervisor associated with training at South West London College, University of London Goldsmiths College and the Centre for Stress Management, London. A former features editor of *Counselling*, the BAC journal, she now writes on various aspects of counselling. *Time to Listen to Children* (with Birgit Carolin) is in press (Routledge). She is a consultant director of the Centre for Problem Focused Training and Therapy, London.

Stephen Palmer PhD is Director of the Centre for Stress Management and also of the Centre for Problem Focused Training and Therapy, London. He is an Honorary Visiting Senior Clinical and Research Fellow, City University, London. He has written and edited over fifteen books and training manuals, and edits a number of professional journals. He is a chartered psychologist and a certified supervisor for training in REBT.

Foreword

The main aim of this series is to focus on different approaches to stress counselling and management. It is intended that the books will link theory and research to the practice of stress counselling and stress management. Leading counselling, clinical and occupational psychologists, biologists, counsellors and psychotherapists will report on their work, focusing on individual, group and organizational interventions.

The books will interest both undergraduate and postgraduate students as well as experienced practitioners in the helping professions, in particular those who work in the fields of counselling, psychology, psychotherapy, sociology and mental and occupational health.

This book, *Integrative Stress Counselling*, is the third book in the *Stress Counselling* series. In contrast to some other forms of counselling, this approach helps clients to focus directly on solving or managing problems that are a cause of their distress. In addition, this integrative approach facilitates the discovery and subsequent change of underlying thinking styles that help to exacerbate stress. It is hoped that this book will provide the reader with a useful insight into how the problem-focused approach has been applied to the fields of stress counselling and stress management.

Stephen Palmer
Centre for Stress Management, London

Preface

Confronting and solving problems is a painful process which most of us attempt to avoid. And the very avoidance results in greater pain and an inability to grow both mentally and spiritually.

M. Scott Peck (1983) *The Road Less Travelled*

'Stress' is news and according to the media, modern life is permeated with it; sometimes it appears that it may achieve epidemic proportions. Yet many people still rely on their common sense and much of the time engage in positive and adaptive ways of responding to fatigue and stress. Difficult times are still dealt with effectively by getting a good night's sleep, taking a break, 'going fishing', or perhaps talking to friends or colleagues.

We do not wish to 'talk up' the stress of our times, nor underestimate people's own resources and ways of dealing with the pressure of their lives. We do, however, recognize that modern times are presenting more people with situations which stretch their ability to cope beyond its normal elasticity, not just once or twice, but repeatedly. It is when our normal coping resources are over-stretched more frequently than usual that we may see an imbalance between the demands of the particular situation and our current ability to cope. Stressful situations become problems when we perceive that our current ability to cope is not adequate to the demands of the situation, as we see it.

The integrative problem-focused counselling approach to such a dilemma is to help clients to increase their capacity to cope or to develop ways of reducing the demands of the situation. Both these ways of coping interact. If people are able to increase their ways of coping, they will not only feel differently, but will be likely to see the demands of the stressful situation as less threatening or overwhelming. Similarly, reducing or changing people's perception of the demands upon them increases their feeling that they are better able to cope.

These are simple, common-sense statements. However, they are not merely short cuts which concentrate on changing symptoms, but form part of the continuing work of self-understanding and self-discovery which all counselling involves.

We seek to integrate the rational optimism of cognitive behavioural and social competence philosophies within a skills-based, supportive, emotionally congruent, humanistic relationship. Our approach generally works to modify behaviour and attitudes, rather than change them radically, so that, for example, clients who are depressed may become better able to tolerate depression and develop the cognitive and emotional skills to recognize and work through periods of depression if they recur. Clients may learn to be more assertive in the course of their counselling, but they will still have to work hard to retain their assertion in times of future stress. The maxim 'in times of stress we all regress' need not bring despair but can be a source of hope – 'I have been here before and I know how to cope'. Thus, conflicts which clients have found stressful they may learn to avoid or to handle differently.

SEARCH FOR A COMMON LANGUAGE

There is a tendency for cognitive behavioural literature to be presented in a specific, technically oriented language, which, at its most grandiose, may be quite abhorrent to humanistic counsellors, who generally prefer a simpler, more expressive style of communication, which itself may be too lacking in focus and rigour for the cognitive behaviourist! To illustrate our language dilemma, one author (Stephen Palmer) can readily accept a description of specific problem-solving skills which states that: 'At an immediate level of specificity is a set of relatively specific problem-solving skills each of which has a distinct contribution to make toward a successful outcome in a particular problem-solving situation' (D'Zurilla, 1986: 15).

The two authors are different personality types and Pat Milner has an adverse reaction to this form of language, preferring to describe specific problem-solving skills in a different way: 'Several specific skills are needed to solve or manage a problem situation effectively and each of these skills makes its own distinct contribution to success.'

We have attempted, with varying success, to use language which does not dilute the specific order of cognitive behavioural work, but makes it more accessible to humanistic counsellors.

Finally we want to emphasize the importance of three things: (1) seeing the integrative problem-focused approach as one whose success depends upon its use within a positive therapeutic relationship; (2) seeing it as an active, coping process which rests on the interaction between a person's cognitive, emotional and behavioural aspects; (3) and recognizing when other ways of working are more appropriate for a particular client.

Our combination of a client-centred relationship, multimodal assessment, problem-focused stress management and a rational emotive approach to emotional blocks, with a consideration of the influence of personality on people's reactions to stress is an integration which seeks to work from their strengths rather than emphasizing those factors which differentiate them.

The authors would like to acknowledge the influence of A. Bandura, A. T. Beck, T. Burton, W. Dryden, T. J. D'Zurilla, G. Egan, A. Ellis, A. A. Lazarus, R. S. Lazarus, M. Neenan, C. R. Rogers and B. Wasik in the development of this approach.

CHAPTER 1

A Working Model of Stress and Coping

What's the use? Yesterday an egg, tomorrow a feather duster.
Mark Fenderson (1873–1944) *The Dejected Rooster*

Although numerous counsellors, psychotherapists and stress management trainers may attempt to help stressed clients manage stress or deal with negative life events, we question how many have a good systematic working model of stress that underpins their practice. Before we introduce our integrative problem-management approach to stress counselling, we will share our conceptual model of stress and coping. A personal anecdote (Stephen Palmer) may help to clarify some of the factors involved (see Palmer, 1991b).

EXAMPLE OF HOLIDAY STRESS

Life was going well. The night before departure, Maggie (my wife) was arguing with Kate and Tom (our teenagers) and not me. By coming home late from work I had escaped the usual row. I was not the focus of the usual pre-holiday free-floating anxiety. I congratulated myself. I was smug. I had cracked it. I was applying a systems approach to managing holiday stress. I was cheating by avoiding the system! We were off to a great start. We had broken years of tradition; we were still communicating with each other and it was midnight.

The next morning Maggie and I left early. This had two major benefits. Firstly, we did not have to place a guard by the car whilst loading up. Well, it is street parking in London and a number of our neighbours had lost their belongings whilst foolishly leaving their cars unattended in similar circumstances. Secondly, we would avoid the usual London rush hour in which most vehicles slowly travel at 5 miles per hour. It's strange that we call it a 'rush' hour!

Back to the story. As I engaged first gear and drove up the hill, I thought that the omens were good. So far so good as the phrase goes. Ridiculous! A therapist with strong cognitive leanings using magical thinking. 'Whatever next?' I asked myself. I challenged this thought by the time I reached third gear. I was quite proficient in recognizing and subsequently disputing my own self-defeating thinking. However, it was only seconds later when I became stressed, or to be accurate, anxious and angry. As I pointed the car towards the M25 motorway, our holiday destination being Cornwall, I clearly visualized Kate, Tom and their friends wrecking the home. 'Damn it. What will we return to?' I thought. This was the first time we were leaving them in charge of the house. The banned parties would take place. The new 'wall to wall' carpet stained with red wine beyond repair. We had waited eight years before we could afford this carpet. Perhaps we should have left the floors bare? I remember thinking at the time how quickly it was possible to feel stressed. Nothing had actually happened yet I was stressed and anxious. My neck muscles felt tense, there was an unpleasant feeling in the pit of my stomach and my mind was racing.

I wanted to be able to leave my worries behind me in Blackheath, London. I tried thought stopping. It didn't work. I could hear my supervisor's words in my head. 'This technique is only usually effective with the educated middle class.' I started to question who and what I was. He must be wrong. It only goes to show that 'supervisors should not overgeneralize,' I thought. I searched for other techniques. What about using a cognitive distraction exercise? I quickly rammed a Leonard Cohen tape into the cassette player. For the uninitiated, he is rather a sorrowful singer. Not surprisingly, I started to think about death. Yes, this technique was working. I decided that there are far worse things in life than a wrecked home. 'It would not be the end of the world if the carpet was damaged,' I thought. I was successfully de-awfulizing the situation. I started to calm down and later we stopped at a Happy Eater cafe, which was an excellent distraction. As we were making good time, Maggie suggested that a slight detour over Dartmoor would not go amiss. It was a beautiful sunny day and the views over the moors would be exhilarating. In my mind's eyes, I could see a clear picture of the wild horses on the moors and I could hear the silence. With this relaxing scene, my earlier anxieties just drifted away and I was no longer suffering from physical tension. We continued our journey and looked forward to our holiday.

We will now use this real example to illustrate the nature of stress and coping. I had predicted that if I had gone home at my usual time I would have become part of the pre-holiday squabbles. Although this was an avoidance technique, it did appear to work and therefore I congratulated myself. Next morning we left early to avoid loading difficulties and the rush hour traffic jams. This was also a coping strategy which would help to reduce potential stress. I was still pleased as I had appeared to have dealt with customary holiday problems and the 'omens' were good. I recognized that I was doing magical thinking.

The next phase is more interesting. Even though in reality absolutely nothing externally had occurred I became stressed, anxious and angry. I could see an image of Kate, Tom and their friends wrecking the home (anxiety). Seconds later I thought, 'Damn it (anger). What will we return to? (anxiety)' Almost immediately I started to feel physically tense, had unpleasant feelings in my stomach and my mind was racing with many thoughts. This was the stress response. The image and my thoughts were sufficient to activate the fight and flight response and thereby stimulate the release of adrenaline and noradrenaline from my adrenal glands. In this example the most prolonged emotion was anxiety as I prediced a negative outcome and I could not do anything to stop the teenagers wrecking the home in my absence. I did not believe that I was in control of the anticipated situation.

The last phase focused on my attempts to cope with the apparent stress scenario. Thought stopping did not appear to work. However, listening to music was a good distraction and as Lenoard Cohen sang about death, I quickly de-awfulized my predicted future event and realized that on a scale of life events even if Kate and Tom did wreck the house it would not be the end of the world. I started to calm down and later when I had a picture of Dartmoor in my mind's eye I felt very relaxed.

This example illustrates how an imagined stress scenario can trigger the stress response and how coping strategies can switch off the stress response. My body reacted as if the situation had really occurred even though it was just a figment of my imagination. In fact, when we returned home two weeks later the house (and more important, Kate and Tom) were fine. To quote Hamlet:

> Why, then 'tis none to you; for
> there is nothing either good or bad but
> thinking makes it so.

MODELS OF STRESS AND COPING

Historically, a number of different models of stress have evolved. Before we describe our integrative transactional model, we will briefly look at the earlier theories.

The engineering or stimulus variable approach conceptualizes stress as a demand or noxious stimulus that is externally imposed upon an individual which can lead to ill health. In this model stress can also be caused by too little or too much external stimulation.

The physiological or response variable approach is based on Selye's (1956) three-stage model: the initial alarm reaction (sympathetic–adrenal medullary activation), the stage of resistance (adrenal–cortical activation) and the stage of exhaustion (final reactivation of the sympathetic–adrenal medullary system). This response is commonly known as the general adaptation syndrome in which the individual will suffer from the physiological 'diseases of adaptation' to stress caused by noxious or aversive external stimuli if the last stage of exhaustion is reached. The model overlooks the fact that some aversive stimuli such as heat do not necessarily trigger the stress response.

Both the engineering and physiological models are mechanistic and based on the stimulus–response paradigm which ignores the effect of personal perceptions, thoughts (cognitions) and attitudes that an individual may have in any given situation. These cognitions can help to inhibit, moderate or exacerbate the activation of the stress response in any given potential stress scenario. It is now generally recommended that the interaction between the external and the internal worlds of the person needs to be incorporated into any practice-based theory of stress to produce a less mechanistic and more person-friendly model.

The psychological or interactive variable approach to stress endeavours to overcome the deficiencies of the earlier models. There have been a number of proposed psychological theories: the interactional and the transactional. The interactional theories focus on the match between the person and their environment (e.g. Bowers, 1973), or the ability to make decisions and job demands (e.g. Karasek, 1981).

The transactional theories of stress and coping centre on the ways people think and feel about their experience of interacting with their external environment and the coping styles they may adopt or lack (Palmer, 1996a). In developing a transactional model of stress, Lazarus and Folkman (1984) defined stress as resulting from an imbalance between demands and resources. They assert that a person continuously monitors or evaluates a particular incident, demand or ongoing situation and analyses whether a problem or threat exists. This process is known as primary appraisal. The next stage, secondary appraisal, follows when the person evaluates his or her options and resources. Unlike the earlier models of stress, one of the key issues involved is whether the individual recognizes that a problem exists. Once recognized, if the demands are greater than the perceived resources and the situation is of personal significance to the individual, only then does stress occur. If the individual perceives that his or her resources are greater than the demands then the situation may be viewed as a challenge and not a stress scenario. Interestingly, if an individual is too inexperienced to recognize that a particular problem exists then this would not be considered as a stress scenario until it became obvious that he or she could not cope. Hence, it is the subjective and not the objective assessment of any given situation that may trigger the stress response.

Cox and Mackay (1976) developed a five-stage transactional model of occupational stress which was later developed by Palmer (see Palmer and Dryden, 1995) into a multimodal–transactional model of stress to help multimodal counsellors and stress management practitioners apply stress theory to stress counselling practice. We have now collapsed this model further into a simpler integrative–transactional model of stress and coping. Before we discuss this model which underpins the counselling practice advocated in this book, it may be helpful to look briefly at 'coping', which is an important factor in any transactional theory of stress.

Coping has three main properties (Cox, 1993; Palmer, 1996a: 532)

1. It is a process involving what the person thinks and how the person behaves in a stressful situation.
2. It is context-dependent as it is affected by the specific situation or initial appraisal of it, and then by any resources the individual has to deal with the situation.
3. Coping as a process is 'independent of outcome', that is, it does not depend upon whether it does or does not lead to a successful result.

Coping can be divided into task-focused and cognitive-emotive-focused strategies, which include developing better skills and competency to deal with the specific problem, seeking social support, information seeking, denial, rationalizing/reappraisal of the problem, de-awfulizing a problem, delaying action by using relaxation/ distraction, and symptom management. Essentially, coping can be seen as a problem-solving strategy which starts with 'recognition and diagnosis (analysis) followed by actions and evaluation through to re-analysis' (Cox, 1993: 21). It is worth noting that this cycle of action may actually make a situation worse if a person uses the wrong interventions or strategies. Self-helping behaviour is regarded as developmental, whereas self-defeating behaviour is defensive in nature and includes procrastination, displacement behaviour, problem denial and substance abuse. The more self-helping and goal-directed the coping strategies are that people use, the less likely they are to suffer from stress-related disorders. Therefore our approach to stress counselling and stress management seeks to ensure that clients receive adequate problem-solving skills training and cognitive–emotive skills training to help them deal with adverse demands.

INTEGRATIVE–TRANSACTIONAL MODEL OF STRESS AND COPING

Our model of stress and coping is transactional as it centres on how a person appraises any given situation and then considers his or her coping resources versus the external demands or stressors. Therefore the psychological processes are central to the model. Life's problems and ways of managing or solving them are a transaction. We have called it an integrative model as the areas assessed match the possible interventions included in our integrative approach to counselling and stress management. Figure 1.1 illustrates the new integrative–transactional model.

The model can be separated into five discrete stages.

Stage 1 occurs when a potential external pressure or demand is recognized by a client. For example, Jane, a deputy headteacher, being asked to give a presentation to the board of governors for the first time. Jane may or may not have the coping resources to deal with the potential problem. Coping resources can include specific skills and the time available to prepare and undertake a task. There are day-to-day physiological and psychological necessities to meet in order for us to survive, such as food and water. Many people also demand human company, therefore being alone for prolonged periods can become a potential stressor too.

In *Stage 2* Jane considers the situation and decides whether the demands exceed her ability to cope with it and whether the situation is of personal significance. This is called an 'appraisal'. The latter can be an important influence on the stress response. For example, if Jane does not care if she gives a poor presentation to the board of governors then she is less likely to appraise the situation as threatening. Whereas if she has high expectations of herself, such as 'I must always do well at work otherwise I'm a useless teacher', then she is more liable to perceive even an innocuous situation as a stressor. These internal pressures usually affect a person's appraisal of a situation in addition to the individual's assessment of their coping resources to deal with any potential problem. At this stage if Jane does not view the situation as threatening but she still needs to deal with it, then she will proceed onto the next stage of this model *without* triggering the stress response. She is more likely to decide what steps she needs to take, or in technical terms to apply coping problem-focused strategies to deal with the situation. However, if we assume that Jane perceives the situation negatively then we progress onto the next stage of the stress model. Incidentally, appraisal does not always involve talking to oneself in one's head with thoughts (internal cognitive dialogues) such as 'it's awful', as sometimes we can hold a negative picture in our mind's eye of a disastrous outcome.

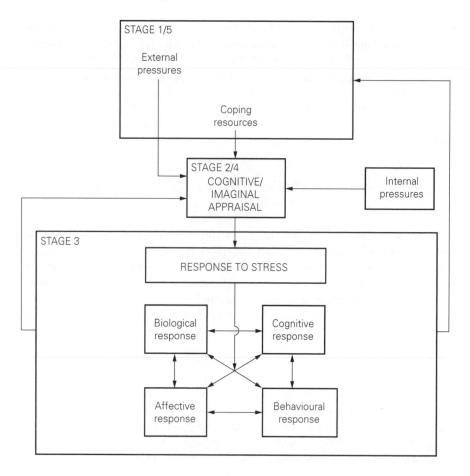

Figure 1.1 *The integrative–transactional model*

This picture would often be sufficient to trigger the stress response especially if she had a previous similar negative experience where she failed to live up to her (or others') expectations.

If Jane thinks that the situation is threatening then in *Stage 3* the stress response is triggered. This involves a variety of psychophysiological changes. There is normally an emotion or combination of emotions, which may be anger, anxiety, guilt or shame. These emotions usually have a combination of physiological, cognitive and behavioural aspects. Returning to the presentation example, Jane may feel anxious that she might fail to perform well; have physiological symptoms of anxiety such as butterflies in the stomach, increased heart rate, clammy hands; have cognitions such as 'I must perform well otherwise the board of governors will think I'm useless. Perhaps they will even demote me'; and have images of being laughed at by the governors. Behaviourally she may start tidying her desk and making a cup of tea as a way of temporarily reducing her anxiety (displacement behaviour). However, she may choose to take a more problem-focused approach to the situation. For example, cognitively she might tell herself that 'All I can do is my best. If I do badly it will not be the end of my world. Anyway, perhaps I should concentrate on preparing my notes and acetates.' She could mentally rehearse giving her presentation by using imagery. Behaviourally, she could start to prepare her notes and also ensure that she has checked with the head what she is expected to lecture on. This self-helping approach is likely to reduce her anxiety and physiological symptoms.

At *Stage 4* a person assesses the effect of his or her responses during Stage 3 upon the stress scenario. Essentially, is the approach actually helping to deal with the problem? This reappraisal of the situation can either completely switch off the stress response if it is seen to be helping the person to deal with the situation, or it can maintain or re-trigger the stress response if it appears that the strategies applied are not working and the person truly believes that that demand must still be met. In our example, Jane may have prepared sufficiently well in her estimation to believe that she will give an adequate presentation. Or she may have reduced her internal pressures by lowering her high standards and expectations.

Stage 5 is more concerned with the effect of the person's actions upon the pressures. If the strategies employed have been ineffective, then the individual may experience prolonged stress, which can adversely impact upon the external and internal pressures and exacerbate an already difficult situation. For example, if Jane made a bad presentation, then the board of governors could decide to put pressure on her to improve her performance and also investigate other areas of her work such as school budget responsibilities. This could become an additional occupational stressor and feedback into her stressful environment and also become another burden (see Figure 1.1). Prolonged stress can have many psychophysiological consequences which can lead to serious physical and mental illness including burnout.

The integrative–transactional model of stress highlights the importance of the internal and external worlds of an individual. In many examples of stress the external stressor is not necessarily the main factor that triggers the stress response. Jane's example is quite common – many individuals would suffer an extreme stress reaction if they had to give an important presentation whereas experienced presenters may stay relatively calm. Experienced individuals who view themselves as possessing adequate coping resources to deal with a specific situation have what is known as 'self-efficacy'. It is a major cognitive component in the appraisal of future events as non-threatening and therefore *not* stressful. They may hold beliefs such as: 'This will not be a problem. I've done it successfully before.' 'I'm in control. I can do it.' 'This is a challenge and not a stressor.' These beliefs and internal self-helping dialogues often prevent the individual from triggering the stress response in Stage 3 of our model in which the coping strategies are applied. The integrative model of stress counselling and management can help the client to intervene at any of the five stages of our model of stress and coping.

Before reading the next section, it might be a useful exercise to re-read the personal example of stress at the beginning of this chapter and attempt to relate it to the integrative–transactional model of stress.

PHYSIOLOGY OF THE STRESS RESPONSE

In our experience our clients have found it useful if they can understand the physiological aspects of the stress response. Often clients suffering from stress fear that they may be 'going mad' (Palmer and Dryden, 1995). Clear physical explanations about the nature of stress can allay fears and also later help the client to understand why certain activities such as relaxation suggested by the counsellor may be beneficial. In this section we will cover the stress response in some depth and in physiological language. However, it will probably be necessary to adapt and simplify the explanation depending upon your client's needs and level of understanding.

There are two physiological systems involved in our response to stress. The first is the autonomic nervous system (ANS) which is responsible for controlling the lungs, heart, stomach, glands and blood vessels. The ANS consists of two sub-systems: the parasympathetic nervous systems (PNS) and the sympathetic nervous system (SNS). The PNS aids relaxation and conserves energy. It increases bodily secretions such as gastric acids, mucus, saliva and tears which aid digestion and help to defend the body. The PNS sends its messages by a neurotransmitter called acetylcholine, which is stored at the nerve endings. If at Stage 2 of the integrative–transactional model of stress an individual appraises a situation as threatening then messages are conveyed along neurones from the cerebral cortex (where the thought processes occur) and the limbic system (associated with the emotions of anger and fear) to the hypothalamus. The anterior hypothalamus triggers the sympathetic arousal of the ANS. The main sympathetic neurotransmitter is called noradrenaline, which is released at the nerve endings. The SNS prepares the body for action. In a stressful situation, it rapidly does the following:

- increases heart rate
- increases fat and sugar levels
- increases strength of skeletal muscles
- increases perspiration
- increases mental activity
- reduces intestinal movement
- inhibits digestive secretions and tears
- dilates the pupils
- relaxes the bladder
- decreases blood clotting time
- inhibits erection/vaginal lubrication
- constricts most vessels
- dilates vessels in heart/leg/arm muscles

The adrenal gland is involved in the production of stress hormones. The SNS is directly connected through a nerve to the central part of the adrenal gland, the adrenal medulla, which produces noradrenaline and adrenaline. Contingent upon the respective levels of these two catecholamines, which are released into the blood supply, the organism is prepared to either fight or flee. Noradrenaline is associated with anger and the fight response, whilst adrenaline is associated with the fear and the flight response (see Henry, 1980; Henry et al., 1976).

The second physiological system involved in our stress response is known as the pituitary-adrenal cortex or endocrine system. In this system the hypothalamus instructs the pituitary to release adrenocorticotrophic hormone (ACTH) into the blood which then activates the adrenal cortex (the outer layer of the adrenal gland). The adrenal cortex synthesizes cortisol, which aids glucose and fat mobilization, reduces the inflammatory response, lowers allergic reactions and can decrease lymphocytes that are involved in dealing with invading bacteria or particles. People suffering from prolonged stress and who feel depressed, often experience raised levels of cortisol which eventually reduces the effectiveness of the immune system leading to increased susceptibility to minor colds and to more life-threatening diseases. Such people tend to believe that they have a lack of control over external events. The adrenal cortex also releases aldosterone which increases blood volume and thereby increases blood pressure. Prolonged arousal over a period of time due to stress can lead to hypertension.

The pituitary also releases vasopressin and oxytocin, which contract smooth muscles such as blood vessels. Vasopressin increases the permeability of the vessels to water, thereby increasing blood pressure. Oxytocin causes contraction of the uterus. The pituitary also releases a thyroid-stimulating hormone which stimulates the thyroid gland to secrete thyroxin. Thyroxin increases the metabolic rate, increases respiration/heart rate/blood pressure/intestinal motility, and raises blood sugar levels.

If the individual reappraises the threatening situation as non-threatening then the PNS restores the individual to a state of equilibrium. If the individual has suffered from a severe trauma such as an assault, this is less likely to occur immediately after the threat is over. Prolonged stress reduces the body's immune system and can raise blood pressure leading to headaches and hypertension. The adrenal glands may malfunction, which may result in general fatigue, muscles feeling weak, sleep disturbance, dizziness, and digestive difficulties with a craving for sweet, starchy food.

STRESS RESPONSES

It is helpful for counsellers and stress management practitioners to take a systematic approach when assessing the responses to stress that a client in stress counselling may be suffering. The following list places the responses into categories which correspond to the integrative–transactional model of stress described earlier. This may assist a counsellor in the assessment and subsequent development of a therapeutic programme for a client.

Cognition:
'If I fail, this proves that I'm a total failure'
'I must be in control'
'I must be certain of the outcome'
'I must have what I want'
'I must perform well'
'I/others must obey "my" moral code and rules'

'It's awful, terrible, horrible, unbearable', etc.
'Life should not be unfair'
Low frustration statements, e.g. 'I can't stand it'
'Others must approve of me'
self/other downing statements, e.g. useless, worthless, stupid, idiot, bastard, waste
   of space, etc.
'This is a threatening situation'

Images of:
accidents/injury
becoming a bag lady/man (or tramp)
dejection, rejection
failure
helplessness
isolation/being alone
losing control
nightmares/distressing recurring dreams
persistent daydreams
physical/sexual/mental abuse
poor self-image
self and/or others dying/suicide
shame/humiliation/embarrassment
visual flashbacks

Affect:
anger
annoyance
anxiety
concern
depression
envy
guilt
hurt
morbid jealousy
regret
remorse
sadness
shame/embarrassment
suicidal feelings

Biological/physiological:
abdominal cramps
aches/pains
allergies/skin rash
asthma
biologically based mental disorders
butterflies in stomach

cancer
chronic fatigue/exhaustion/burn-out/rust-out
clammy hands
cold sweat
diabetes
diarrhoea/constipation/flatulence
dry mouth/skin
epilepsy/seizures
oesophaegeal spasm
feeling faint/dizziness
frequent bouts of influenza/common colds
frequent urination
headaches
heart beat increases
high blood pressure/coronary heart disease (angina/heart attack)
hypertension
indigestion
insomnia/sleep disturbance
lowered immune system (reduction in lymphocytes and eosinophils)
migraine
nausea
numbness
palpitations
poor nutrition, exercise and recreation
premature ejaculation/erectile dysfunction
rheumatoid arthritis
sensory flashbacks
spasms in stomach
tension
tinnitus (noises in the ears)
tremors/inner tremors
vaginismus/psychogenic dyspareunia

Behaviour (including interpersonal):
accident proneness
aggression/irritability
alcohol/drug abuse
anorexia/bulimia
avoidance/phobias
checking rituals
clenched fists
co-dependency
comfort eating
competitive
compulsive behaviour
crying frequently
gossiping

impaired speech/voice tremor
impulsive behaviour
increased absenteeism from work
increased nicotine/caffeine intake
loner
makes friends with difficulty/easily
manipulative tendencies
nervous cough
no friends
over-eating/loss of appetite
passive/aggressive in relationships
poor driving
poor eye contact
poor time management
puts others' needs before one's own/placatory productivity
restlessness
sex addiction
sexual activity decreased/increased
sulking behaviour
suspicious/secretive
sycophantic behaviour
teeth grinding
tics, spasms
timid/unassertive
type A behaviour, e.g. talking/walking/eating faster; hostile competitive, heightened awareness of time
unkempt appearance
withdrawing from relationships

The list of responses to stress should only be used as a rudimentary guide although it does give some indication what to look for in each of the four key modalities. Individuals who have been suffering from stress over a period of time may eventually develop problems of a physiological or organic nature such as diabetes, hypertension, tension headaches or coronary heart disease. Integrative problem-focused stress counselling and management may be directed towards helping the client deal with the external stressor such as work overload as well as physiological disorders such as raised blood pressure, the latter under the guidance of a medical practitioner. The approach attempts to look at the *whole* person not just the presenting problem.

In the next chapter we look at an overview of the integrative problem-focused approach to stress counselling.

CHAPTER 2

Integrative Problem-Focused Stress Counselling

The most savage controversies are those about matters as to which there is no good evidence either way.

Bertrand Russell (1950) *Unpopular Essays*

Controversy has characterized the field of therapeutic work since Freud's disputations with his colleagues over the development of psychoanalysis.

Currently disputes erupt in the professional counselling journals; for example, between a person-centred practitioner and a psychodynamic psychotherapist about the non-existence or the reality of differences between counselling and psychotherapy (Ellingham, 1995; Naylor-Smith, 1994). Or a psychodynamic psychotherapist may take issue with a solution focused therapist's deliberate exclusion of the past history of clients (Goddard, 1993; Wilgosh, 1993). However, disputes can develop into dialogue, such as the creative interaction between John McLeod and Sue Wheeler (1995) about psychodynamic and person-centred counselling. These examples were published in *Counselling*, the journal of the British Association for Counselling (BAC), and are included in *Counselling: The BAC Counselling Reader* (Palmer *et al.*, 1996).

Dialogue may subsequently develop into some form of integration and the integrative approach is sometimes viewed as a move to combine good ideas from the various forms of counselling and therapy, so as to identify a set of converging themes, or those principles, approaches and methodologies which make up the essence of helping.

WHY AN INTEGRATIVE APPROACH?

The various theories supporting counselling are being reappraised as counsellors acknowledge both the inadequacies of any one system and the potential value of others. There is a growing consensus that no one approach is adequate for all clients and situations; neither the techniques nor the theories are adequate to deal with the complexity of psychological problems. Therapeutic reality calls for a more flexible perspective and the move towards integration reflects growing dissatisfaction with single theory approaches. Dryden and Norcross (1990) propose five factors behind the current move towards integration of the therapies:

- proliferation of therapies
- inadequacy of single theories
- equality of outcomes
- search for common components
- socio-economic contingencies

Proliferation of therapies

In the late 1950s, 36 distinct forms of therapy could be identified; by the mid-1970s, 130 therapies stacked the 'therapeutic jungle-place' and in the mid-1980s, Karasu (1986) estimated 250–400 different schools of psychotherapy. The rival claims which emanate from this proliferation have been characterized as 'confusion, fragmentation and discontent' (Norcross, 1986). From this staggeringly wide choice no single theory has been able to corner the market on validity or utility.

Inadequacy of single theories

In a wave of sceptical self-examination leading members of several major schools have criticized their own theories and the assumptions behind them. As psycho-analysts query whether free association is plausible, behaviour therapists question their own over-reliance on observed behaviours, and cognitive therapists doubt that cognition precedes affect and behaviour and acknowledge the difficulties in dispelling dysfunctional thinking. 'Obviously no single theory has a monopoly on truth or utility and the integration movement, to some extent, reflects dissatisfaction with single approaches' (Dryden and Norcross, 1990).

Equality of outcomes

The quality and the quantity of research into counselling continue to improve and increase but the most specific outcomes seem to indicate that there are certain factors common to successful outcomes and that it is possible to synthesize useful concepts and methods from different therapeutic traditions.

Search for common components

'The identification of common change processes or therapeutic factors has been called the most important psychotherapy trend of the 1980s' (Dryden and Norcross, 1990: 6). It is not so much the apparent differences between therapies which are impressive but rather what they have in common. Prestige and economics emphasize the successes of rival approaches, which pushes attention to identifying shared components into the background.

As early as 1936, Rozenzweig indicated four factors which were common to different methods of psychotherapy: catharsis; therapist personality; theoretical consistency of the therapy; and provision of an alternative explanation of the problem (cited in Kramer, 1992).

Dryden and Norcross (1990) illustrate more recent definitions of the processes which produce change in therapy, citing those of

- Garfield (1980): the relationship; catharsis; explanation; reinforcement; desensitization; information; time
- Frank (1982): an emotionally charged, confiding relationship; a healing setting; a rationale or conceptual scheme; a therapeutic ritual
- Karasu (1986), who identifies three methods of change shared by all therapeutic approaches: effective experiencing; cognitive mastery; regulation of behaviour.

The integrative problem-focused counselling approach we propose combines elements of all the above processes.

Socio-economic contingencies

As the counselling field expands and an increasing number of counsellors emerge from mushrooming training courses, there is concern about quality of training and adequacy of practice. To date counsellors have had the luxury of much individual freedom within their profession, but political and economic pressures are mounting for accountability and a clear statement of practice geared to meet the needs of clients. 'If therapists are not to lose their credibility, it is incumbent upon them to state clearly and unambiguously the nature and type of services offered. The client has a right to more than vague platitudinous assurances' (Laungani, 1995: 113). It is the prediction of Dryden and Norcross (1990: 8) that the escalation of external demands will see an increase in the spirit of open enquiry and therapeutic integration.

INTEGRATIVE OR ECLECTIC?

Is there a difference between integrative and eclectic approaches? For the purpose of this book we offer the following very broad, working definitions based on Connor (1994: 17).

Counsellors who are integrative have a core theoretical model or approach forming the essence of helping, or, as in our problem-focused approach, the counselling foundation, as the basis for their counselling work. It is within the framework of this essential core model that other theories or approaches are introduced. We suggest that because integration focuses on the essence of helping it goes beyond eclecticism.

Again for purposes of definition, counsellors who are eclectic draw good ideas from a variety of theories and approaches as they seem appropriate to the ongoing work, without necessarily having any reference to a core model or theory.

A random borrowing of ideas resulting in a 'pick and mix' approach is eclecticism at its most unprofessional and least helpful because it leads to an incoherent approach to clients and counselling and leaves the client at the mercy of whatever approach the counsellor feels like trying out. However, an approach which is systematic, rather than random, such as the technical eclecticism of Lazarus's (1989) multimodal therapy, does produce an effective eclecticism.

We agree with Dryden and Norcross (1990: 11) that 'integration' is used to denote a conceptual synthesis of diverse theoretical systems. Our problem-focused approach to stress counselling is a humanistic, cognitive behavioural, personality integration which attempts to answer the question 'What works for this client?'

THE INTEGRATION OF PROBLEM-FOCUSED STRESS COUNSELLING

Problem-focused stress counselling is integrative both in spirit and application in the sense that its counselling foundation rests on any one of the skills-based integrative models already taught and practised in the counselling field. These are represented by the skilled helper problem management framework of Gerard Egan (1975, 1982, 1986, 1990, 1994, 1998); the integrative skills model of Sue Culley (1991, 1992); the lifeskills counselling approach of Richard Nelson-Jones (1994, 1995, 1996), the integrating skills theory and practice of Ivey (1993), and the intentional model of Ivey (1995).

Upon such a counselling foundation we have placed a sub-structure of the CABB integrative–transactional model of stress covering cognitions, affect, biology and behaviour, which informs the CABB assessment profile process adapted from that of Lazarus (1981, 1989). Integrated into the CABB model is a five-star framework for emotional problem-solving based on the work of Albert Ellis (1962, 1994, 1996).

Central to the whole structure is a seven-step problem management outline derived from the social competence work of D'Zurilla (1986). Interwoven throughout the counselling process is a practical application and understanding of individual personality differences.

Figure 2.1 illustrates the problem-focused stress counselling model.

Thus the integrative stress counsellor is not using a new form of therapy, but rather a combination approach which is specifically built on a proven, skills-based counselling relationship framework, using a technically eclectic assessment process. This leads into a problem-focused stress management model, supported where necessary, by a cognitive–emotional stance towards those thoughts and feelings with which clients either generate stress, or prevent themselves from working to reduce it.

The integration is made in the service of clients, with differing personalities, whose lives are generating more stress than they can handle with their current knowledge and resources.

The integrated problem-focused approach is based on the assumption that clients troubled by stress which they are not able to manage using their current resources, want at some level to be enabled to take intentional action that will help them reduce their stress by managing their life better.

The approach also posits that although effective action is usually preceded by awareness, insight and clarification, none of these alone will effectively reduce stress without some kind of action.

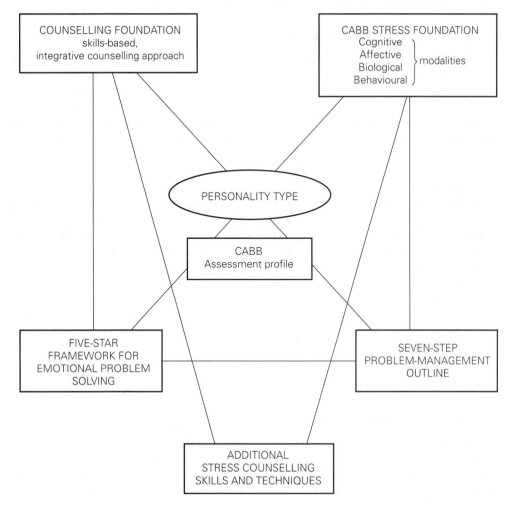

Figure 2.1   *The integrative problem-focused stress counselling model*

FIVE FUNDAMENTAL ASSUMPTIONS ABOUT INTEGRATIVE PROBLEM-FOCUSED STRESS COUNSELLING

1. Integrative problem-focused stress counsellors are professional and accountable for the quality of their work.
2. Work with clients is at the heart of all integrative problem-focused stress counselling.
3. Integrative problem-focused stress counselling is about learning and teaching; it is a collaborative learning encounter.
4. Acknowledgement of individual differences, particularly of personality and learning style, is inherent in the approach.
5. Power is shared in the integrative problem-focused approach.

(Based on Connor 1994: 27.)

Professional and accountable

We are all less than perfect and we do have days which do not go well and clients with whom we do not work as successfully as we would like. This is a normal part of being a counsellor. Because the counsellor often has a directive role in our approach, we need to be particularly aware of our own contribution to those occasions when things do not go according to plan. When our work with a client does not appear to be moving to our joint satisfaction, of course we look at the client's part in the process. However, it can be a temptation in all counselling to look for causes of unsuccessful work only in the behaviour and personality of clients. Both partners in the therapeutic working relationship contribute to the outcomes of counselling work; we emphasize that counsellor self-reflection and evaluation in supervision, plus joint evaluation with clients, is the professional and accountable way forward even when things are going well. These approaches are essential if things are going badly. As counsellors, we may assess a client's problems incorrectly, be insensitive to some aspects of their presentation, or too hasty in our eagerness to make progress. Our therapeutic skills may not be adequate for the particular complexities of a certain situation and if this is the case we have a responsibility to behave accountably and review or possibly refer a client elsewhere. We recommend that counsellors subscribe to and practise the British Association for Counselling Code of Ethics for Counsellors (BAC, 1992, amended 1993, 1996, 1998; see p. 268.)

It is not professional to accept clients for integrative problem-focused stress counselling who do not need it, or who are unlikely to be helped by means of it.

Clients at the heart

The problem-focused nature of our approach should not mislead readers into assuming that it is a way of working which is totally oriented to problem solving. We cannot emphasize too strongly that in this work problems do not exist apart from the clients who bring them. Clients are differentiated in terms of age, gender, education, socio-economic status, social skills, cultural background and of course, personality. They are completely individual, and it is this uniqueness which is at the heart of our approach. It is true that a client's problems are focused upon, but always within the individuality of their person. Taking a solar system view, the client is the sun and their problems occupy the position of revolving planets, not the other way round. We believe that clients respond positively to affirmation and high expectations and that they are capable of achieving change which will ameliorate their stress.

Learning and teaching

People who consult an integrative problem-focused stress counsellor do so because there are circumstantial, situational, experiential, emotional, relational and often physical aspects of their lives which they intimate they need help to change for something better. The implication in this consultation is that the stress counsellor will have knowledge and experience not yet possessed by clients and will share their knowledge and resources and teach clients the necessary skills to enable them to bring about change in their own lives. Thus there are times when the counsellor occupies the role of 'teacher' in providing information, handouts, exercises and skills for coping with stress.

In addition to working with a client to establish a therapeutic working relationship, the counsellor is responsible for generating a climate which will be conducive to learning for each individual. 'Flexibility is the key that will open different doors in different ways for different learners' (Connor, 1994: 22). Within these 'givens', it is an assumption of the integrative approach that:

- clients are able to take responsibility for their own learning
- that they learn about themselves both within the experience of counselling itself and through their work and life outside, to change the situations and relationships of their everyday lives
- that they also learn new lifeskills.

Individual differences

Our stress counselling model assumes the importance of individual differences and acknowledges their effect on the process and outcomes of counselling. It pays particular attention to the ways in which people differ from each other in terms of their personality and the influence that this has on the ways in which they learn and the ways in which they are affected by stress (see Chapter 10).

Although our model is prescriptive, unless the work is collaboratively generated with each person, individually, it will not result in gains in the quality of their everyday lives, nor will there be better understanding in the counselling sessions or in the client's situations and relationships outside it. Working to enable clients to understand their own individuality is a mutual endeavour and a joint responsibility.

> [M]uch of the physical pain and stress in our world is the result of misunderstandings among generally well-intentioned people and is not occasioned by irreparable disagreements. . . . great gains in the quality of everyday life should be possible for each of us through a better understanding of ourselves and of how we gather information, process it, come to conclusions or decisions and communicate our thoughts and wishes to others.
>
> (Myers and Myers, 1995: Preface)

Sharing of power

Our model has the client at the heart of the counselling process and as a partner in the therapeutic working relationship. However, the model is unilateral and does not assume that the client knows best in matters of handling stress. Clients consult a stress counsellor precisely because they have been unable to mitigate the stressful situations in their lives without help. Counsellors using this approach are explicitly directive and active participants in the relationship. They acknowledge that they have skills and resources to pass on to clients. In that sense they have knowledge and that knowledge is powerful. Nevertheless it is clients themselves who have the most power to effect change in their lives and the counsellor's resources are impotent without the action of the client. We suggest that the model is most effective when counsellors and clients openly cooperate in their knowledge and power-sharing.

STAGES OF THE MODEL

The counselling foundation

The reasons for choosing an existing skills-based counselling foundation are first to facilitate and sustain the therapeutic working relationship which they espouse and upon which the efficacy of the integrative problem-focused approach depends. The second reason is that a counsellor already experienced in skills-based work will find themselves more at ease with the development of the CABB strategies we propose, than would a counsellor who is neither familiar with nor appreciative of the skills-based counselling process.

We do not infer that counsellors using models other than those we have mentioned cannot use the integrative problem-focused approach in working with stressed clients, but do wish to point out the possible adjustments which may be required. One of the authors (Pat Milner) comes to integrative stress counselling from an early background of person-centred work. We are aware of the hotly argued, current debate on whether or not it is desirable to introduce other methods into classical person-centred therapy. The usefulness of our model may be recognized by those person-centred practitioners who wish to move towards the inclusion of active skills for work in specific areas such as stress counselling. This is a controversial view when set against the philosophy and tenets of the person-centred approach, which is not a series of specific technical competencies, but a general framework for understanding individual people (Mearns and McLeod, 1984).

It is the belief of both authors that the skills of the behavioural sciences offer a myriad of strategies and techniques for managing stress and that these are not of prime importance to others, such as person-centred therapists, as Clarke (1996: 41) suggests. It is the experience of one author (PM) that the person-centred approach is highly effective in accompanying clients in their important search for self-identity, but that it lacks experiential credibility as a means of helping clients to manage their stress. However, the same author also has experience of working with former clients of cognitive behavioural therapists, who report the feeling of being imprisoned in a pedantic, power-hungry, jargon-obsessed, impersonal network of strategies and techniques. Of course both experiences may reflect upon the counsellor more than they do upon the approach. In the integrative problem-focused approach we attempt to combine the effectiveness of cognitive behavioural work with the fundamental humanity and flexibility of the person-centred tradition.

Model for the counselling process

Our model of stress counselling rests on a foundation of one of the integrated skills-based frameworks which draw upon both humanistic and behaviour theory at different stages of the counselling process. The work moves from a 'client-centred' focus in the here and now to a future-centred focus and the behavioural stages of goal setting, action planning and action itself. However, it is crucial that counsellors remain both 'client-centred' and 'problem-focused' and a distinction is drawn between being directive and drawing from behavioural strategies in a way that influences the process, but leaves the client in charge of the content.

The problem-focused model rests well on a foundation such as that of Egan's (1975, 1982, 1986, 1990, 1994, 1998) skilled helper approach, because it too can be accessed at any point which is appropriate for the needs of the client. The steps form guidelines for practice, not rigid formulae and the model essentially integrates person-centred principles with pragmatic problem-solving outcomes in a flexible framework which offers a map for the counselling process.

Theory

Various aspects of counselling theory support the integrative problem-focused stress counselling model. In this approach:

- people are viewed from both a humanistic and a behavioural framework and both these concepts are emphasized and integrated throughout the stages of the work
- growth develops from the facilitating conditions of the therapeutic working relationship, the structured experience of counselling and the client's action in their external environment to generate learning and change
- there is integration of applied developmental and cognitive behavioural psychology (with its understanding of the negative and positive aspects of the learning process)
- there is integration of areas of convergence and recognition of divergence in counselling approaches
- applied personality theory is an essential consideration in the development of individual stress management programmes for individual clients (see Chapter 10)
- an underpinning of social psychology is used to understand people in their own social systems, and the ways in which these affect their personal growth and movement towards change.

(Based on Egan and Cowan, 1979.)

Therapeutic process

The concepts of underpinning the counselling process are those of a therapeutic relationship providing the core conditions for growth and change, integrated with the assumptions and explanations which underlie a problem-management process. This integration interweaves the development of a client's personal and environmental resources with the setting and realization of appropriate and realistic individual goals for the management and relief of their stress. The therapeutic relationship and the problem-management process in combination form the therapeutic working relationship at the heart of the integrative problem focused approach.

Therapeutic working relationship

The counselling process unfolds over time and counsellors and clients encounter different challenges in the early phase of the work from those met during the middle and ending stages, even when the work is as brief as one session of crisis counselling. Particularly during the early phase, the interpersonal connectedness between counsellor and client that forms the bond between them has its roots in the person-centred tradition (Rogers 1961, 1980). This shows that clients tend to move towards psychological growth when they experience the counsellor as:

- showing an empathic understanding of their concerns
- being genuine in the therapeutic relationship
- showing respect or unconditional acceptance of them as persons.

The skilful communication of these attitudes forms the basic work of person-centred counsellors (Mearns and Thorne, 1988). However, for cognitive behavioural counsellors, the importance of these attitudes is that they set the stage for the problem management strategies which follow (Trower *et al.*, 1988).

In the integrative problem-focused approach the core conditions are used throughout all stages of the work, but the focus for the work is the management of the problems which generate stress for each individual client. The constructive counsellor qualities and interventions of empathy, respect and genuineness are intended to help a client to develop:

- trust in the counsellor (and the process)
- feelings of safety in the relationship
- faith in the counsellor as a person who can help them change.

There are of course clients who have little trust in people and find them threatening to be with and those who have little faith in counselling as a means of bringing about improvement in their lives. Here the counsellor's task is to emphasize certain attitudes and soft-pedal others in order to establish the most productive and therapeutic bond with each client. Dryden (1989) suggests that the counselling bond is enhanced when the interpersonal styles of counsellor and client form a good 'fit' and is threatened when the fit is poor. He cites an example of a productive 'fit' in the rapport building early stage as happening when the counsellor's style is 'dominant-friendly' and the client's style is 'submissive-friendly'. An example of an unproductive fit occurs when the counsellor's style is 'passive-neutral' and the client's 'submissive-hostile'. The implication of his point is that:

> the counsellor's initial task is to modify his or her personal style to complement the client's style in order to initiate the therapeutic alliance. Once such an alliance has been firmly established, the counsellor can begin to consider ways of slowly changing his or her style in the service of initiating client change.
>
> (Dryden, 1989: 3)

A pragmatic partnership

The relationship between counsellor and client is a working alliance requiring hard work for both sides to create a pragmatic partnership – one related to results. Different clients have different needs and differing personalities and these are best accommodated through different kinds of relationship. Effective counsellors use a mix of skills and techniques tailored to the kind of relationship that is right for each client. A client who fears intimacy may be greatly discomfited and stressed by a counsellor who communicates a great deal of empathy and warmth, yet might respond better to one who is more objective and business-like (Egan, 1994: 48).

In our model we emphasize the nature of the relationship between counsellor and client because it is through this relationship that clients begin to trust, challenge and take responsibility for themselves. It is the quality of the therapeutic working relationship which enables counsellor and client to collaborate in using the integrative problem-focused stress counselling model effectively.

However, it is equally important to emphasize that if too much focus is placed on the relationship itself this can prove a distraction and a denial of the real work of this approach to counselling. It is time to move on to action.

THE MODEL IN ACTION

CABB assessment profile

The beginning stage of integrative problem-focused stress counselling is one in which the counsellor balances the qualities and process of relationship building with the skills of assessing the stress problems presented by a client, while also considering possible therapeutic interventions. Our emphasis is on short-term work, which means that an initial contract of perhaps five counselling sessions could be agreed. However, some clients may require one or two sessions only, whilst the counsellor may review progress with others and make a mutual decision whether or not to extend counselling with re-negotiated goals.

We have described in Chapter 1 the Cognitive, Affective, Biological and Behavioural model of stress which underpins our stress counselling approach. The CABB Assessment Profile is a method of structuring and recording with (and usually for) a client the ways in which their thought and behaviour patterns and their emotional and physical reactions have come together both to affect and express their current levels of stress.

Research indicates that there are a number of life events and changes which are liable to generate stress and it is useful to recognize them in order to include the relevant ones in a client's CABB profile. We have included an example of the holiday stress of one author (SP) in Chapter 1. In addition to that generated by holidays, stress may be caused by the following events:

- Christmas or anniversaries of various kinds
- death of a partner, a close member of the family or a friend
- divorce
- illness or injury
- retirement
- pregnancy or addition to the family
- child leaving home
- relationship difficulties
- unemployment or redundancy (lay-off)
- prison sentence

- sex problems
- new, large mortgage
- mortgage foreclosed
- personal achievement

If there is a cluster of such events or changes in a short time this could have a cumulative effect and increase the likelihood of a person suffering from a stress-related illness. Not only are these events often intrinsically stressful, but they also increase the number of everyday problems or hassles with which we must cope.

We now look in more detail at the four modes of the CABB profile.

COGNITION

Stress may depend on how you look at life

Throughout the assessment process it is important to keep in mind the fact that whether an event is stressful or not depends very much on how it is viewed by the individual client. One person may see taking out a large mortgage as a crippling burden, while another may be quite excited by the prospect and not view it as a problem. Retirement may signal an empty life ahead or an over-the-moon opportunity to use one's time in long-awaited ways. Cognitions or ways of think-ing about things are affected by habit, learning, circumstances, emotions and personality (Banduna, 1986). Ellis (1976) also suggests that biology/genes could affect the ways in which we think. Thus the manner in which people think about and imagine themselves and their lives can actually increase or decrease their levels of stress. It is because thought processes or cognitions have a great influence, for good and ill, on stress levels that we place them first in our CABB model. In doing so we do not seek to diminish the importance of the other modalities, each of which has its recognized place in the model. However, cognitions not only increase or decrease stress but also affect a person's ability to solve the very problems generating that stress (Lazarus and Folkman, 1984). It is in recognition of the power of thinking that we initially pay attention to cognitions and thought processes in our model of stress and the integrative problem-focused approach to counselling which runs parallel to it.

Thinking which hinders problem solving

Some of the ways of thinking which frequently hinder problem solving are described below:

focusing on the negative (and ignoring the positive):

'So many things are going wrong in my life and nothing good is ever going to happen to me.'

discounting the positive:

'I only got an 'A' grade in my exam because I was lucky and the examiner was feeling generous.'

all-or-nothing (with no middle ground):

'I hate my boss, there is nothing decent about her at all. My only option is to leave this job.'

labelling:

'Failing my driving test proves that I'm stupid and a complete failure.'

mind-reading:

'He pretended not to notice me in the road today, we're obviously not friends any more.'

fortune-telling:

'The weather is bound to be awful on our holiday'.

magnification:

'If I lose my job it will be the worst thing that could ever happen to me.'

minimization:

'Although I scored three goals they were all absolutely diabolical.'

emotional reasoning:

'She made me angry, therefore she must have treated me badly.'

personalization (blaming yourself for something when you are not really responsible):

'My students have not passed all their exams, I've only myself to blame.'

blame:

'Where are my keys? Which one of you has moved them?

over generalization:

'What's the point of applying for any more jobs? I've already been rejected by five employers.'

shoulds, musts, have tos and oughts:

'I must always do well at whatever I am undertaking.'
'My children should always get good marks.'

(adapted Palmer and Strickland, 1996: 9–10).

Thinking errors, commonly known amongst cognitive behavioural therapists as 'cognitive distortions', are mistakes in our mental processing which are illogical – the outcome does not necessasrily follow from the premise – and are often stress related. Such thinking is very common and needs to be given attention in the client's assessment profile and recorded as a thinking errors issue to be addressed during the problem management work.

Challenges to thinking

A key role of the counsellor in this model is to challenge illogical, unhelpful thinking and those beliefs, attitudes and behaviour which interfere with a client's ability to solve their problems. This does not require the counsellor to take a confrontational stance; it is the thinking that needs examining and challenging, not the person directly. The timing of the challenge, however, is vital. In the development of a therapeutic working relationship, the aim is to enable the client to speak freely with the minimum of intervention; that is what Egan (1994) calls 'telling their story'. Once problems have been defined the counsellor's task is to help a client reassess their position, and it is at this stage that challenges to stress-related thinking, feeling and behaviour, which have become habits taken for granted by a client, are helpful.

> [S]upport without challenge is often superficial and challenge without support can be demeaning and self-defeating. It is important to understand the client's . . . point of view even when it is evident that it needs to be challenged or at least broadened. . . . challenge at the service of a new perspective . . . is best woven into the fabric of the entire helping process. Helping clients challenge themselves with respect to goals, action strategies and action itself, is part of the process.
>
> (Egan, 1994: 27)

(Some of the skills which are helpful in challenging stress related thinking are developed in Chapters 3 and 6.)

AFFECT

> Affect refers to the feelings and emotions that proceed from, lead to, accompany, under-lie or give colour to a client's experiences and behaviours.
>
> (Egan, 1998: 68)

The five-stage model of stress presented in Chapter 1 illustrates that it is at stage 3, when a person has acknowledged a situation as negative or threatening, that their stress response is triggered, involving a variety of psychophysiological changes. The triggering of the stress response results in the person becoming aware of one or more emotional responses such as anxiety, embarrassment, anger or guilt. Our model proposes that these emotions have physiological, cognitive and behavioural components. Consequently in integrative problem-focused stress counselling, emotional responses are addressed not solely as feeling reactions which are explored for their own intrinsic value, as in classical person-centred work, but rather as an intrinsic part of the person's whole response to stress. Life's problems are often stressful and the emotions they evoke have a significant influence on the process of managing our stress.

Emotions which hinder problem solving

We have described some of the cognitions or ways of thinking which hinder problem solving and we look at ways of helping clients to recognize and change these in Chapter 6. However, it would be extremely naive to see the effective management of people's stress as just a question of ironing out misunderstandings in thinking. There are times when the consequences of our thinking invoke emotions so powerful that they completely block our capacity to change our thinking or attend to our problem solving. When this is the case we argue that a counselling model which pays attention to the links between our thinking and our emotions provides the best way forward.

This parallels the thinking of Egan (1994) who suggests that one of the goals of the helping process is to help clients to release themselves from the burden of disabling feelings and emotions; to learn to control their emotions without becoming lifeless. 'The best way to control emotions is to control the thoughts that provoke them. If I let myself dwell on the ways in which you have wronged me, I will inevitably get angry. But I can actively refrain from dwelling on such thoughts' (Egan, 1994: 70).

Consequently we have integrated a five-star thinking–emotions framework into our counselling model (see Figure. 2.1). This is based on the work of Albert Ellis (1994) and his ABCDE model.

Emotional problem solving

In the early stages of counselling the use of our seven-step model of problem solving, described later in this chapter (and in Chapter 5), may need to be post-poned in situations where a client is unable to deal with a particular problem because of high levels of stress and anxiety. This is particularly pertinent if a client is largely distressed or disturbed due to her or his thoughts or beliefs. The cornerstone of cognitive behavioural (CBT) and rational emotive behavioural approaches (REBT) to stress counselling is crystallized in the view that reactions to life events or stressors are largely determined by our perceptions, that is, meanings and evaluations of these events, rather than by the events themselves. There are of course times when our perceptions are accurate reflections and these can be stressful, but frequently our distress is not the direct result of the prob-lems we encounter, but arises from the misguided assumptions we make about them. When this is the case, the five-star framework can be used to teach clients how to establish cognitive control over their emotional reactions. Indeed Ellis (1994) developed his five-stage model of emotional 'disturbance' and change to help people to understand this process (Palmer 1997d, adapted Dryden and Gordon, 1993):

A = activating events – situations, experiences (actual or inferred past, present or future occurrences)

B = beliefs – the assumptions we make about the events, often rigid and unqualified demands in the form of musts, shoulds, have to's, got to's, oughts

C = consequences – emotional, behavioural and physiological disturbances resulting in stressed behaviour

D = disputing – (cognitive, behavioural, imaginal) of those assumptions or beliefs which have produced stress and prevent us from working on our problems. (Called 'disturbance-producing, problem-interfering beliefs)

E = effective, efficient and flexible new approaches to the problem which reverses the stress noted at C.

Using the model

When a problem or stressor triggers a high level of emotional disturbance or avoidance the five-star model can be used to help clients. Neenan and Palmer (1996: 5) emphasize that it is a client's beliefs (B) about the stressful events at (A) which lead to their emotional, behavioural and physiological disturbances at (C). By disputing (D) the disturbance-producing and problem-interfering beliefs in a variety of ways, the client can learn to internalize a new outlook that reduces their stress and help them to develop a more effective and flexible outlook and philosophy.

The five-star model is briefly covered below and broken down into discrete parts to help understanding. (A more substantial explanation is given in Chapter 6.)

Step 1. A problem or stressor is agreed and noted down in concrete terms (A).

Step 2. The counsellor asks the client how she or he feels about the problem.

Step 3. The counsellor then uses a technique known as inference chaining to discover which aspect of the problem (A) the client is really disturbed about. Often the initial problem mentioned by the client is not the real underlying fear. In inference chaining the client's fears are not challenged and, temporarily, it is assumed that they could occur.

Step 4. Once the aspect of the activating event (A) that the client is really disturbed about is agreed, the counsellor then assesses the beliefs which produce the client's disturbance and interfere with their ability to work on their problem. The client's self-defeating beliefs are noted down and become the focus for challenge (called disputation). It is usually a good idea to write the problem down in ABC terms on a whiteboard in the session, so as to share with the client exactly what the focus of the session is.

Step 5. The next step is to examine and dispute these beliefs. There is a variety of ways of doing this. One of the most commonly used methods to help clients to change or modify their beliefs is through the use of questions. Three major arguments used to dispute irrational beliefs are:

- Empirical: There is no evidence that if you fail at something, therefore you are a total failure.
- Logical: It is not logical to conclude that if you fail at a task therefore you are a total failure.
- Pragmatic: If you carry on believing that when you fail at something you are a total failure, you will stay stressed and anxious.

Step 6. Once the beliefs have been challenged sufficiently, then counsellor and client are in a position to develop more helpful, flexible and problem-focused beliefs. Then they can discuss together a new more effective, efficient and flexible approach to dealing with the problem.

Integration of the two problem-solving models

In brief problem-focused stress counselling the five-star model is integrated within the seven-step model and is used whenever a client has revealed disturbance-producing and problem-interfering beliefs that effectively block them from staying focused on their stress problem. Occasionally while using the seven-step model a client may mention a problem-interfering belief as an aside. The full five-star approach may not be needed here, but the belief can be challenged and then the focus of the session can return to the seven-step model.

Positive and negative emotions

The emphasis attached to emotions in the integrative problem-focused counselling model concentrates on their relationship to stress. While some counselling purists may claim to perceive emotions as value-free, there is now sufficient evidence from everyday life and from personality theory that:

- emotions affect some people more than they affect others
- some emotions have positive effects on a person and some emotions have stressful or negative effects
- although some emotions are stressful or negative in their effects, some are more negative and unhelpful than others
- some negative emotions do not necessarily distract a person from the job in hand, whereas others are more self-defeating and prevent a person from achieving their aims and goals
- some negative emotions may actually help to motivate the person to achieve their aims and goals.

Table 2.1 *Positively and negatively productive emotions* (Clarke and Palmer, 1994a)

Perceived situation	Emotion	Positively (PP) Negatively (NP) productive
Threat or danger	Anxiety	NP
	Concern	PP
Loss; failure	Depression	NP
	Sadness	PP
Breaking of moral code (self)	Guilt	NP
	Remorse	PP
Breaking of moral code (another)	Damning anger	NP
	Annoyance	PP
Display of personal weakness	Shame	NP
	Regret	PP
Betrayal of self by other	Hurt	NP
	Disappointment	PP
Threat to an exclusive relationship	Morbid jealousy	NP
	Non-morbid jealousy	PP

Source: adapted from Palmer and Dryden (1995)

The concept that emotions have powerful behavioural consequences and that there are positive and negative aspects to emotions is fundamental to the integrative problem-focused stress counselling approach. The unifying factor is that both aspects contribute to our energy flow, rather like the positive and negative poles of an electric battery. The difference between them is that those emotions which are considered positively productive are characterized by flexible and realistic thinking involving preferences, wishes, desires and wants. Conversely, those which are considered negatively productive or stressful are characterized by over-evaluative, dogmatic, rigid and unrealistic thinking involving 'musts', 'shoulds', 'oughts', and 'have to's'. To illustrate this further, Table 2.1 summarizes some of the main positively productive and negatively productive emotions and links these to some typical situations in which these emotions tend to be generated.

Some of the skills integral to challenging stress-related negative emotions are developed in Chapter 6.

PS

As a postscript to our thinking–emotions alliance, we freely acknowledge that some people need help to learn to express their emotions in the service of enriching their humanity. The problem-focused stress counselling approach may not be the most helpful for these people.

BIOLOGY

In addition to considering the psychological concomitants of stress responses, the integrative problem-focused stress counselling approach aims to help clients to understand some of those physiological aspects of their stress outlined in Chapter 1.

We have found that if people understand something of the effects of stress on their body the physical responses produced are often less fearful to them and this understanding can itself help to reduce anxiety levels. We also recognize that a greater understanding of those physical responses of a serious nature may increase stress levels and where that happens the effects of this will be acknowledged in the relationship and included in the problem-solving process.

As well as enabling clients to understand the physical symptoms of stress, the model proposes physiological means to control stress which work directly on the body and can have a very positive effect on the way people feel about themselves. This proposal is based on the premise that if people are healthy, maintain a good diet, take regular exercise and allow time for relaxation they are likely to be better prepared for adversity. For people who are already in the throes of adversity, whose bodily condition is affected, an improvement in their fitness and health, allied to consideration of the other stress areas, can lead to improved physical resources to deal with stress. The old-fashioned concept of a healthy mind and a healthy body has an important place in stress work.

Stress, performance and pressure

The relationship between stress and performance is generally an inhibiting one. Contrary to the belief of some counsellors, it is not stress than enhances work performance, but pressure. While the precise amount of pressure needed for good performance obviously varies from one individual to another and from one situation to another, we seek to emphasize that too much or too little pressure is invariably experienced as stressful. The relationship between pressure and people's ability to cope can be illustrated through an optimum performance curve (see Figure 2.2).

Stress can be reduced by helping people to cope more effectively with an overload of pressure. However, specifically dealing with the physical effects of stress is an integral backup to the cognitive, affective and behavioural work. Some of the ways of helping people to cope with the physiological effects of stress are developed in Chapters 7 and 8.

BEHAVIOUR

What we actually do when we are stressed is in some ways our most obvious response. Other people cannot read our unexpressed thoughts, nor, unless they are very empathic, relate to our private feelings and our physical reactions may or may not be obvious to others or ourselves. A steadily rising cholesterol level may creep insidiously round our body, leading to a build up of plaque on the artery walls, until its presence is dramatically announced by a heart attack.

Our model of stress in Chapter 1 includes a wide range of examples of behavioural responses to stressful experiences, from accident proneness, through poor time-management to withdrawing from relationships. This list of behaviours illustrates the extent to which our behavourial stress reactions can affect our physical well-being, our work performance and/or our personal lives. The integrative problem-focused stress counselling model uses behavioural methods of problem management

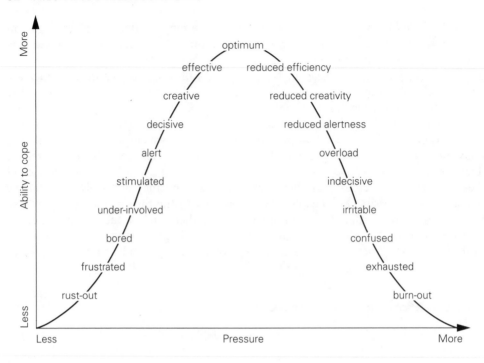

Figure 2.2   *Optimum performance curve* (Clarke and Palmer, 1994a)

to examine and deal with these difficult situations in a constructive and positive way. These usually consist of practical approaches to reduce stress at work (see Chapter 8) and at home by learning to manage time more effectively, or learning to develop supportive networks and relationships to help deal with stress through increasing the development of social skills.

It is easy to assume that we automatically become adept at dealing with life's problems and develop social competence through everyday living. This is not the reality for many of us. Students frequently arrive at college after experiencing thirteen years of formal education, only to discover that they have neither the study skills nor the social competence to meet the demands of their new situation. This is not a criticism of students, but rather a realistic acknowledgement of the limitations of 'learning through living', unless we pay conscious attention to our experiences and focus on our skills. This in the service of behaving as active, thinking, problem-solving human beings who interact with our environment rather than reacting passively to it.

The integrative problem-focused stress counselling model clearly includes a behavioural content which uses a step-by-step approach to help people to change their behavioural responses to stress. Some of the skills and techniques of this content are developed in Chapters 4, 5, 6 and 7.

SEVEN-STEP PROBLEM MANAGEMENT OUTLINE

Problem management is the name we give to the process through which a person:

- approaches the stressful problems in their life
- works to discover effective remedies or coping responses
- acts to put these into practice
- evaluates the results.

Coping refers to those things we do in order to reduce, minimize or control our stress.

Step 1: identify the problem

Stress often builds up over long periods so that by the time clients consult a counsellor about their situation it can have developed into a multi-layered mixture of thoughts, feelings and behaviour in which the real issue may be far from clear. Both the counselling foundation of the integrative stress counselling model and the CABB assessment profile are intended to be developed to help a client to put the counsellor, and often themselves, 'in the picture', or in Egan's terms to 'tell their story'. Throughout this step the counsellor is working on two levels: one to maintain the therapeutic working relationship upon which the counselling rests, the other to gain the clearest possible understanding of the issues as the client sees them.

Although step 1 of the seven-step management outline is simply described as identifying the problem, actually understanding the problems a client brings and helping them to clarify the issues involved is often complex. There may be several reasons for this lack of clarity such as a genuine confusion about what is wrong, which a client encapsulates in a vague reference to 'things not going right for me at all'.

Another client may be so overwhelmed by the complexities of life that they look at the counsellor helplessly and say, 'I don't know where to begin, it's all too much.' Sometimes clients are reluctant to disclose what the difficulties are and there may be others who present a combination of all these factors.

Experienced counsellors will be quite familiar with all these presentations from clients and will have their own ways of responding. Some will respond with empathic silence, others will explore the feelings involved. In our model the first task is to work with the client to map out the issues as clearly as possible, because until they have been defined with some clarity, they defy both management and resolution. This does not mean that we ignore the feelings of clients or ride over them, but we do remain problem focused.

Step 1 ends when both client and counsellor are aware of:

- the range of the problem
- the key people and issues involved
- the relative importance of all the interconnected issues.

Step 2: select realistic goals

Helping clients to select realistic goals is the beginning of their move towards change. Realistic goals are those:

- within the client's personal capabilities
- within the client's environmental resources
- specific
- substantial – not too easy, not too hard
- verifiable – can be evaluated by both client and counsellor together.

It is preferable that goals originate from clients themselves. We are wary of ever suggesting goals for clients because they learn best from working these out for themselves, with help, but this is a directive approach and we will not watch clients struggle interminably when we think we can make a suggestion which will get them started. There are occasions when clients get into a seemingly intractable, stuck position in which the best and the worst the counsellor can do is to suggest a goal in line with the client's aspirations and values. For effective change it is crucial that clients can own their goals and recognize them as something that they want, whether the goal originated from themselves or the counsellor. Unless we can give our personal commitment to change we are unlikely to harness the work and resources needed to achieve it, whether in counselling or in life generally.

Step 2 is completed when a client has selected one or more goals to help them manage their stress differently and has framed them in the most realistic and helpful way possible.

Step 3: explore options

The task of step 3 is to encourage the client to produce the most creative possible ways of achieving their goals, rather than being limited to the more obvious and orthodox routes. Although the goals need to be realistic, at this point the options for getting there can be quite fanciful or even outrageous – on the premise that giving reign to creativity can release both talent and stress.

Clients are also encouraged to identify their existing personal strengths, resources and support networks, personal, social and environmental.

Step 4: consider the consequences

Before acting on the goals selected, through the various ways of reaching them which have arisen from the work of steps 2 and 3, the important auditing strategy of step 4 is brought into focus. Auditing consists of evaluating the possible consequences of the chosen courses of problem-solving action which are being considered as ways of managing the client's stress. Gaining a systematic and clear view of the pros and cons of each proposed action often uncovers points which might otherwise be missed and can act as a guard against failure.

Step 5: take decisions

Theoretically, by working through steps 1–4, a client should be in a position to choose ways of reaching those goals which will manage their stress in the most feasible way – with the greatest gain and the least negative consequences. The planned solution chosen from those identified in the earlier steps is likely to be one which is calculated to resolve the problems generating stress, while at the same time maximizing a client's personal and emotional well-being with the minimum of time and effort.

Step 6: taking agreed action

The management solutions chosen will have no effect on a person's stress unless they take positive action to change the situation which is generating that stress. The final choice of action is likely to be more effective if it is:

- described step by step
- focuses on achievements rather than behaviour
- a goal which is achievable – not too hard, not too easy in order to generate success
- characterized by identifiable gains
- within the resources of the client to achieve
- supported by an in-built monitoring system.

Step 7: evaluate the strategy

The final stage of the problem management process seeks to help the client to evaluate the action that they have taken as a result of their collaborative work with the counsellor and the personal choices they made in steps 1–6.

Evaluation is not a test, it is a review of what happened.

Clients sometimes achieve the goals they set themselves and sometimes they do not and become discouraged. The counsellor's role is to help both partners in the therapeutic working relationship to make good use of the learning which is present both in achievement and in an apparent lack of success, in achieving stress management goals.

Contra-indications

Although integrative problem-focused stress management counsellors work to a model which requires supreme optimism, we are experienced enough to acknowledge that not all stress can be resolved by the model we outline. An absence of progress may indicate the limitations of counsellor or client, or the presence of more deep-seated difficulties which will not be reached by working briefly in the way we have outlined, but may require referral to psychiatric resources.

Hawton and Kirk (1989) offer several reasons why a problem-solving approach, on its own, may fail or be unsuitable. It may be that a client has problems which are unrealistic or cannot be stated clearly enough to be worked on. A client's problems may reflect difficulties which are very long-standing or they may have a severe, acute psychiatric illness.

The basic problem-solving approach does require clients to have a reasonable grasp of the realities of life and will not be successful with people who suffer from the delusions of severe schizophrenia. Those who endure the distress of agitated depression or people with severe learning needs may have great difficulty in focusing on the tasks inherent in the work. Falloon *et al.* (1993) have used a problem management approach with less severe schizophrenia; Hawton and Kirk (1989) have worked in this way with less depressed clients and Hawton and Catalan (1987) with suicidal clients who are not thought to be at high risk.

CHAPTER 3
Spectrum of Core Counselling Skills

The counsellor is not an all-knowing, psychologically superhuman being . . .
such a view is too divine and unrealistic, as is the idea that anyone whose heart
is sympathetic can counsel effectively.

Milner (1974, 1980: 166)

What effective counsellors usually bring to their work with clients is a fount of
knowledge through experience, a repertoire of skills and, of course, themselves.
Integrative problem-focused stress counselling is a skills-based and skills-dependent
model, as the content of this book shows.

SYSTEMATIC INTEGRATION OF SKILLS

Fundamental factors basic to choice of skills

Our approach is not a further system of therapy to be added to those already in
existence, which now run into hundreds (Karasu, 1977). Rather it is an orientation
in which the counsellor integrates certain existing skills, strategies and techniques of
choice in a systematic way. This is done with the aim of helping clients to
understand, manage or change those aspects of their thinking, feeling, health,
behaviour or environment which contribute to their individual stress.

The counsellor's choice of response or technique takes account of five fundamental
factors:

- client qualities
- counsellor qualities
- counsellor skills
- counselling relationship
- the specific nature of the chosen technique or intervention.

Relationship of choice

We have emphasized the importance of the therapeutic working relationship based on person-centred principles. In addition we incorporate the concept of the counsellor as an authentic chameleon (Lazarus, 1993), who, in addition to considering the skills and strategies of choice, also adapts to the counselling relationship of choice. Such an adaptation involves developing differing styles of interaction with different clients, which may require the counsellor to decide when and how to be non-directive, directive, supportive, warm, reflective, gentle, tough, formal, informal or humorous. The stance of authentic chameleon demands informed decisions on when a client prefers a warm empathic counsellor and when they prefer the therapist to take the stance of a trainer, teacher or provider of information. The counsellor using such a multi-faceted approach is obliged to provide a rationale to underpin their choice of intervention to fit this client's specific problem at this particular time. It is essential that the client is given the opportunity to understand the counsellor's rationale for using a chosen strategy or technique and to agree (or disagree) with it. Thus a legitimate question for clients is 'Why have you chosen this way of working with me just now?' The integrative stress counsellor needs to have a clear answer.

Authentic flexibility

The key concept of the integrative chameleon is authentic flexibility in the counselling relationship. If during the CABB assessment process it is shown that the client wants support through a recent stressful event such as a close family bereavement, the counsellor's understanding, active listening and empathic reflection of the client's thoughts and feelings will be genuinely present in the relationship. The same client at a later stage in the problem-management process may need to use more active techniques such as brainstorming or role-play, requiring a more directive yet equally authentic approach from the counsellor.

This way of working tries to be tailor-made, not off-the-peg, in suiting client needs and problems, which is why it includes attention to personality differences (see Chapter 10). This is in line with recent writing which indicates that matching different approaches to clients may be better than trying to use one model with all clients and all issues (Inskipp, 1996).

Expectations of integrative stress counsellors

Much is expected from integrative counsellors, not only a wide range of skills and strategies for dealing with stress, but also personal qualities such as open-mindedness, flexibility, creativity, acceptance of others, adequate intelligence, wide-ranging general knowledge, social knowledge and life experience, together with humour, assertiveness, communication skills, the ability to think quickly and an interest in helping people. A tall order, but a necesssary one!

The incidence of media reported difficulties attributed to stress has increased significantly in the past few years, leading to a decided 'band-wagon' roll in the development of stress counselling which we can rightly be accused of riding. If we do not write about an effective approach to stress counselling when stress is 'in the air' so to speak, when else would we do it?

Integrative skills spectrum

Our work is supported by a range of skills and techniques which enables counsellors to help stressed clients. We define a skill as a practised, knowledgable ability in doing (something); for example, it is essential for counsellors to have effective skills in listening, responding and challenging. A technique on the other hand is a method or way of intervening which is particularly useful in stress counselling and management, such as thought stopping, or anxiety management, which we hope will be used with skill (see Chapters 6, 7, and 9).

We have described the integrated model as having a skills-based counselling foundation which sustains the therapeutic relationship and have rooted that relationship in the person-centred tradition. This alliance combined with the problem-management process forms the therapeutic working relationship which is at the heart of integrated problem-focused stress counselling.

We propose that the personal characteristics of the counselling relationship, namely empathy, respect and genuineness, are likely to be effectively learned and shared if they are expressed through the practice of specific skills. Strictly speaking the classical person-centred approach based on the work of Carl Rogers is not itself skills based, but relies more on the personal qualities and abilities of the counsellor in establishing the counselling relationship based on effective communication of the core conditions. Because our integrated approach is evolved for use by counsellors of differing humanistic or cognitive behavioural persuasions, we have grounded the core conditions in a skills-based model. Our reasoning is that people who by personality and inclination are not drawn to the classical person-centred approach can, through learning certain counselling skills, develop the positive therapeutic qualities of this way of working.

This is of course not a new proposition. Robert Carkhuff (1967, 1969a, 1969b) in the 1960s, Gerard Egan (1975, 1982, 1986, 1990, 1994, 1998) since the 1970s, Richard Nelson-Jones (1988, 1989, 1996a) since the 1980s and Sue Culley (1991, 1992) are among those who have advocated the merits of a skills approach based on the therapeutic relationship promoted by Carl Rogers (1961, 1980).

Richard Nelson-Jones (1996a) describes his relating and life skills model as an attempt to 'bring together the soft and gentle nature of the humanistic approaches (to psychology) and the incisiveness of the behavioural and cognitive approaches'. This might also be a description of our integrative framework.

The skilled helper approach of Gerard Egan (1975, 1982, 1986, 1990, 1994, 1998) has been particularly influential in this context and he has refined his work consistently over a twenty-year period into a substantial three-stage skills-based model of problem management in which the skills of each stage add on to those of the previous one(s).

Thus the core skills have been written about extensively over the past thirty years and we do no more than briefly outline these while giving more attention to a range of cognitive behavioural strategies for helping with stress conditions.

This chapter and the four which follow provide a compendium of skills and a guide to strategies and techniques upon which a counsellor using the integrative problem-focused stress model can draw in the service of their role as authentic chameleon.

QUALITIES AND SKILLS IN THE COUNSELLING RELATIONSHIP

The counselling interaction is primarily a two-way street of listening and responding in which the basic skills of interpersonal communication are a more sophisticated extension of those skills which are helpful in developing relationships in everyday life. Since they are so basic and have been written about quite extensively in the counselling literature over several years, it may seem superfluous to repeat them here. However, stress and the anxiety which often accompany it have the effect of distorting or impeding much of our communication and of rendering our relationships ineffectual or even destructive. It is a premise of integrative work that clients need help first to understand what stresses them and then to develop or perhaps re-activate their skills in acting to change things for themselves.

Counsellors model both personal qualities and communication skills from their first contact with clients, whether that is by telephone, face-to-face or, less frequently, by letter. Sometimes a fundamental help we can offer stressed clients is support with their own damaged interpersonal communication. It is as much to remind counsellors of this client need as for their own 'back to basics' that we outline fundamental skills in this chapter. These skills are used to develop the therapeutic working relationship, to facilitate client and counsellor understanding and to encourage action.

Listening and responding

The quality of our listening as counsellors is transmitted to our clients by the quality of our responses, both non-verbal and spoken. Complete listening is a contextual, active, responsive undertaking and our first responses convey, without words, 'I'm working to understand what you are saying, I accept it, I don't challenge it.' We offer a reassurance that we are willing to look at the person and the issues, as they appear to the client.

Attentive involvement

The early stages of counselling involvement is very much a product of our capacity to pay attention, to show, without words, in our posture and social–emotional presence that we are alert and interested. It is a demonstration of our active listening. Egan (1998: 63–4) offers the acronym SOLER as a model for attending and showing our willingness to be involved while we are listening and before we become verbally engaged.

S arranging the physical counselling space to face a client squarely helps us to observe each other more readily
O sitting comfortably, but alert with an open posture suggests our accessibility

L flexibly, responsibly, subtly being involved through tending to lean towards the client

E maintaining a gaze which is steady and direct, but not obtrusive or staring; eye contact which accommodates client's discomfort, anxiety or cultural rules

R relaxed posture, calm, accepting, available. Gentle nods of the head show our continued attention and occasional larger, repeated nods suggest our understanding.

Non-verbal communication is dynamic and two-way and although non-verbal messages all have a meaning, that meaning is contextual – relating to the client and their individual context – not universal. Although Desmond Morris (1994) has written a whole book about body talk, in counselling such messages can most helpfully be explored and read, rather than interpreted.

Bodily tension, movements, gestures, facial expressions, voice-related expressions – sometimes called paralinguistics (such as speed of speaking, loudness of voice, tone, inflection, emphasis, pauses, silences) – can all be more communicative than what we actually say; this can be to the extent that when our facial expression is inconsistent with the our words, our facial expression is more likely to be believed (Mehrabian, 1971).

Culley (1991) reminds us that individual differences call for tentative exploration: one client might smile when talking about a painful experience, another might use an angry tone of voice, while a third might hunch their shoulders and look away. All these non-verbal accompaniments to a client's story speak to us about them as individuals and have implications for the ways in which they deal with their stress.

Non-verbal responses

MINIMAL ENCOURAGERS

We have seen that gentle nods of the counsellor's head can act as an encouragement to clients to continue with their story and occasional larger repeated nods can convey our understanding of what is being said. Palmer and Burton (1996: 20) give the name minimal encouragers to the wide range of short sounds which often accompany our nods and which we use to indicate that we are paying attention. Such sounds include:

- Umm
- Ah-ha
- Ye-es
- Uh-huh.

The tone of voice, the manner in which it is said, the point at which it is uttered, together with a gentle nod, help to maintain contact in an atmosphere that is relaxed, unhurried and accepting.

> *George:* My wife complains that I'm paying too much attention to this language student that is staying with us.

Co: Uh-huh. (minimal encourager)

George: She says that I shouldn't take her a cup of tea in bed in the mornings, but I take one to my wife and daughter.

Co: (nodding) Mm.

George: The thing is my wife is getting really upset about it and I think it's ridiculous.

LISTENING IN SILENCE

Communication continues even when clients fall silent. In social settings silence is often regarded and used in a negative way and it can be greatedly feared. The American musical partnership of Simon and Garfunkel once produced a song called 'Sound of Silence', in which they included the phrase 'silence like cancer grows'. Because of this social attitude to silence as being like a malignant vacuum, which must be filled if it is not to be fatal, the positive therapeutic use of silence is a skill to be learned. A client–counsellor dialogue can be improved by the judicious use of silence.

Peter: I just don't know where to go from here. (Pause) Things have been getting so difficult lately. (Falls silent and seems distressed)

Peter's counsellor has a wide range of responses available at this point and the one chosen will depend very much on how well-established the relationship is, what has gone before, and the differing personalities of the client and counsellor. A prolonged silence early in counselling may be interpreted as rejection, whereas later in the process it may be a natural pause at the end of a stage, or a contemplative prelude to some important work. Accepting the silence can give both Peter and his counsellor time to reflect on the situation, help them to develop trust, and help Peter to understand that the direction of the counselling session is under his control.

However, since Peter is indicating through his body language – sighing, hunching his shoulders and looking at the floor – that he is experiencing some distress, applying a rigid rule of never breaking a silence, which some counsellors have, may not help Peter to proceed.

Counsellor responses in such a situation will vary and according to Palmer and Burton (1996: 23, adapted) may include the following:

- Giving Peter the responsibility for moving the session forward by waiting for him to start talking, no matter how long that is.
- Supporting Peter through the silence by a brief verbal intervention such as:
  - Waiting for a few moments and then asking, 'Do you want to say more?'
  - Waiting for a few moments and then prompting him, 'Things have been getting difficult.'
- Actively moving the session forward by a specific enquiry: waiting for two or three minutes before asking, 'How are you feeling now?'
- Waiting for two or three minutes and saying, 'You look really weighed down and unhappy. I wonder what's going on for you?'

Listening to silence creatively means achieving a balance between enabling clients to continue, providing space for them to reflect or helping them to face their discomfort.

Clients are usually less accustomed to using silence creatively than their counsellors. Many people have had the experience of silence being used against them as a form of punishment by other important people in their lives and it is vital that counsellors do not repeat this experience with clients, however inadvertently. Conversely it is also unhelpful for counsellors to interrupt silences to make the time more congenial for themselves.

CORE CONDITIONS OF THE THERAPEUTIC WORKING RELATIONSHIP

Non-verbal communication characterizes the attentive involvement of the early stages of the therapeutic relationship which is counselling. Both the non-verbal skills and the active responding skills which follow are set within the core conditions of genuiness, respect and empathy. Rogers *et al.* (1967) suggested that the order in which these three therapeutic conditions occur is of special significance because of their interlocking nature. Genuineness is the most basic element and once the authenticity of the counsellor as a person is established, communication of respect for the client evolves as the second effective quality. When the relationship is characterized by genuineness and respect, the actual work of counselling is helped by the empathic understanding of the meaning, significance and content of the client's experiences and feelings. Milner (1974, 1980: 146)

Genuineness: being yourself

The quality of genuineness, sincerity, transparency, not putting on an act, not hiding behind the role of counsellor, being simply and without pretentiousness yourself requires a particularly high level of self-awareness. This authenticity is one of the most challenging of counsellor attributes to develop. Because it is usually less common among people in general, who often need to be more defensive and protective of their work, their person and status, we usually do not come to counselling training with a naturally high level of genuineness. Feedback from others tells us how we come across and once our counselling training is over, such feedback has to be sought rather than being offered regularly. It is the responsibility of counsellors to seek it through ongoing training and supervision and through contact with other counsellors.

Genuineness may be represented by the computer term WYSIWYG, 'What you see is what you get'. Openness, consistency and respectful spontaneity, being comfortably yourself in your interactions require the courage to unlearn and relearn in the cause of self-awareness. This takes time and can be illustrated by a learning progression, as Bill the counsellor, works with Brenda.

> *Brenda:* This whole counselling thing is a waste of time. I don't want to keep coming and talking to you and still feeling so stressed all the time.
> *Bill being a defensive counsellor:*
> Well, you will feel stressed if you don't do the homework.

Bill being a timid counsellor:
> Well that's your decision.

Bill becoming more skilled and more genuine:
> It seems as if you don't feel you get any reward for coming here. You come and keep working and nothing changes. Let's see if we can look at a specific example of what you mean.

Respect: helping someone feel important

Like genuineness, respect is not so much a skill to be learned as an attitude or disposition towards others and oneself, which can be developed. Respect includes being non-judgemental, open and receptive – though not gullible, treating people with the consideration which conveys that they are worth listening to. Those 'natural' counsellors, bar staff and hairdressers, who take a polite interest in our problems and our point of view and do not contradict us, whatever they may think, generate a practical respect (Cowen, 1982). Some of the ways we show our respect as counsellors include:

- observing confidentiality
- being on time, prepared, available and working hard in sessions
- enabling and encouraging clients to be self-responsible and to develop and use their own resources
- refusing to manipulate clients with the powerful skills and techniques in the integrative stress counselling compendium
- helping clients through the pain – not helping them to find ways of avoiding it
- being competent – being caring but incompetent as a counsellor is totally disrespectful.

Respect places demands on clients to deal with their stress, but it also offers help in meeting that demand. Egan (1994) suggests that we can respond with respect in quite different ways:

> *Co:* Where would you like to start?
> *Edith:* I don't know what to say. It's all so confused and I can't sort things out. It would help if you just asked me some questions, that's what my doctor does.
> *Co:* Right. Well let's start with what made you come here?

The counsellor responds to Edith's request in an attempt to help her to get started, rather like finding an end in a tangled ball of wool.

It would also be showing respect to Edith's own abilities to gently challenge her to move away from dependence on questions and answers and to introduce her to the different interactive dynamics of the counselling alliance.

> *Co:* Yes, I can see that your doctor helps you in that way. Perhaps we could talk about that because I feel that if I ask you questions we'll get a lot of information that I think is important, but I won't know what you think is important. It's new for you to talk about yourself in this way and it seems quite different and a bit strange.

A counsellor who assumes that a client's basic difficulty is a lack of information and recommends appropriate books, without giving the client the opportunity and encouragement to talk freely about the things she or he wishes to raise, is showing little respect. Whether it takes two minutes or five hours, making acceptance and respect clear to the client is essential (Tyler, 1969).

Empathy: seeing it their way

Seeing things the client's way, understanding and communicating the thoughts, feelings and actions which combine to make up their experience, with respect and genuineness, characterize the quality and skill of empathy. These three strands, when interwoven, produce that strength of relationship which is the foundation of our integrative approach.

Empathy is the quality and the ability to sense and to say what you understand it is like to be another person at a particular time.

A sympathetic response to a man whose wife has recently died might be, 'I'm very sorry to hear about your wife, why don't you come round and have a meal with us on Friday night. My wife will make you very welcome.' This is a practical, realistic response from a friend or neighbour which communicates something like, 'I know what is troubling you, you are lonely, let me help.'

An empathic response is more of a reflection from the inner emotional world of the recently widowered man, which conveys, 'It feels as if the world is a very lonely place for you just now.' A response which conveys, 'I feel and share your loneliness.'

Empathy communicates an understanding of what the client says, implies, hints at and also makes connections between seemingly isolated statements. It invents nothing and is helpful only to the degree to which it is accurate.

The combination of respect and empathy is paramount because of the emotional content of many empathic messages. Naming, revealing and discussing feelings is a threat for some clients and it may be more helpful to focus on experiences and behaviours – what people did or thought as a prelude to talking about feelings. Certain feelings are easier than others for some clients: anger may be easier to acknowledge than hurt, or vice versa. Empathy includes the emotional capacity and the ability and skill to pick up these individual differences.

In the integrative approach empathy does not have the pivotal place which it occupies, for example, in traditional person–centred work, because the approach offers many practical skills for helping clients with stress. We are, however, in no doubt that counsellors unable to feel and therefore to communicate empathically will find our approach, or any other, less effective.

> As a way of being and a communication skill, empathy should be integrated into a helping model that provides the kind of understanding challenge and support that clients need to do their part in establishing a working alliance and moving forward in the problem management process.
>
> (Egan, 1994: 120)

Skills of empathy

REFLECTION

The capacity to reflect, to present back, to mirror attitudes, thoughts, feelings or behaviour with empathic understanding is the powerful basis of classical person-centred work. It is important to remind counsellors not familiar with the person–centred approach that mere reflection itself is not empathy. Thus, the following is a reflection of content, but it is not empathy: 'You feel distressed because you have been diagnosed as having bone cancer.'

This is a simple reflection, or naming of a feeling, plus a descriptive reason for that feeling. Such an explanatory reflection may well be helpful at a later stage of the stress work, when the 'because' formula provides contextual framework for helping the client to act. However, in the early relationship and trust building stage of the integral model such a response is not appropriate. It is not an empathic response because it shows no appreciation from the counsellor of what experiencing that distress means for the client in terms of intensity, conflict with other emotions, or consequences. Although accurate, such a simple reflection is grossly inadequate to the intensity of the client's anxiety and distress and the counsellor does need to go well beyond the mere recognition and naming of a client's feelings and to explore their causes and implications for the client's stress.

A less bleak response in the early stages of the relationship might include, 'That feels absolutely shattering news. It seems such a shock after being given the all clear last year. It's really hard to actually take in what's happened.'

An empathic response shares some of the discomfort, disappointment and uncertainty about the future and does not try to rush the client on to action before they are ready, but helps them to explore their feelings and concerns more fully.

Barbara, aged 38, has returned to work in the financial services department of a national bank. She has been retrained and is a popular, successful member of the computer department. Her self-confidence has been boosted by her experience of returning to work. However, she is unhappy with her current relationship with her partner: 'Brian mollycoddles me all the time, looking after me, meeting me from work, treating me like a child . . . he suffocates me. He just doesn't realize that since I've come back to work I'm independent and strong, I don't lean on him any more.'

Barbara has talked to some of her friends and they have made various comments such as: 'Men are all the same – you don't need them'; 'It really must be hard for you'; 'It's as if he doesn't understand how you've changed and still treats you like he used to. That's really irritating.'

Barbara's counsellor responds, 'I sense you're angry that Brian doesn't understand that you've changed, that's really powerful . . . but, I wonder . . . you look as though you're trembling . . . is that your anger, or is there something else going on for you as well?' After a prolonged silence Barbara says quietly and tearfully, 'Yes. I'm really frightened that I might lose him now I'm different.'

Reflection is tied to attending and listening because accurate and sensitive responses depend on a counsellor's understanding of the nature of the client's stress. It is also a significant way of communicating respect and genuineness to the extent that as the counsellor reflects attitudes and feelings accurately and sensitively, they show sincere interest in the client and help to create a positive therapeutic relationship – the foundation for the future work of managing stress.

TENTATIVENESS

Tentative accuracy in reflection can help the client on the receiving end. One client who frequently makes very self-critical statements can be devastated by a counsellor who reflects, accurately from what they have heard, 'So you really can't do anything right.' Whilst another client may welcome such a response as a jolt of adrenalin to move them on.

A reflection which is equally accurate but less likely to be received as critical and disapproving by the first client is, 'So whatever you try doesn't seem to work out very well.'

Reflection then is a safeguard against misunderstanding and misinterpretation. It can help counsellors to check that they have understood correctly and can help clients to become more aware of patterns in their behaviour and their situation which they may not previously have recognized.

REFLECTION TRAPS

Selective minimal mirroring of a word or phrase helps to:

- reassure clients that they have your attention
- stay with the client's perspective
- enable clients to keep a clear focus
- build up trust.

Yet it also serves as a trap for the inexperienced or unwary counsellor. The key is in selectively mirroring a word or phrase as an economical way of encouraging clients.

> *Karen:* . . . I felt so angry.
> *Co:* (nodding) Angry? (mirroring)
> *Karen:* Yes, I don't feel any different from the other students, but they tease me and I get so lonely.

Karen emphasized the emotionally laden word 'angry' and the counsellor's echoing of it, with an implicit question mark, encouraged Karen's further response which revealed her loneliness. (To ask directly 'What do you mean by angry?' or 'What sort of angry are you?' would have been too obtrusive and taken attention away from the flow of Karen's story. However, at a later stage, it is helpful not just to reflect the anger, but also to explore its nature. See Chapter 6.)

The reflection trap is sprung if the counsellor continues the minimal mirroring.

> *Karen:* . . . I felt so angry.
> *Co:* (nodding) Angry? (mirroring)

Karen:	. . .Yes, I don't feel any different from the other students, but they tease me and I get so lonely.
Co:	(nodding) Lonely?
Karen:	Sometimes I want to run away.
Co:	You want to run away?
Karen:	Yes, I want to run away this minute, I feel so lonely now!
Co:	You feel lonely now?

This is an example of the parroting parody so beloved of critics of the traditional person-centred approach and it is right to be critical of such an insensitive mockery of the skill of reflection.

FURTHER REFLECTIVE SKILLS

Paraphrasing

The skill of paraphrasing lies in re-phrasing or making an accurate precis of what you understand to be the core content of a client's message in an accepting and non-judgemental way. This can help them to clarify their issues and concerns and can help you as the counsellor to understand your client more fully.

Sam:	I've got this offer of a place at university and I can't make up my mind about it. I'm useless. Sometimes I think it's a wonderful chance and I'd be mad not to take it. Then I think, no, it's not what I want.
Co:	You're undecided. Now you've got the place you're not sure that you want it?
Sam:	(Pause) Well, no, not really. I do want the place, but I'm not sure I can cope with it. I'm really scared of failing.

The counsellor is not offering any special insight, but is simply expressing in different words and more concisely what Sam has already said. Sam's response suggests that this is helpful; he is reassured that he has been heard and understood and it helps him to pause briefly, to take stock and to get in touch with the fear of failure which accompanies his success and which is generating his confusion.

Summarizing

This is a further way of helping clients to gain some coherence and order by giving a more comprehensive review of the core content of what they have been communicating. Culley (1991: 48) suggests that summaries can be particularly helpful at the beginning and ending of sessions, and also to:

* clarify content and feelings
* prioritize and focus
* review the work
* move the counselling forward.

Russell:	I just feel stressed in so many ways at the moment, I just don't know which way to turn. I've just been promoted to a new job, which I really want to do well at,

but it will mean more travelling. My father is 88 now and is getting very frail and absent minded . . . he's lost a lot of weight . . . (sighs) and sometimes . . . well, he just doesn't seem to know what's going on. (Long pause. Takes a deep breath.) I think he'd like to come and live with us, (speaking more quickly) but neither of us want that. Some things like the new job are very exciting. (Looks back at counsellor.) But the thought of my father coming to live with us is very frightening. (Looks away.)

Co: It seems that of all the new demands and changes you're facing, the one you feel most concerned about is caring for your father. You sounded anxious when you talked about him. Is that the way it seems to you?

Russell: Well he is really on my mind. I know I can handle the new job, but I feel so torn about my dad and would really like to feel I had some different possibilities for looking after him.

Co: Would it be useful to look at that today? To explore your ideas and fears about looking after your father?'

The counsellor uses a short, tentative summary to focus on what seems to be the core concern in Russell's present situation, the one which appeared to generate most feelings and most difficulties for him (adapted Culley, 1991: 48).

PROMPTS AND PROBES

The skill of encouraging clients to be specific or to consider other aspects of their story which have not been mentioned is the skill of prompting and probing (Egan, 1994). This is an area of counselling which can be one of the most contentious since it involves the use of questions. Questions are the world's way of obtaining information and they invade every aspect of people's lives. Trainee counsellors are often taught to avoid asking questions because it is in their human nature to ask too many, thus distorting the direction of the client's work in pursuit of the counsellor's goals. Having learned to avoid questions, counsellors then need to relearn the skill of presenting them differently. Many of the questions which illuminate counselling work are really more in the nature of queries, or responses which a counsellor uses to check their understanding. A query question is a shared responsibility because it starts with what the client has presented and is thus less likely to distort the direction of the work.

Queries and questions

Questions fall in a range between the open and the closed variety. The more closed a question, the closer it is to inviting a 'no' or a 'yes' response and the nearer the counsellor is to slipping into the 'question and answer' trap. Even those in between questions which invite a 'maybe' or 'perhaps' answer are more closed than open, in that they offer an interpretation or an answer and invite the person questioned to agree or disagree with it.

'You're upset aren't you?'   closed question
'How are you feeling now?'   open version

| 'Have you been doing this for a long time?' | closed question |
| 'How long have you been doing this?' | open version |

| 'Were you angry when that happened?' | closed question |
| 'What were your feelings when that happened?' | open version |

Restrictive open questions:

'When did you stop eating well?'
This question is burdened with assumptions:
  • that the person has stopped eating well
  • that they understand what you mean by well
  • that they can actually remember when their eating problems began.

'Why do you penalize yourself like that?'
'Penalize' is a loaded word and may not describe the way the person feels about their behaviour. The question is restrictive because it is full of quite emotive assumptions. Sometimes counsellors do feel that clients 'penalize' themselves in which case perhaps a more acceptable way of conveying this is to use reflection and to be more tentative. For example, 'It feels as if you are being very hard on yourself . . . it almost feels like punishment.'

The more open a question the less demands it appears to make and the more like a query it becomes. Queries can be more acceptable and less threatening to clients.

Rationale and follow-up for questions

Generally counsellors ask more questions or pose more queries in the early stages of the integrative approach and particularly in the CABB assessment stage, which derives from its cognitive behavioural roots. Nevertheless, questions should have a rationale and some helpful follow-up if they are not to emphasize factual matters over feelings and experience, and thus lead to a question and answer style of interaction which over-emphasizes the role of the counsellor in what is a collaborative relationship.

Questions may need to be asked when there is inadequate information about something important:

  • how long stress problems have been troubling client
  • what seems to precipitate them
  • how they have dealt with them in the past
  • how they have felt during the past week
  • how they progressed with plans for change.

Such questions need to be introduced as part of the natural flow of dialogue, not as interruptions to it.

Quite precise questions can be a help when certain clients are unresponsive and say things like 'OK', 'All right', or 'I don't know'. Sometimes young people particularly resent questions as an invasion of their privacy and we are probably all familiar with the classical adult/adolescent interaction:

'Where have you been?'   'Out.'
'What did you do?'   'Nothing.'

Yet behind this intractability is often a longing to be able to say more, without losing face, which may, if there is sufficient trust be helped by some precise queries, if that is not a contradiction in terms.

Co:	How are things going?
Philip:	All right. (shrugs shoulders)
Co:	Could you tell me what happened when you went home with your boy friend last night?
Philip:	My mother threw a wobbly.
Co:	Mm . . . mm. What did your mother say?
Philip:	She just screamed abuse at us . . .
Co:	That must have felt . . .
Philip:	Bloody awful.
Co:	Ye-es . . . what did you do?
Philip:	We marched out and went back to Martin's place.
Co:	So you got out pretty quickly. What were you thinking?
Philip:	I don't know, I just don't think my mother will ever accept that I'm gay and I want to live with Martin.

This very structured form of enquiry opened up an initial ambiguous response from Philip.

INVITING QUESTIONS

'Could you tell me about the problems at home?'

'You say you've been rather frustrated recently, will you say more about what that's like?'

'It seems that you've been working really long hours for the past month, shall we look at that?

'How are things going?'

These are all examples of questions which invite responses in a general area – home, frustrated behaviour, working long hours, or an open enquiry about things in general. Their aim is to open up an area for discussion.

DISCERNING QUESTIONS

Once an area of discussion is focused on it may take many different directions. A client may be reluctant to say more or alternatively unlock a cascading tangle of problems, feelings and experiences. This introduces the need for discerning questions, which aim to clarify what is happening and narrow the focus.

Possible questions for the client who is finding it difficult to get started:

'Could you explain that in more depth?'

'What is it about . . . that you are anxious about?'

'Will you tell me a bit more about that?'

Possible questions for the client who is overwhelmed with material:

'You've described what's been happening to you for a while, can you now focus on what you believe is the event that you are most upset about?'

'I am beginning to understand the general picture. Could you give me one or two recent examples?'

SPECIFIC UNDERSTANDING QUESTIONS

In the initial stages of counselling, clients often tell their story using broad, general statements. This allows them to ease their way into the relationship and into what, for many, is the rather strange, new experience of talking about themselves. However, if stress problems are to be managed the general story needs to be focused into specific and concrete examples. Sensitive questions can gently guide clients to more specific understanding.

> *General statement:*
>   'They want me to leave.'
> *Co:*   'Can you tell me a bit about who these people are?'
> *Specific response:*
>   'I overheard Mary and Joseph in the kitchen saying that they thought I was untidy.'
> *General statement:*
>   'Losing my house would be the end of the world.'
> *Co:*   'When you say the end of the world, can you tell me what you mean?'
> *Specific response:*
>   'I couldn't stand it. I'd rather kill myself.'

The aim of specific understanding questions is to move the story on and to help the client move to a different, more concrete level of their story. When that shift in perception has been made several times, many clients begin to talk in more specific terms without prompting from the counsellor. Probing too intensively makes the shift in levels from general to specific too radical and is likely to be counterproductive, whereas a gradual narrowing of the focus keeps the perspective manageable.

BEING SPECIFIC TO MANAGE STRESS

Helping clients to be more concrete and specific is an essential step in enabling them to manage their stress problems. As clients express themselves more clearly they often reveal aspects of their thinking, believing and attitudes which are inconsistent, discrepant, negative, passive or in other ways contributing to their stress. Such aspects cannot responsibly be ignored by an integrative counsellor who is, for example, compelled by the nature of the approach to challenge the false assumption that clients are powerless to change their stress situation. For some clients the prospect of managing their stress may seem as impossible as putting the toothpaste back in the tube. Although the two situations vary greatly in importance, the skill in both lies in changing the pressure. It is possible to get some of the toothpaste back in the tube by changing the pressure from the middle to the side. It is possible to manage stress problems by changing the pressure brought about by our ways of thinking, feeling, behaving and our approach to our health, as outlined in the CABB profile.

Counsellors make an assessment – how realistic is this client being and do they really need to face the things which are being denied or evaded – before embarking on the 'tough love' course of challenge (Egan, 1994: 58).

Challenging skills

Egan (1998: 146–99) offers a comprehensive account of all the aspects of challenging which is strongly recommended for readers who seek a more in depth account than we can give.

Challenge is an extension of authentic empathy, not an attack on the client and while it may help them to move from a defensive place, it should not make them feel defenceless. It has been suggested that the 'right' to challenge clients is earned through the work which the counsellor has put into building a good therapeutic working relationship, one which gives clients some confidence that the counsellor intends to be helpful.

Challenging is a form of reality testing. The rapport created by empathic understanding and permeated by respect and genuineness often brings a client some respite, in that they feel better about their stress through having been listened to and supported, but they still have their stress problems. It is at this point in integrative work that clients need an invitation to challenge themselves to change.

While clients' perceptions of their stress are real and need to be understood by themselves and by the counsellor, they are sometimes distorted, that is, they do not square with the facts and realities of their lives. In order to be both client-centred and problem-focused, it is important for counsellors to be reality-centred and tough minded in their understanding, so that they can detect gaps and distortions and are able to name them, describe them and challenge them at an appropriate time. In our work understanding a client's point of view is not the same as accepting it, but we agree with Egan (1998) that it is crucial to see things the client's way as comprehensively as possible before challenging them.

The integrative problem-solving approach combines empathy with challenge to help stressed clients to re-frame their often seemingly intractable problems, in ways which will give them some possibility of resolution. Clients who are stressed are trapped in a way of thinking or feeling which leads them to talk about their problems as incapable of resolution. This is what stress means, the demands on us look greater than our available resources. Problems stated in unsolvable terms are plights and whereas problems can be managed, plights can only be endured (Egan 1994: 163).

GUIDELINES FOR CHALLENGING

If they are not to exacerbate stress, challenges need to be:

- preceded by the development of mutual trust (earning the right to challenge)
- made tentatively, bearing in mind that you may be wrong, yet also
- made with commitment, because you take the challenge seriously and want the client to do so
- checked for bias (an automatic reaction to views which differ from your own)
- structured to encourage clients to challenge themselves
- presented as a two-way process, so that the client understands that it is acceptable to challenge the counsellor and to encourage clients to challenge themselves.

SOME BELIEFS THAT UNDERPIN CHALLENGING

- People can make changes if they choose to
- People can alter their attitudes and behaviours
- People have more resources for managing their stress than they assume
- People sometimes overestimate their psychological frailty.

DISCREPANCIES MAY BE CHALLENGED

A man who says he gets on well with everyone but also mentions having considerable difficulties with several people can be helped to be clearer about the discrepancy between what he thinks and feels about relationships and what he says actually happens. Such a challenge is an invitation to explore, understand and act.

DISTORTIONS MAY BE CHALLENGED

When we cannot face things as they really are, we can protect ourselves by distorting them and this is often an indication of our needs. For example, I am afraid of someone and I see them as aloof, although in reality they are a caring person. Or I am myself a stubborn person, but I readily turn this into the virtue of commitment.

One way of helping clients to deal with distortions is to suggest a different 'frame of reference', or way of looking at themselves or their world.

- Life can be seen as a challenge, rather than just pain.
- A mother's care for her son can be experienced as smothering rather than nurturing.
- Intimacy can be rewarding rather than just demanding.
- 'You talk about getting close to people as a burden for you. It takes up your time, people let you down and make unreasonable demands on you. I wonder whether you have experienced any rewards in your friendships?'

EVASIONS MAY BE CHALLENGED

We avoid real issues because they are often painful:

'I did try to give up smoking pot, but I just can't.'

'Can you tell me some of the things you've tried?'

Challenging is a way of pointing out to clients things they would probably prefer to ignore and insisting on facts they would like to leave comfortingly vague. Apathy and passivity can be great harbingers of stress and generate statements such as:

'It's not my fault, things happen to me and I can't do anything about it.'

'I'm ill, so I don't have to think about that.'

The challenge lies in identifying the consequences which flow from these patterns of thought.

Chapter 6 covers in detail the importance of challenging negative patterns of thinking, especially with anxious or depressed clients, particularly their:

- need to be perfect
- perception of their misfortunes as major calamities
- readiness to predict disaster.

Immediacy as challenge

When a client's interpersonal relationships have been affected by their stress problems they can be helped through the use of what Carkhuff (1969a) called 'immediacy' and what Egan (1994: 186) calls 'you–me' talk. This use of direct mutual talk is based on the belief that an important aspect of maintaining an effective relationship can be to talk to each other about how you relate.

Using immediacy is a move by the counsellor to use some dimension of the client–counsellor relationship itself as the focus of challenge. Immediacy takes three forms: personal feedback responses from counsellor to client, relationship immediacy and here-and-now immediacy (Egan, 1998: 180–86).

Personal feedback responses from counsellor to client may be positive challenges which offer support and encouragement, particularly early in the relationship.

Co: Approaching your manager to talk about your work showed a lot of courage.

They may also be more negative in tone and therefore more directly challenging.

Co: I am quite surprised that you didn't send in the application for the job you talked about last week. What happened?

In traditional person-centred counselling responses which involve the personal feedback of the counsellor are generated through the quality of genuineness in the relationship. Rogers himself uses the example of confronting a client with his own persistent feeling of being bored and having difficulty in staying awake during sessions.

> *Rogers:* I don't understand it myself, but when you start talking on about your problems in what seems to be a flat tone of voice, I find myself getting very bored.

This was Rogers' genuine way of not beating about the bush and when his client had recovered from the shock, he was able to say,

> *Client:* You know I think the reason I talk in such an uninteresting way is because I don't think I have ever expected anyone to really hear me.
>
> (Adapted Landreth, 1984: 323; cited in Egan, 1998: 183)

Rogers' confrontation helped the relationship to move forward.

RELATIONSHIP IMMEDIACY

'Let's talk about how we have been relating to each other' is about the counsellor's ability to discuss with the client, not the work in hand, but where they stand in their relationship. This may be because the relationship has become stuck, or it may be as a way of helping the client to take positive learning into other relationships.

> *Co:* You've talked about difficulties in your relationship with your head of department. Let's just look at our relationship. I feel we respect each other and there has been some give and take between us. You've been angry with me sometimes and I've been impatient with you, but we've worked it out. I wonder what our relationship has that is missing in your relationship with your head of department?
>
> *Margaret:* Well, you listen to me and he doesn't. I listen to you, but I don't listen to him at all. I think he's inadequate and he probably knows that.

From talking about her head of department being responsible for everything that is wrong in their relationship, Margaret begins to focus on the contribution she makes to their difficulties.

HERE-AND-NOW IMMEDIACY

'Let's talk about what's going on between you and me, now, as we talk' is about the counsellor's ability to talk about a specific interaction, not the whole relationship. This is something that people in general often avoid and the effects of that omission are cumulative. You feel offended by something your partner says, but say nothing, swallow your feelings and go quiet for a few days. Your partner notices, wonders what's going on, but says nothing. The 'saying nothing' on both sides eventually accumulates until a huge argument over something quite small leaves both of you wondering what it was all about.

> *Co:* I'd like to stop a minute and just look at what is happening now, between you and me.
>
> *Gary:* (sharply) What do you mean?

Co: Well, we started today in quite a lively way and now we seem very subdued. I feel quite tense and wonder if I might have said or done something wrong.

Gary: I don't know.

Co: Gary, is it just me, or do you feel that things are a bit strained between us?

Gary: Well, a little bit maybe.

Co: I have been challenging you quite strongly about your way of thinking about things. How has that affected you?

Gary: It's difficult, sometimes you talk to me as if you are really interested in me and what I'm doing and then you start to boss me around, just like my father, and I really resent that.

Co: Is it the fact that I push you now and then?

Gary: No, if you didn't push me I wouldn't get anywhere, but it's the way you do it sometimes, too strong.

Co: Hm. It sounds as if I am too keen for you to do well. I'll stay more in touch with where you are.

Gary: Yes, but don't stop pushing me altogether because I need your encouragement.

The skills of immediacy are emphasized here because the integrative approach uses stress management strategies and techniques in a directive way. Monitoring the effect of this on individual clients and on the relationship is vital to the effectiveness of this way of working.

Addictive challenging

Some counsellors can become addicted to challenging clients; the adrenalin flow which it generates encourages them to challenge too frequently, which leads to serious problems, including disputes, clients leaving counselling, or retreating into empty talking but not participating. However, lack of courage to state unpalatable truths or to insist upon the discussion of vital but embarrassing or distressing topics can also lead to disastrous consequences and can be seen by clients as a form of betrayal. Passivity by counsellors is experienced by certain clients as a lack of concern. If the people in your life who have cared about you have given you a hard time and you suddenly find yourself with someone who does not engage with you in a lively way, you can legitimately wonder whether or not they care a fig about you.

Challenge to change and motivate

Challenge and reassurance go hand in hand in the work of encouraging people to contemplate change and helping them to achieve it. The first hurdle in promoting change is motivating clients to attempt it. Change is never made without inconvenience, even from good to better, and there may be pain and discomfort in change which are not lessened because the client has chosen it. An explicit recognition of the feelings of reluctance, resistance and hesitancy experienced by many stressed clients may be a helpful place to start the process of motivation.

It is here that the concept of the counsellor as authentic chameleon comes into its own. The transition from an empathic assessment of a client's stress situation to the more active phase where change can actually be envisaged and brought about may be helped by a distinct change in the counsellor's physical posture, choice of language and manner of speech. Leaning forward and speaking more incisively can helpfully signal the traversing of such a transition. Clients who are rendered depressed and apathetic by their stress need a lot of encouragement to take even the first step.

We recognize that some humanistic counsellors will feel reluctant to make any approach which involves giving direct instructions to a client, because it seems to be intrusive and they believe that they do not have the right to 'tell clients how to live their lives'.

If such counsellors wish to use the integrative model they will need to look at their own learning blocks by cognitively considering the place of problem management in helping clients who are in a state of perplexity, confusion and distress (which they desperately want to change), because their own ways of coping do not meet their needs. Another consideration for such counsellors is to recall situations in their own lives in which they were stressed and the effects upon them of understanding but passive friends and of understanding but active ones. In more specific terms a person who says that they feel desperately suicidal receives one kind of support and motivation from someone who conveys 'Well, life is so full of pain and hopelessness for you, it's hard for you to hang on to it.' They receive a different kind of support and motivation from someone who conveys 'Well, life is full of pain for you, nevertheless suicide is a permanent solution to a problem which is temporary and which we can work to change.'

Never is it more crucial to consider the advantages and disadvantages of a decision for change than when that change is from life to death.

Reassurance in our approach is an aspect of a confidence building function which helps people to see that their worst fears are realistically unjustified. This does not mean saying that things will be all right when there is the possibility that they may actually go wrong. It does mean reassuring clients that the steps they are about to take, in the counsellor's experience, give them the best possible chance of making successful changes in their lives.

Inexperienced counsellors often underestimate the degree of anxiety which clients experience, particularly at the start of counselling. A client needs reassuring that they are valued as a person and need not feel ashamed of seeking help; that they are not odd, isolated, blameworthy or sick; and that the stress they are experiencing can be particularly appreciated. Such recognition works to reduce that anxiety which accompanies the decision to come for counselling, which may in itself be an additional source of stress.

CHAPTER 4
Assessment in Integrative Problem-Focused Stress Counselling

The beginning is the most important part of the work.

Plato *The Republic*

In Chapter 2 we gave an overview of the integrative problem-focused approach to stress counselling, and in Chapter 3 we introduced a spectrum of core counselling skills. We now look at the beginning phases of stress counselling, starting with the therapeutic working relationship, then moving on to the important area of assessment and matching the approach to meet individual client needs and expectations. Early, accurate assessment of a client's difficulties and problems helps the counsellor to work in partnership with the client to develop an appropriate therapeutic programme. Our view of stress is that it is manifested to some extent in all the CABB areas and therefore each area needs to be reviewed in the CABB Assessment Profile. However, the extent to which stress makes its presence felt in these areas varies considerably and the profile assessment needs to be tailored to the client rather than being applied as a blanket process. The comprehensive assessment and the subsequent psycho-educational mediation in the client's patterns of stress form the basis of their individual therapeutic work.

THE THERAPEUTIC WORKING RELATIONSHIP

Relationship is the bond that gives vitality, warmth and sustenance to the work between client and counsellor. Without the foundation of the counselling relationship, integrative problem-focused work would be a process of cool reason only, whereas with it, the process is enlivened and infused with the emotional satisfaction and support that make the effort worthwhile. Experienced counsellors of different orientations are in broad agreement that the relationship between client and counsellor is of fundamental importance to the efficacy of the work in which they share. Counselling approaches vary in many respects: counsellor activity and directiveness or non-directiveness; focus on behaviour or on the client's inner world of feelings and attitudes; emphasis on the client's present life or their childhood history; which aspects of a client's current difficulties are looked at, together with the many procedural differences in the work. Yet almost every approach to counselling and therapy recognizes the central place of the relationship in client change. The 'better' the relationship, the more open a client is about feelings and situations, and the more likely they are to explore these openly and to listen to and learn from the counsellor and the counselling experience; that is, the more likely the client is to change.

In person-centred work, the relationship is all, as Mearns and Thorne (1988: 21) emphasize:

> The distinctive feature about the person-centred approach is that it does not just pay lip-service to the importance of the relationship but actually takes that as the aim of the counselling process with every client. In the person-centred approach there is no withdrawal from the relationship and retreat into exercises, interpretation or analysis of the client's behaviour.

Yet Goldstein (1975: 16) a behavioural psychologist suggests that:

> a positive or 'therapeutic' relationship may be defined as feelings of liking, respect and trust by a client toward the helper from whom he [sic] is seeking assistance, combined with similar feelings of liking, respect and trust on the part of the helper toward the client.

The beneficial effect of a positive relationship is not confined to therapeutic work – learning in education depends in part on the teacher–student interaction; how well medication serves its effective purpose is partly a result of the relationship between the person who prescribes the drug and the one who takes it. Caring and respect, love (in one of its many faces), social exchange and affirmation are characteristics of a potent counselling relationship. In times of helplessness, vulnerability and stress, the need for these peculiarly human forms of nourishment is intensified. A person feeling stressed, resourceless, and empty handed in the face of a problem needs and wants connection with someone who combines caring with the knowledge, power and ability to help. Consequently we have built our approach on the foundation of a relationship characterized by positive feelings and interpersonal attitudes held by counsellor and client.

We recognize that there are people in need who have lost the trust in other human beings that makes relationship possible. We have all had anxious clients who display their difficulties in responding mutually in a positive relationship by behaving in ways which are aloof and non-committal, defiantly independent, demanding, clinging or over-intense in their feelings for the relationship or the counsellor. This is the way such clients are and the relationship needs to be tempered to meet them where they are. One of the dangers of a problem-management approach, even in the hands of experienced counsellors, is that problems have a habit of demanding solutions with an irresistible force and counsellors can become 'addicted' to problem solving at the expense of their client and the therapeutic working relationship. Establishing trust and building rapport may happen fairly immediately in the relationship or it may be a longer minefield process of tests and trials by a client. If the relationship is proving to be hard won, it can be a temptation for a counsellor to set aside the hassles it generates and move on to the more exciting work of problem management, with the comforting thought that, after all, this is what the client is really here for. It is neither necesssary nor helpful for us to cast ourselves in the role of a 'representative of reality' before our clients are ready. It is not necessary because clients are, in some part of themselves, well aware of their world and its realities. It is not helpful because by disregarding the insecurity clients feel in our relationship, we alienate ourselves from them and therefore from their willingness and ability to change, without which all our problem-management skills are as dust.

THE RELATIONSHIP AND THE PROBLEM

Relationship cultivates and warms the intelligence, sustains the spirit and carries the client forward in what might otherwise be a cool, detached, rational process. It is what differentiates problem-focused work in counselling from problem solving as a purely intellectual process. When Helen Harris Perlman published her *Social Casework: A Problem Solving Process* in 1957, it was assigned to the library shelves in the University of California at Berkeley in the section marked 'Mathematics'! Perlman (1970: 131) herself comments:

> Problem solving as a casework process is not a manipulation of people or objects or circumstances to bring them from disorganisation to order, from dilemma to resolution. Problem solving is not a series of strategies by which a 'fixer' or arranger moves by the laws of logic and abstract reasoning from some difficulty to its dissolution. Problem solving is not a game by which the person who knows its rules guides and controls the person who is in trouble and moves him [sic] into a marked-out goal called 'home' or 'cure' or 'there now'. It is none of these.

Perlman is describing a social work approach, but there still persists among some counsellors the notion that to focus on problems means some intellectual, logical, rational process through which a problem is attacked, subdued and tidily resolved. The clients of integrative problem-focused counsellors do not leave counselling with a neatly packaged parcel marked QED.

What we are describing is a process, a forward-moving series of transactions between two active people – client and counsellor – in an active environment – the life circumstances in which they are involved. The problem or stressor, meaning the difficulty that is at the centre of concern at any given time, is felt, carried and experienced by the client. It is the client with their own subjective reading of and reaction to their problem who must be their own problem-solver, but relationship is the continuous context within which problem solving takes place. It is not only the emerging product of the mutual efforts of client and counsellor, but is also the catalyst in the shifts and changes in the client's sense of trust, security, self-worth and self-confidence. The supportive rewards of the relationship make it possible to tolerate the frustrations and compromises that problem-focused work involves. Of course the client comes to talk about their problem, but how it is talked about is both the content and the outcome of the relationship.

We consciously focus on stress problems and their resolution in order to educate clients in the use of their own problem-solving skills and abilities. This focus enables clients to become their own decision makers and to cope more competently on their own with the stress problems of everyday living. The support of the counselling relationship is an important factor in this learning process. Living is itself a problem-solving process and this approach aims to improve rather than worsen the systematic rather than disordered ways by which we may live, enhance and enjoy our lives. People who are stressed turn to counselling at a time when their own usual means of solving problems are, for whatever reasons, inadequate, inappropriate or inaccessible to them. Egan's (1994) implicit assumption is that the person's inability to cope alone is due to some absence of:

- motivation to work on the problem in appropriate ways
- capacity to work on the problem in appropriate ways
- opportunity of ways or means to mitigate the problem.

Integrative problem-focused stress counselling involves client and counsellor working together to replace this inability with a considered, active, individual therapeutic programme and this purpose is built into their joint understanding from the beginning.

CLIENT–COUNSELLOR WORKING UNDERSTANDING

We have tried to find a simple, straightforward name to describe the 'contract' between counsellor and client in our integrative approach. The word contract is already used in counselling and is incorporated into the British Association for Counselling's *Code of Ethics and Practice for Counsellors* (BAC 1998, see p. 268). Many aspects of everyday life are now characterized by 'charters' of various kinds which set out the aims and standards which those who issue them will attempt to achieve, in relation to their clients or consumers. We have charters for NHS patients and users of gas and electricity, for example. Many places of work now have written 'mission statements'. What all these contracts, charters and mission statements seek to do is to make explicit provisions and circumstances which had formerly been implicit. These forms of agreement have formal and legal connotations which, although valid, do not quite suit the joint enterprise we are describing in our integrative work. Those counsellors who have anxieties about litigious outcomes from counselling may wish to make formal written contracts with their clients. There are certainly eminently sensible and respectful reasons to afford clients a clear statement of what they and their counsellors will act together to achieve in the form of a client–counsellor working understanding. We have chosen the word 'understanding' because it describes exactly what both client and counsellor need to attain for integrative problem-focused stress counselling to be effective.

The understanding between client and counsellor has traditionally been an implicit one, with clients being expected to accept what the counsellor has to offer without necessarily understanding what it was. This has meant that the expectations of clients may differ from those of their counsellor without either being aware of the fact. Increasingly professionals are being expected to discuss the fundamentals of their work in the form of a 'contract' with clients, as we have seen in the adoption of charters and the BAC *Code of Ethics for Counsellors* (see p. 268).

The integrative problem-focused working understanding may be a written statement which forms part of or accompanies a written 'contract' between client and counsellor or it may be agreed in a structured, verbal agreement. Much will depend upon the setting and circumstances of the work and the needs of the client and counsellor. Egan (1998: 55) reminds us that 'if helping is to be a collaborative venture then both parties must understand what their responsibilities are' (see Appendix 1).

Outline of client–counsellor understanding

We offer one outline of such an understanding, adapted from Egan's (1994: 62–5) client–helper working charter.

The aims of client–counsellor working understanding in the integrative stress counselling model are:

- to help clients to be
  – more informed about the process
  – more collaborative in the process
  – more pro-active in managing their problems.
- to help clients by
  – reducing their initial anxiety and reluctance
  – providing a sense of direction
  – enhancing their freedom of choice.

Our working understanding depends upon certain shared information and the counsellor's contribution includes the following:

- brief overview of the integrative stress model
- brief overview of the counselling process
  – flexibility of the process
  – how the relationship is to be structured
  – kinds of responsibilities clients and counsellors have
  – procedural issues
  – techniques to be used
  – how it will help in the long run.

We are not recommending academic lectures, but one sentence descriptions or possibly a simple handout of the model. Whether the information is verbal or written it is important that it:

- does not overwhelm the client with distracting detail
- does not take the place of establishing the therapeutic working relationship
- is not used with highly distressed clients as a means of containing their anxiety or distress rather than acknowledging and understanding it.

If stressed clients are to be collaborators they need an outline map of their counselling journey and some indication of their destination (Egan, 1994).

Brief overviews, as Egan (1994: 62) also suggests, can include descriptions as short as:

'We begin by getting a picture of what is happening in your life to make you feel stressed.'

'Generally people seem to get stressed when the demands on them are greater than the resources they feel they have available to cope. Does that fit your particular situation?'

'Some of the things that affect how stressed we become include the ways in which we think and feel about our life and the people in it, our general health and the ways we behave. We can look at these areas of your life to see how you might change them.'

'In counselling everything we do should help you to manage the demands on yourself better, so that you feel less stressed.'

'Stress counselling isn't just about talking but about doing things differently. If people are to manage their stress they usually have to act differently. I'd like to help you to find ways to do that, but I can't do it for you.'

'I want to understand the things that make you stressed. As you tell me about them we will both come to understand them more clearly and be in a better position to do something about them.'

'If I see you trying to avoid doing something which I think might help you feel less stressed, I will tell you about it, but I won't try to force you to do anything.'

Summary

The focus of integrative problem-focused stress counselling is initially on the person of the client, for the purpose of helping them to reveal themselves to themselves, as it were, and to their counsellor by talking about their currently recognized stress. This includes their feelings about it, the wishes and hopes they bring for its resolution and their reactions to the present possibilities. This first help is to enable the client to want and to use the ways and means of dealing with stress which are offered by an integrative counsellor. It is when the person has been fully acknowledged that the problems and their involvement in them can begin to be unfolded and examined.

ASSESSMENT

Our integrative model clearly has a problem-focused assessment structure, but it is a client-centred process in that the counsellor uses their ability to understand clients, to spot what is happening with them, to see what they do not see and yet need to see, to make sense of their variable and sometimes chaotic stressed behaviour and to help them to make sense of it. Egan (1998: 116) suggests that assessment is a form of 'reality testing listening' in which counsellors as they hear the client's story also hear more than the client's point of view. He quotes the example of a client who describes a deep conviction that he is 'not an alcoholic' whilst at the same time the counsellor notices the trembling hand, smells the alcohol-laden breath and hears the desperate tone of voice.

The purpose of the empathic and active listening of assessment is not to place the client in a diagnostic category, but to enable the counsellor to be open to information and understanding in an interplay between assessment and intervention that will enable them to help the client.

Assessment is part of all stages of the integrative problem-focused stress counselling model, nevertheless some initial assessment of the seriousness of the client's concerns is called for.

ASSESSMENT PROCEDURES

The assessment procedures used in the integrative model are similar to those used in some forms of structured therapy. We have emphasized the central function of the therapeutic working relationship in dealing effectively with stress and this applies from the beginning to the end of counselling. However, we also emphasize that this is a therapeutic *working* relationship, that the work is active and pragmatic and also begins right at the beginning of counselling with good assessment. It follows therefore that in the initial counselling phase in addition to establishing a good therapeutic alliance, an integrative problem-focused counsellor will be concerned with assessing presenting problems.

The parallel process of keeping the client at the centre while retaining a working focus on their stress problems is the essence of our approach.

Present-ing problems and focus on the present

We need to state clearly that in our model present-ing problems tend to be taken at face value. This is in contrast to those counselling approaches in which 'presenting' problems are seen as an acceptable and safe way for a client to approach a counsellor without revealing too much of themselves too quickly. By using a 'presenting' problem the client has the option of withdrawing from counselling when their presenting problem has received attention, or remaining to work on other things if they feel safe enough to do so. Experienced counsellors will be familiar with the established definition of a 'presenting' problem and know its place in counselling work.

The place of the past in integrative work

Because we are dealing with problems of stress which 'present' themselves in all the CABB areas of a client's life, we use the assessment to focus on the problems which the client brings, and refer to them as present-ing problems, with the focus on the present, rather than the past. We consider that 'how' the past is discussed is more important than whether or not to discuss it. As Egan (1998: 128) states:

If the past can add clarity to current experiences, behaviours and emotions, provide clues as to how self-defeating thinking and behaving can be changed now, let it be discussed. However, if the past becomes the principal focus of the client's exploration, helping is likely to lose the name of action.

We recommend that counsellors help clients to review the past, learn from it and use the learning as a basis for change in the future. We talk about the past to make sense of the present, but we do not emphasize it. An adult client who recently started having panic attacks while travelling on trains will not be asked questions about her or his childhood unless they themselves believe that the origins of their problem stem from childhood. A potentially dangerous logic can support discussions of the past in which the person becomes trapped in a circular argument: 'I am what I am because of my past, since I cannot change my past, how can you expect me to change myself?' It is not helpful to talk about the past and be cast under its spell; it is helpful to talk about the past to be liberated from it and to use it to understand the present and plan for the future (Egan, 1998: 128).

Client expectations

An area to be explored early on in the work is that of the client's expectations of counselling and his or her beliefs about their ideal counsellor. There are confused ideas in circulation about counselling and many clients lack both experience and accurate knowledge of what to expect. 'What are this person's expectations of counselling?' is one of the counsellor's first concerns. In our experience, some clients expect that counselling should be short term and they do not wish to remain in counselling for very long. Typically they want help with their most pressing problem(s) and once these are resolved they want to leave therapy. Others believe that counselling should last longer and expect to remain in therapy for perhaps two years. In Britain the rate of attrition (early ending) in therapy is generally high with clients dropping out of most forms of therapy within a few sessions (Palmer, 1997b).

To mitigate against an early ending to therapy arising from misunderstandings, we believe that it is important for the counsellor to adjust their therapeutic approach and interpersonal style to meet the client's expectations, personality and therapeutic needs. To do this it is necessary to:

- know what the expectations are
- have some working understanding of personality differences
- assess the client's problems and therapeutic needs.

In developing a programme which is adaptive to a particular client's personality and needs counsellors may find it helpful to:

1. Decide whether the client prefers a formal or informal relationship (which will depend to some extent on their personality).
2. Monitor the client's response to directive and non-directive intervention from the counsellor.

3. Discover how the client responds to the counsellor's use of humour (because humour may be is used later in the model).
4. Establish how the client responds to counsellor self-disclosure (this is also used in the integrative model).
5. Subsequently match counsellor behaviour with client expectations.
6. Consider whether or not the environment is appropriate for the client and alter if necessary (and possible); for example, formal office surroundings may be indicated or contra-indicated for certain clients.
7. Consider the counsellor's sartorial influence – what is the effect of the counsellor's clothes on particular clients? For example, casual wear may be considered inappropriate when counselling senior managers; suits may be intimidating to young clients who may associate them with intimidating authority figures; 'mini' mini skirts may not help certain clients to keep their mind on their work.

We are not suggesting that counsellors have a 'stage wardrobe' but that they take account of the effect they have on individual clients (adapted from Palmer and Dryden, 1995: 24).

Additional considerations

We have also found it useful in the initial counselling phase to consider additional areas which we outline below. It is important to emphasize that this information is derived from what the client communicates during the early sessions; it is a reminder list for the counsellor, not a list of compulsory questions to be checked off.

This is an integrative approach to stress counselling which structures counselling sessions around information about the client's current life. We want to point up a danger of our 'aide memoire' lists. In the hands of unskilled counsellors, these can become merely an interrogatory approach liable to generate hostility and defensiveness in clients because it becomes too rigid to allow them to tell their story in their own way. Having expressed our reservation, we recommend early consideration of the following areas:

1. Has the client any previous experience of counselling, therapy or relevant stress training? If yes, what was the outcome? Was it a positive, negative or neutral experience and why?
2. Why is the client seeking counselling now and not last month or last year?
3. What are the persisting stress problems and what seems to precipitate and exacerbate them?
4. What appear to be the important prior factors – those which have led up to the stress problems?
5. What or who seems to be maintaining the client's visible and hidden stress problems?
6. What are some of the client's positive strengths and attributes?
7. Are there signs of physical illness or any disturbed motor activity?
8. Are there signs of psychosis?
9. Is there evidence of depression, suicidal or even homicidal tendencies?

10. Are there any indications as to whether it would be in the client's best interests to be seen individually, as part of couple work, in a family unit or in a group?
11. Can a mutually satisfying relationship ensue or should the client be referred elsewhere for help.

(Adapted Lazarus, 1987; adapted Palmer and Dryden, 1995: 19)

At this initial stage the counsellor is gathering relevant information and assessing whether or not counselling would help this particular client. We have found it useful to discuss any previous experience of counselling with clients. The problems they have encountered and the things they found helpful previously can guide the integrative counsellor in adopting a suitable interpersonal style and working with the client to develop a therapeutic programme.

As we have suggested in the client–counsellor working understanding, a clear explanation of the ways in which the integrative stress approach differs from others and an account of how it can help a particular person are important, especially if the client has had a previous negative experience of counselling. A client who shows signs of serious health problems or psychosis, which are not supported by medical resources, may, or may not, welcome a judicious referral to a general practitioner or a source of psychiatric help. In some cases other forms of help such as group counselling, stress management training, family or couple therapy may be more appropriate (see Chapter 9). These issues may be discussed during the initial counselling session or at a later date, if and when an alternative becomes an obvious option of choice. If there is a mismatch between a particular counsellor and client, perhaps in the area of personality (see Chapter 10), which may lead to an unproductive relationship, the client may be better helped by referral to a more suitably matched counsellor. For example, some clients believe that they can only relate to their 'confidante' or counsellor if he or she is of a specific gender, or within a certain age range; it will help to have this belief out in the open.

CABB ASSESSMENT PROFILE

Client assessment is underpinned by our integrative–transactional model of stress. Therefore unless a client is in an immediate crisis, or feeling suicidal, an assessment of the four CABB areas is usually interwoven with the building of the therapeutic working relationship. However, if the counsellor is working in a time-limited setting, assessment may need to be more restricted. The information in the CABB profile may be obtained gradually over a period of time; it is neither necessary, nor desirable to pack the first interview with enquiries about all four different modes. Some of the key areas are presented in the list below. We emphasize that these are intended as a guide for the counsellor, not a rigid template or a game of twenty questions. Depending upon the problem(s) the client presents, different CABB areas can be explored. The purpose of the assessment is to present the person of the client, and the relationships and circumstances of their life, which contribute to their stress but may also be a resource for reducing it. Thus we are trying to see and understand our client through the following aspects: cognition helps to provide a picture of the person as a thinking, believing, imagining human being; affect helps to provide a picture of the person as an emotionally aware human being; biology/physiology helps to provide a picture of the person in sickness and in health; and behaviour helps to provide a picture of the person as an active, interactive and social human being.

Cognition and imagery:
What are your main wants, wishes, desires and preferences?
What are your main musts, shoulds, oughts, have/got to's?
In what situations do you say something similar to, 'I can't stand it,' 'It's awful/ horrible/terrible.'
Do you ever call yourself or somebody else, 'completely useless' (or worthless/ stupid)?
What are the beliefs you consider are important?
What are the main values you believe are important?
In key areas of your life, what basic philosophy do you hold?
What perfectionist beliefs do you hold?
If you could use one word to describe your main current problem, what would it be?
What are your major intellectual interests?
What are your hobbies/interests?
What expectations of others do you have?
What expectations do you think significant others have of you?
What expectations do you think society has of you?
Which people have been important in your life?
Which people are now important in your life?
Who has been the most significant person in your life, (and why)?
Who has said something to you that had/has a considerable effect on your outlook?
Can you describe your self-image (or body-image)?
What images do you have that you like?
What images do you have that you dislike?
When you have these negative images, do you feel less or more anxious (or depressed, or guilty)?
Can you describe any recurrent dreams or nightmares you may have?
Can you describe any pleasant/unpleasant flashbacks (or memories) you may have?
Can you picture any scene that you find relaxing?
What do you picture yourself doing in the immediate future?
In moments of solitude, do you picture any particular event from your past or have any fantasy about your future?
What do you picture yourself doing in two years (and/or five years, ten years, twenty years and/or fifty years) time?
How do your beliefs, attitudes and images affect your emotions (or behaviour, or health, or sensations, or relationships)?

Affect (emotions):
What do you get anxious about?
What do you get angry about?

What do you cry about?
What do you laugh about?
What do you get depressed about?
What do you feel sad about?
What makes you happy?
What do you feel guilty about?
What do you feel hurt about?
What do you get envious about?
What do you feel jealous about?
How do the significant people in your life affect your moods?
Do you persistently have recurring negative emotions?
How do your emotions affect your health (or behaviour, or thoughts, or images, or sensations, or relationships)?

Biology/physiology (health):
What are your main concerns about your health?
Are you on medication? (If so, what type of medication.)
Do you take drugs?
Have you undergone major surgery?
Do you smoke? (If so, how many a day.)
Do you receive adequate sleep?
Are you experiencing sleeping difficulties?
How much alcohol do you drink in a week?
Can you describe your diet?
Have you tried to lose (or gain) weight? (Were you successful.)
What type of exercise, if any, do you do?
Have significant others set you a good/poor health-related role model?
How do the significant people in your life affect your health?
Are you interested in improving your general health?
Do you believe that if you are taking regular exercise and eating a balanced diet you will feel better about yourself?
What do you like to see? What do dislike seeing?
What do you like to taste? What do you dislike tasting?
What do you like to hear? What do you dislike hearing?
What do you like to touch? What do you dislike touching?
What do you like to smell? What do you dislike smelling?
What unpleasant sensations do you suffer from, if any (e.g. tension, tremors, light-headedness, pains)?
How do you feel emotionally about any of your sensations (e.g. do you become anxious about your pain)?
How do your general health and physical sensations affect your behaviour (or relationships, or thoughts, or images)

Behaviour (actions and relationships):
What would you like to start or stop doing?
What is preventing you from doing things that you want to do?
What do you avoid doing?

When do you procrastinate?
Do you procrastinate because you are afraid of failing?
Do you have any phobias? (If so what are you phobic about.)
What behaviours are preventing you from being happy?
Are the significant people in your life doing things you would like to do?
What skills would you like to develop further?
How assertive (or passive, or aggressive) are you?
When are you most likely to be assertive (or passive, or aggressive)?
What social situations do you avoid (and/or prefer)?
To what extent are you either a loner or highly gregarious?
How do the significant people in your life affect your behaviour?
How does your behaviour affect your relationships (or emotions, or thoughts, or images, or health, or sensations)?
How does your behaviour affect your mood (or thoughts, or images, or health, or sensations)?

(Based on Lazarus, 1981; Lazarus and Lazarus, 1991;
Palmer and Dryden, 1995; Palmer, 1997b)

CABB assessment need not be a protracted process and the time it takes will depend on the client, their problems and whether or not they are ready and able to work. With experience in using the model, the counsellor will become more adept at choosing which areas to consider at which time and more skilful in integrating the assessment and the development of a good therapeutic working relationship. This means that when a client mentions feelings of sadness, for example, the counsellor might empathically ask 'What is it that you get sad about?' It is important to both acknowledge the sadness and, in this approach, to discover its source. Similarly a client who says that they do not consider good health to be important may be asked about significant people in their lives who may be the source of their lack of interest in health.

The integrative counsellor directs the client's attention to the CABB areas but in a flexible way which integrates the assessment into the relationship.

The purpose of the CABB assessment profile is to provide client and counsellor with a focused analysis of identified problems which appear to contribute to the client's levels of stress. This serves as a working hypothesis which can be revised or modified as counselling proceeds and new information arises. Sometimes the CABB profile can be used as a counsellor *aide-mémoire* only; for example, to prevent overwhelming a depressed client, or someone who has dyslexia. A simple profile can be developed with a client on a whiteboard during counselling, while the counsellor develops a more in-depth version for their own use. Circumstances alter cases and it is important not to add to a client's stress in a counter-productive way.

Client CABB assessment

Some clients are more interested in the assessment process than others and there are those who want to make their own profile, outside the counselling session, as a homework task. We encourage this interest through a written handout (Box 4.1) for

Box 4.1 *Personal CABB stress assessment profile*

C *Cognition and imagery:*
Which thoughts, ideas, values, opinions and attitudes seem to contribute to your stress or get in the way of your happiness.

Make a list of unhelpful things you tell yourself (e.g. 'I'm useless and worthless.' 'I must always do a perfect job.' 'People should treat me fairly.')

Do you have any memories of sound or speaking that you keep on hearing and that are a problem (e.g. sad music etc.)

Note down how these thoughts and ideas influence your feelings, behaviour and physical well-being.

Write down any recurring dreams or vivid memories which bother you. Include any negative features about your self-image (the way you see yourself). We are looking for 'pictures' or vivid scenes from your past, present or future, that may trouble you. If your images arouse any significant actions, feeling or sensations, add these to your notes on feelings, behaviour and physical well-being.

A *Affect (emotions):*
This refers to emotions, moods and strong feelings. Which emotions do you experience most often? Write down your unwanted emotions (e.g. anger, anxiety, depression, guilt, shame, embarrassment etc.)

Note under behaviour what you tend to do when you feel a certain way (e.g. avoid friends when feeling depressed).

B *Biology/physiology (health):*
Write down any health and medical concerns and illnesses you have or have had. Include whether you want to improve your diet, lose or gain weight, or take more exercise, or stop smoking or reduce caffeine/alcohol intake.

Make a list of all drugs that you are taking, whether prescribed by a doctor or not.

Seeing, hearing, touching, tasting and smelling are our five basic senses. Make a list of any negative sensations which apply to you (e.g. blushing, butterflies in the stomach, dizziness, pain, tension, sweating). If any of these sensations cause you to feel or act in certain ways, put them down under feeling (affect) or behaviour.

B *Behaviour (actions and relationships):*
Behaviour refers mainly to the things you do which you can observe, such as habits, gestures, actions, responses and reactions.

Write down those behaviours you would like to increase and those you would like to decrease.

What would you like to stop doing?

What would you like to start doing?

Write down any difficulties with other people (e.g. friends, relatives, colleagues at work, a lover, acquaintances etc.) which bother you.

Concerns you have about the way people treat you or how you treat them can be written here.

Check through the items you have written under thoughts, imagery, feelings, physical sensations and behaviour to see if you can work out how each of these influences and is influenced by your interpersonal relationships.

Source: based on Palmer and Dryden (1995: 26–7)

two reasons: first, that the client's profile can usefully be compared with that of the counsellor; and second, that it helps the client to accept homework as an integral part of the counselling process.

Integrating client and counsellor CABB profile information

Traditional assessment procedures using verbal dialogue do not necessarily give sufficient specific information to enable the client and counsellor to negotiate a therapeutic programme which will deal with the client's stress. The additional information provided by those clients who are interested in completing their own stress profile, as a homework assignment, can usefully be integrated with the information gained by the counsellor during the sessions.

From what the client says in telling the story of their stress and in response to the more structured enquiries of the CABB assessment, we begin to get a picture of what is happening in four major areas of a client's life to contribute to their stress.

WHAT IS THE PERSON THINKING?

Stressed people do find themselves falling into errors of thinking and negative imagery, as we saw in the example which opens Chapter 1. These ways of thinking actually increase their stress levels and often reinforce each other. When that happens they need attention.

WHAT IS THE PERSON FEELING?

Clients are often unsure how to define different emotions and have difficulty in exploring and expressing them. It is not just the feelings themselves, but all the issues involved with them – the links between emotion, thoughts, behaviour and the client's health which provide insight into the causes of their stress.

HOW IS THE PERSON'S HEALTH?

We have frequently noticed that clients may not initially want to work to improve their health. Doing so seems to be another intolerable burden to add to their already stressed life. Since stress can have a life-threatening aspect, health is one of our important considerations and we keep it under review throughout counselling. However, as clients learn to increase their tolerance of frustration through the integrated approach, they do gradually come to see giving up smoking, for example, as less of an ordeal and may choose to build a behavioural stop-smoking programme into their therapeutic work.

WHAT DOES THE PERSON ACTUALLY DO?

The things we do or avoid doing when we are stressed often become self-defeating. Since problems are not always easy to recognize and can be stressful, we have a tendency to avoid them to protect ourselves from anxiety and threat. However, having done this we are left with the negative consequences of the unsolved problem in the form of emotional distress, or perhaps an inability to work effectively, or difficulties in our relationships. It is then all too easy to label this consequence as 'the problem' without recognizing what the real or underlying problem is. We aim to focus on disabling stress behaviour as a means of identifying fundamental problems and enabling clients to cope with them effectively.

CABB PROFILE AND ACTION PLAN

If clients are to make changes in their lives the CABB profile has to be combined with a therapeutic action programme which will include psychological, physiological and behavioural ways of managing, reducing or, in some cases, eliminating their stress.

Psychological actions focus on how a person perceives a situation or life event. Some people magnify the importance of stress in their lives and manage to elevate what others see as molehills, into mountains. Sometimes high expectations produce additional pressures and stress when a person's work is less than perfect. Psychological action enables people to assess situations more realistically and change their responses to potentially stressful situations through the use of a variety of thinking and imagery skills.

Physiological actions focus on the reduction of the physical effects of stress and may include relaxation, meditation, exercise, diet, behavioural and self-help programmes.

Behavioural actions focus on ways of helping to change a situation, or, better still, prevent a stressful situation from happening in the first place. Such action may include assertion, time management and changing thinking patterns. (The skills associated with the integrative problem-focused counselling action plans are explained in chapters 5, 6 and 7.).

Table 4.1 gives an example of a CABB profile and overall action plan for Tom.

The overall therapeutic plan can appear to be a creator of stress when seen in its entirety, but it is put into practice in a step-by-step approach to the problems and challenges. We emphasize that the steps need to be client-sized for it is the client's feet that have to walk in these particular shoes and they need to be hand-crafted to their personal last.

In this example both the five-star model and the seven-step problem-solving model were recommended to help Tom to deal with his work-place problems. Additional skills such as relaxation were included to aid him in this process. It was important that he also decided to work on his biology mode by stopping smoking and reducing his weight.

Table 4.1 *Tom's CABB assessment profile and action plan*

Assessment mode	Stress problem area	Therapeutic action plan
Cognition	I must not arrive late I must perform well If I fail then I'm a total failure Failure would be awful Low frustration beliefs, e.g. 'I can't stand it.'	Examining and dispute self-defeating beliefs Use five-star (ABCDE) problem-solving forms
Imagery	Pictures failing at tasks	Coping imagery
Affect	Anxiety Depression	Dispute self-defeating and problem-interfering beliefs
	Anger	Self-calming statements and breathing exercises
Biology	Smokes 20 cigarettes a day	Behavioural stop-smoking programme – self-hypnosis tape
	Tension in shoulders and neck	Neck self-massage
	Frequent migraine	Relaxation technique Biofeedback Modify stress-inducing beliefs Check diet; medical referral
	Lack of exercise	Medical referral for permission to start exercise programme
	Overweight	Suitable exercise and nutritional programme; examine beliefs
Behaviour	Procrastinates	Challenge problem-interfering beliefs and then focus on seven-step problem-solving model
	Overprepares	Discuss 'pros' and 'cons' of over-preparing
	Avoids giving presentations	Challenge problem-interfering beliefs, model appropriate presentation skills, use seven-step problem-solving model
	Spends too much money	Discuss financial management skills and displacement shopping
	Relationships:	
	Passive-aggressive in relationships	Assertion training
	Most 'friends' are work colleagues	Discuss 'pros' and 'cons'

CHAPTER 5

A Problem Management Approach to Stress Counselling

If therapy is to end properly, it must begin properly – by negotiating a solvable problem.

Haley (1976: 9: cited in Egan 1998: 160)

We have chosen to integrate problem management into our model because this is a way of helping clients who have problems which are amenable to a practical solution and those who have problems which distress them emotionally. This makes it ideally suited to stress counselling and in the Chapter 2 overview we outline the seven-step problem-management process that is used to help clients develop a structured approach to their stress problems. Through this step-by-step process, clients can be helped to discover effective remedies or coping responses upon which they can act. These responses may include attempts to change the stressful situation and/or their own personal reactions to it and may be described in cognitive behavioural terms as their 'coping performance', or in more humanistic terms as 'effective action for change'.

In this chapter we will also show how and when we integrate the five-star framework for emotional problem solving (see Chapter 6), where necessary. The case study of Jane is used to illustrate this integration.

SIMPLE FRAMEWORK

Wasik (1984) and Palmer (1997c) offer a simple framework of questions which can help clients to understand the working of the seven-step problem-management model without too much difficulty.

Step	Questions/action
1 Identify the problem	What is my concern?
2 Select realistic goals	What outcomes do I want?
3 Explore options	How can I reach these goals?

4	Consider consequences	What might happen? Weigh up the pros and cons
5	Make decisions	What is the most feasible solution?
6	Take agreed action	Plan step by step. Now do it!
7	Evaluate	Did it work? How successful was it? What can be learnt?

This simple framework is one way of introducing a client to the steps of the model and can act as a lead in to illustrate the way it might work in practice.

CASE STUDY: JANE

Jane is 38 years old and a newly appointed deputy head of a comprehensive school. Hers was an internal appointment: she was formerly head of the English department and previously had pastoral experience as a head of year in another school. Jane is married with two children: Dan, aged 5, and Jodie, fifteen months old. Jane has been asked by her headteacher to make a presentation to the school governors to explain the use of the 'value-added' factor in considering the examination results of students during the previous summer.

Jane and her counsellor have done an initial CABB Profile, which is reproduced below.

Initial CABB profile for Jane
Jane's present-ing problem:
Making a perfect presentation to the governors of her school on the value-added factor in assessing examination results.

Cognitions: What do you think?
- It's so awful
- I must do a perfect presentation
- I can't stand it
- I'm a failure
- Image of school governors looking bored.

Affect: What do you feel?
- Very anxious
- Panicky
- Guilty.

Biology: What happens to your body and health?
- Tensions in neck
- Difficulty with breathing
- Butterflies in stomach
- Headaches
- Insomnia.

Behaviour: What do you do or avoid?
- Avoid or get out of the situation by being ill
- Passive/aggressive at work
- Put off doing things (procrastination)
- Clean the house repeatedly.

The counsellor is now going to introduce Jane to the idea of dealing with her stress in a problem-management way.

Co:	We have done a CABB assessment together which helps us to understand some of the things that you get stressed about. I'd like to introduce you to a way of managing stress problems which takes each of them one step at a time. Do you feel ready to do that?
Jane:	Yes, I'd really like to get started.
Co:	Okay. Each step can be looked at by asking yourself one question. If we go through the questions I think you'll understand the way it works. Ready?
Jane:	I think so.
Co:	We begin by asking for a particular concern that you want help with. Will you choose one as an example?
Jane:	I'm really worried about giving this presentation to the board of governors at school. I've never done this before and I'm so anxious I'm sure to make a mess of it.
Co:	Right. What do you want to happen about this presentation?
Jane:	I must do a perfect presentation because otherwise the governors will think I'm useless.
Co:	So you want to do the best presentation you can. Let's now ask what you think you can do to make that possible.
Jane:	Well, I don't know really, I just feel so anxious, I can't think straight . . .
Co:	It's important then to help you to feel less anxious so that you can think more clearly about things.
Jane:	Definitely.
Co:	So one alternative is to help you relax. We can do that. What other things might you do about the presentation?
Jane:	Well I feel so anxious and my stomach is so upset. I just panic so much when I think about it. I might not be well enough to do it at all.
Co:	Yes, if we work to help you feel less anxious and help with your feelings of panic what else might you do about the presentation?
Jane:	Well, if I really didn't feel so anxious, I could start to plan it and get some ideas down on paper. Perhaps I would have time for that if I were off sick.
Co:	So the possibilities we've thought about so far seem to be to work on your panic and to help you feel less anxious or for you to take time off work because you feel too stressed to go on and that might give you time to plan your presentation. Have I got that right?
Jane:	Yes, that's the way I see it.
Co:	Can we now ask a question about the consequences of each of those alternatives. What might happen if you felt so stressed you had to be off sick?
Jane:	Well, I would feel relieved not to have all the pressure of work, but I think I would get so worried that everything was piling up there that I would get more anxious

and would have that as well as the presentation to worry about. I couldn't cope with that.

Co: So you think that you would feel more stressed about the thought of work piling up and that would stop you using the time to prepare your presentation, which would add to your pressures. What might happen if we were able to reduce your anxiety, to help you feel more relaxed, less panicky?

Jane: If it really worked, I wouldn't need to take time off school because I wouldn't feel so ill all the time.

Co: Okay. So which alternative would you choose?

Jane: I'll see if you can help me to feel less panicky.

Co: You want us to work together on your feelings of panic. When you've made a choice the next step is to act on it and the final question will be did it work?

Jane: And if not, why not?

Co: Absolutely. That was a run through of the framework we work with. You seem to have chosen a very immediate problem as your example. Shall we go back to the beginning and take each step more slowly?

Notice that in this example Jane described a number of thoughts or beliefs which disabled her from dealing with her problem (called problem-interfering beliefs), such as 'I must do a perfect presentation because otherwise the governors will think I'm useless.' Therefore the counsellor may decide at this point to focus on challenging these beliefs, which are self-defeating for Jane and induce her stress, before returning to the seven-step problem-management model.

RAPID PROBLEM SOLVING

As clients become more familiar with the problem-management steps we have sometimes found it helpful to introduce them to D'Zurilla's (1986) Rapid Problem Solving Model (see Chapter 9). Clients can use this as an *aide-mémoire* or prompt either between counselling sessions or once counselling is finished. Problem situations occur unexpectedly in all our lives and these are, by their nature, occasions when we do not have the time for the luxury of the careful, deliberate thought and support which counselling sessions offer. The ability to solve a problem and act under time constraints is a versatile and effective stress-reducing skill.

Undertaking a CABB assessment profile may provide a clear picture of what it is about a client and their life which has led that person to seek stress counselling help. When this happens their problems have already been identified and step one of the problem-management model has been integrated into the assessment. However, even after an assessment, the real problems may be far from clear and client and counsellor can helpfully turn to the simple agenda of the seven steps of problem management.

STEP ONE: IDENTIFY THE PROBLEM

The desired outcome of the first step is for client and counsellor to have a clear understanding of:

- the range of the client's problems
- the key people and issues involved
- the relative importance of the interconnected issues.

We cover some of the difficulties which accompany this stage in our outline of the model in Chapter 2. A further limitation on our capacity to identify problems clearly comes from the way our conscious mind works. It has been suggested by Levine (1986) that in the process of solving problems our conscious mind does three things:

- it receives information from our internal and external environment and interprets it
- it remembers information when we need it (or it does not!)
- it combines this information, adding and subtracting points to help us to understand situations and issues.

However, some of us have more difficulties than others in doing all three of these things at the same time, especially when there is a lot of information involved, and/ or when it is complex information. Our effort to remember the important information involved in a problem sometimes gets in the way of our efforts to combine different parts of that information in order to understand the problem.

Underlying principles of help

There are three underlying principles which we use to help us to sharpen up the ability of our minds in the service of understanding and managing stress problems. These consist of externalizing, visualizing and simplifying information (D'Zurilla, 1986).

EXTERNALIZING

Externalizing is the process of displaying information in an external and visual form whenever possible in order to relieve our mind of the need to re-remember, thus freeing it to concentrate on the more critical activities of interpreting and evaluating. In practice this introduces into counselling sessions the use of a whiteboard, flip chart or notepad on which to record:

- information about the problem situation
- diagrams to illustrate relationships between different aspects of the problem situation.
- alternative solutions and their consequences.

Client and/or counsellor may be the 'scribe' in externalizing and because the details are displayed in a visual way, both are enabled to share the same information.

VISUALIZING

Visualizing should not be confused with the written, that is, a visual presentation of information which is used in externalizing. In visualizing the emphasis is on a different kind of visual presentation and imagery. Visualizing is a powerful medium used quite extensively in different forms of humanistic counselling. We use it to rehearse alternative solutions, using role-play, or in the real problem situation. It is also employed to help clients to free their imagination to visualize situations in their minds as a way of testing or rehearsing alternative ways of managing their stress. Visualizing helps us to remember and understand the logic and relationships between different pieces of information and to describe situations more accurately and often in more depth.

SIMPLIFYING

Clearly a complex problem becomes more manageable if it is broken down into subordinate parts, or sub-problems. It also helps if we focus only on the most relevant information and do not give every aspect the same weighting. Likewise vague, complex or abstract ideas become clearer and easier to understand when they are translated into terms which are simple, specific and more concrete. This is what simplifying is about.

Clearer information or relationship barrier?

There will be those counsellors who will balk at the idea of introducing cognitive skills or pen and paper and also writing, mapping and charting into counselling sessions. Their objections may centre round the belief that to do so will erect a barrier between themselves and their client, thus interfering with the quality and healing nature of the therapeutic relationship. This is a historically valid objection which needs to be acknowledged. However, this objection needs to be balanced against the proven efficacy of putting the three underlying principles of externalizing, visualizing and simplifying into practice in the service of helping clients to manage their debilitating stress. Whether or not the use of cognitive skills and visual aids such as notepads or flip charts becomes a barrier between client and counsellor depends largely on the relationship skills of the counsellor and their ability to put the three underlying principles into practice in an efficient and sensitive way. These in turn will be affected by the personalities of client and counsellor and by their attitudes to approaching such integrative problem-focused stress counselling.

SKILLS IN IDENTIFYING PROBLEMS

Stress mapping

Stephen Palmer's (1990a) stress mapping is a visual technique which gives a clear understanding of the effects of interpersonal and environmental factors on a client's stress, particularly when it arises from an especially complex situation. This way of identifying problems places the client in the centre of a diagram of a specific aspect of their own life – perhaps a work setting, or a relationship. The diagram is then developed to represent the levels of stress which the client believes are generated by other people or by practical situations in that setting, each of which

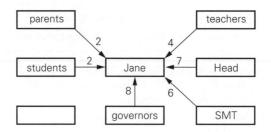

Figure 5.1 *Jane's initial stress map*

is written into a different box. Other aspects of stress such as external demands – new computers at work – or the internal demands clients place on themselves – 'I must do well' – are also displayed on the stress map in relation to the client. When the client has completed the boxes, they are asked to rate the amount of stress each potential stressor can cause them weighted on a scale of 1 to 10, where 10 represents high levels of stress. They then put their score next to the appropriate stressor. A further helpful use of the stress map is for clients to ask themselves how much stress they cause the other people on their map and to note these scores on the diagram. This helps clients to acknowledge their contribution to a stress system.

Example of stress mapping

The CABB assessment profile of Jane, our 38-year-old, newly appointed deputy head, shows that she has been suffering from stress-related disorders for about six months. She suffers frequent headaches and has difficulty in sleeping. She finds her job stressful, but is unclear why this should be so, especially as she feels that she gets on well with other staff and with students; although she expresses some anxiety about her ability to take her place as a 'valuable' member of the school's senior management team. Jane attributes her major source of stress to the presentation which her headteacher has asked her to give to the school governors on the use of the value-added factor in considering the most recent examination results.

Jane's initial stress map is illustrated in Figure 5.1. The first step in the mapping process is to include the people whom Jane works with most closely and to indicate the relative stress levels which she feels they generate for her. Jane can now use the stress map to identify the main sources of her stress at work and her estimate of the level of that stress.

The next stage is to add further lines and numbers to indicate the amount of stress that Jane thinks she is having on others. She is able to see from the stress map where some of her work stress comes from and the effects that she herself has on her relationships at school.

Stress mapping is a useful aid for looking at work, social and family conflict and distress from the personal, subjective view of the client. It can help both client and counsellor to make connections within and between families, work systems and interpersonal relationships. This snapshot view of a client's world aids its exploration and can allow early, yet acceptable challenge of stress-related, self-defeating beliefs (see Chapter 6).

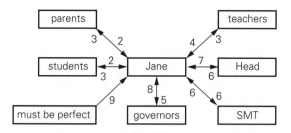

Figure 5.2 *Jane's completed work stress map*

It is important to re-emphasize the subjective nature of stress mapping. It is not a definitive diagnosis of the client's problems and their origins and it does not claim to be objective. Rather its purpose is to:

- enable a client to clarify their view of their own situation.
- enable a counsellor to see the world from the client's perspective and to gain an understanding of the often complex web of relationships which characterize their lives.

Once an initial stress map has been made, it can serve as a reference point in future explorations, which may sometimes challenge the map or suggest revisions to it. A second stress map made after a client has made some changes in their thinking, feelings, biology or behaviour can be a useful aid in the evaluation process of step seven of the problem-management model.

Problem listing

Not all stress-related problems can be illustrated through stress mapping because sometimes the interconnections are too complicated and the visual power of the presentation to clarify a situation is lost, perhaps leading to more, rather than less, confusion and stress. At such times a more helpful outcome of a session which is seeking to identify problems may be a list of issues which client and counsellor have identified together (Palmer and Burton, 1996).

Eric, a 50-year-old manager has recently been given notice that he is to lose his job in two months time when his company is re-organized. As he became very distressed about this, he was referred to the company's Employee Assistance Programme for counselling. Eric and his counsellor drew up the following problem-focused list:

- anxious about the future
- depressed about being made redundant
- irritable with work colleagues and family
- loss of appetite
- redundancy itself.

PRIORITIZING

When a client and counsellor have developed a problem check list they can take it one step further and work together to rate the issues in order of priority, as the client sees it, and also to include the possibilities the client has for influencing the problems.

Prioritizing can help to clarify:

- the extent to which problems are interrelated
- a priority sequence for working on the problems.

Eric's list was re-ordered in terms of priority, as follows:

1. Redundancy.
2. Depressed about being made redundant.
3. Anxious about the future.
4. Irritable with work colleagues.
5. Loss of appetite.

Eric decided that if he reframed 'redundancy' as an opportunity to find another job, then he would become less depressed and also less anxious about the future. However, the counsellor decided to share her thoughts with Eric and suggested that he might also need to focus temporarily on examining those self-defeating thoughts that could be contributing to his depression and anxiety, otherwise he might not be motivated sufficiently to find a new job.

Change of question

A simple additional point which may help to provide specific answers which help to clarify the nature of problems is to ask a client 'What would you like to change?' rather than 'What is the problem?'

Increasing sensitivity to problems

Whilst some clients are clearly aware of the areas of their lives which generate problems for them, we have seen that stress can inhibit a person's normal capacity to both identify and deal with problem situations. When clients are blocked by their stress there are three areas which counsellors can introduce to guide them towards an increased sensitivity.

1. *Using feelings as an indication of the source of a problem.* Rather than looking upon certain feelings as being themselves the problem, such feelings can serve clients by alerting them to explore their situation and behaviour to discover the difficulty which is behind the feelings. Everyday problems commonly generate anxiety, depression, anger or confusion. Empathically remaining with the feelings can be a great source of support, but it can also trap clients in a treadmill of defeating circular thoughts about those feelings which do not offer any hope that things could be different.

2. *Using unsuccessful behaviour as an indication of the source of a problem.* Stress can sometimes have a numbing effect on our feelings, which means that they do not alert us to the possible source of our difficulties. If we go on making mistakes and we are unable to respond effectively to a situation which we are stressed about, we may be better served if we focus on identifying the personal environmental aspects of that particular situation which we are not coping with, rather than labelling our mistake as 'the problem'. Stressed people often find it difficult to organize their time effectively, so rather than repeating the blaming 'I keep on being late for things', it is helpful to look at what it is about themselves and their circumstances which have this result and to work to improve their time-management skills.

3. Once clients are alerted by their feelings or their ineffective behaviour to search for the source of their difficulty, a problem checklist such as the one below (adapted from D'Zurilla, 1986: 106) helps them to pinpoint the area or the specific nature of that problem.

Problem area: Work
- too much or too little work?
- work too difficult?
- work not sufficiently challenging?
- too much or too little responsibility?
- job demands which conflict?
- unhealthy or unpleasant work environment?
- little opportunity for promotion?
- poor communication with colleagues or managers?
- disputes with colleagues or managers?
- travelling problems?
- conflict between job and family responsibilities?

Problem area: Interpersonal – Problems in relationships with:
- partner?
- children?
- parents or other relatives?
- friends?
- lack of social contacts?

Problem area: Health – Problems with:
- illness?
- sleep patterns?
- disability?
- sexual relationships?
- alcohol?
- drugs?
- exercise/weight?

Problem area: Personal – Problems in:
- managing time?

- self-discipline?
- low self-esteem?
- emotional life?
- religious or moral life?

Concerns about: your neighbourhood? community? environment? world problems?

Typical appraisal questions for step one

Have we missed anything important from your problem list?
Does this list really reflect what you want to change?
Are you overwhelmed by this problem list?

STEP TWO: SELECT REALISTIC GOALS

When client and counsellor understand the range of the problem, the key people and issues involved and the relative importance of the range of issues which are interconnected with all of these, the next task is to work together to define and choose ways of changing the situation which is generating stress. Put more briefly it is to select goals.

Which goals?

We emphasize the importance of working within the personal and environmental capabilities and resources of the client, some of which will have become clear during the CABB assessment. In addition, clients will be helped if counsellors encourage them to check that any ways of changing the problem which they identify are:

- specific
- realistic
- substantial
- verifiable
- recognized by the client as their own, whether they came originally from the prompting of the counsellor or themselves.

Example

Jane, the deputy headteacher to whom you were introduced earlier in the chapter, is our example. Jane is very anxious and panics at the thought of making a presentation to the governing body of her school.

SPECIFIC GOAL

Jane said she 'must give a perfect presentation' which is so specific as to be unattainable and at the same time hopelessly unspecific because we have no idea what it involves. 'Give a good presentation' is better, but we still need to question what 'good' amounts to in Jane's eyes. A finally refined goal might be 'to give an adequate presentation, acceptable to me'. Of course this will lead to the next consideration 'what is acceptable to me?' Later to be followed by 'what do I need to do to make a presentation which is acceptable to me?'

We might also examine whether her demand that she 'must give a perfect presentation' actually increases or decreases her stress levels. In our experience this rigid demand increases anxiety and affects performance. A problem-focused belief could be 'I strongly prefer to give an adequate presentation but I don't have to.'

REALISTIC GOAL

'Give an adequate one-hour presentation tomorrow', may be taking things far too quickly, although both authors have experience of clients who put themselves under such powerful, last-minute pressure. In a more ideal world, an initial goal would be less ambitious and less immediate. Clients often need the counsellor's encouragement to take things step-by-step and at a realistic pace as part of managing the stress they put on themselves. Since Jane is not able to rehearse her presentation directly to the governing body because its meetings are not conducive to this, a more productive goal for her may be 'to speak about the value-added factor to the senior management team for ten minutes next week'. This achievement could then be built on over a period of weeks until a full half hour's session is managed.

Egan's (1994: 261) one-sentence summary of what constitutes a realistic goal is clear and all-encompassing: 'A goal is realistic if the client has access to the resources needed to accomplish it, external circumstances do not prevent its accomplishment, the goal is under the client's control, the goal is sustainable and the benefits outweigh the costs.'

Unrealistic goals change the problem from a manageable one to an unmanageable one and are likely to increase a client's stress. There are perhaps exceptional amputees who may achieve an ascent of Everest, but most of us need our own two legs just to climb the more modest mountain of our own particular lives. There will sometimes be goals we want to achieve that are beyond us. There will also sometimes be achievements we can make which we do not believe we are capable of, and part of a counsellor's help lies in helping us to work out which of these is which.

SUBSTANTIAL GOAL

The step-by-step nature of setting realistic goals may lead to clients developing goals that are very easily attained and part of the counsellor's help, as we have suggested, lies in helping clients to be aware that goals which are not challenging enough may prolong the duration of counselling. For example, talking to the senior management team individually would probably not give Jane a sense of real progress towards her goal of giving a presentation to the whole board of governors. However, speaking to certain governor's individually may well do so. Remember our motto: 'challenging but not overwhelming'.

VERIFIABLE GOAL

To aid the problem-focused process it is important for both client and counsellor to have a goal(s) that is easily measurable in observable and behavioural terms. This is so that they can both ascertain what progress has been made later in the work. For Jane to say 'I want to feel more relaxed during my presentation' is in itself unhelpful until she is helped to understand and say what 'feeling more relaxed' amounts to. This might be less tension in her stomach, no feeling of sickness, slower breathing, a slower heartbeat and few images of failure going through her mind.

GOAL RECOGNIZED AS THE CLIENT'S OWN

Counsellors will already be aware that ownership of goals is vital, for unless a client is personally committed to a goal they are unlikely to devote the personal resources needed to make it happen. Egan (1998: 261) calls this ownership a 'higher form of commitment' and points out that a client who says 'I'll do this, it's logical' is making a very different kind of commitment from one who says, 'I'll do this, it's what I really want.'

A client's goals are more likely to be reached if they are in keeping with their own values and chosen by them. A counsellor who takes responsibility for setting goals for a client can expect to be rightly blamed if the goals are not reached and need not expect thanks if they are. However, a client may well need prompting in verbalizing their goals, perhaps with a remark that suggests that other people in a similar position have tried this, this and this, and what do they think? There is a difference between leaving clients stranded and helpless on the shore and helping them to the water.

Some principles of prioritizing

Prioritizing means choosing to work on those particular problem areas whose management will provide a reasonable return on the investment of both client and counsellor resources.

Egan (1998: 210) offers some overlapping principles to guide the work of prioritizing.

- If there is a crisis, first help the client manage the crisis.
- Begin with the problem that seems to be causing pain for a client.
- Begin with issues the client sees as important.
- Begin with some manageable sub-problem of a larger situation.
- Begin with a problem that, if handled, will lead to some kind of general improvement in the client's condition.
- Focus on a problem for which the benefits will outweigh the costs.

Summary of step two

Throughout this process client and counsellor have moved towards selecting one or more goals at which to aim and ensured that these are described in the most realistic, concrete and helpful way possible. They may also have considered ways of approaching these and are now ready to specifically identify and choose possible ways of making the changes that the client wants.

Typical appraisal questions for step two

Do these goals match the problems you want to change?
Are they realistic in terms of the benefits you want?
Are they things you want to achieve?

STEP THREE: EXPLORE OPTIONS

When realistic targets for change have been chosen and understood, the counsellor's next task is to encourage the client to devise methods of attaining these goals, being as creative as possible in the search for alternatives. This is a point at which realism can temporarily be suspended and some additional skills can be added to those of the earlier steps of problem management.

Brainstorming

Brainstorming is a technique which can help the client to develop a wide variety of alternatives in response to any problem, which already has an acceptable place in several different counselling approaches. Clients are helped to ask themselves 'How many different ways are there of getting where I want to go?' While the freedom of brainstorming is particularly creative, it may also be a great challenge to those clients who, having decided what they want, then do the first thing that comes to mind in order to achieve it. While this impulsive rush to action can be seen as laudable, its results may prove to be inefficient, lack effectiveness or actually be imprudent. (Occasionally the results may be highly effective and we also need to allow for that.)

Although brainstorming is a simple way of stimulating ideas, it is not the same as free-association because even the wildest possibilities may be in some way related to the client's problems and stimulated by their goals.

There are certain rules which help to make brainstorming work effectively (Egan 1998: 229–31):

- suspend judgement
- produce as many ideas as possible
- use one idea as a take-off point for others
- let go and develop some 'wild' ideas – lift the normal restraints on thinking
- produce more ideas by clarifying items already on the list.

The counsellor's role in brainstorming is to stimulate client thinking and imagination. One reason why clients are clients is that they are often not very practised and creative at looking for ways of getting what they want and need. In brainstorming, as in helping clients establish their own goals, counsellors may need to help 'stuck' clients by suggesting alternatives, pointing out tentatively that these are some of the things that other people in this kind of situation have tried, and how do they seem to them. It is important that a client works with any such suggestions themselves to make them into their own idea. In order to help clients to brainstorm, counsellors do need to be imaginative and creative in their own thinking and to keep themselves 'brainstorm fit'. We suggest that those counsellors who are not familiar with brainstorming try it for themselves, either with an issue of their own or with the following fun example.

BRAINSTORMING EXAMPLE:

'50 uses of a pen'

You have been asked by a pen manufacturer to develop new, creative uses of a pen which may help them to increase their sales.

Step 1

Write down the problem in the form of a question. Write the question at the top of a whiteboard or a sheet of paper

WHAT ARE 50 USES OF A PEN?

Step 2

Spend 10 minutes suggesting all possible responses to the question. Include every idea, however silly or irrelevant it may seem.

Suspend critical faculties for these 10 minutes. This will give your creativity free rein and perhaps allow some innovative solutions that you would otherwise have dismissed out of hand.

A sample list brainstormed in response to the question 'What are 50 uses of a pen?':

For writing	For poking people with
For drawing	For chewing
Stopping draughts in a keyhole	For sitting on!
For picking up with your toes	For slipping over
For scratching between your shoulders	Something to fiddle with when nervous
Something to break when angry	For scratching heads
For punching telephone numbers	An artistic piece of work
As a ruler	A container
As a stake for house plants	Something to lose
A present	Making a bridge for spiders
Pen watch	Pen calculator

Step 3

Critically review your brainstorm list. It is possible that some suggestions you might have been tempted to dismiss will be worth building on. Here is a shortlist of realistic suggestions:

A container
A pen watch
A pen calculator

These three ideas might become a springboard to the development of new manufacturing lines.

However stupid or irrelevant ideas may seem it is important to list all of them for later review and consideration. Often the exercise is fun but it has serious objectives including encouraging the client to be creative.

Review of resources

The options available to people in finding resolutions to their stress difficulties are limited by their resources, but it is equally important to emphasize that their resources may be greater than they think. Helping clients to identify their resources, particularly those which get overlooked, is one of the integrative counsellor's most fundamental tasks and any realistic assessment of options includes such an identification. When existing strengths and available supports have been explored the additional challenge of learning new skills and developing new sources of support can be faced. Care is needed at this time not to approach new learning when a client's stress is limiting their ability to undertake tasks which may over-extend them.

Explore personal strengths

Palmer and Burton (1996) suggest that there are four major areas to focus on in helping clients to get in touch with their personal strengths. The first highlights the value of learning from past experience and is a consequence of a client asking themselves a series of questions:

1. *Have I encountered similar situations or problems in the past?* If the answer is yes, the counsellor can help a client to probe further by asking themselves questions such as:

How did I cope with them?

What did I do that worked best?

What did I do that worked less well?

Because we all sometimes resort to managing certain problems by avoiding them, it can be salutary to encourage clients to focus honestly on their past experience of side-stepping their difficulties in this way.

2. *Have I coped with similar circumstances in the past by avoiding them?* Again, if the answer is yes, a client can be aided to discover more by the counsellor asking:

How have you avoided stressful situations?

Sometimes past coping has included the avoidance pattern of absenting or physically removing oneself from the situation: it may have included misusing drugs or alcohol in an attempt to remove one's thoughts and feelings from the situation. Of course such avoidance is accepted as having happened, just as other behaviour is accepted rather than censored, but it is important that its overall value is considered. Typical questions a counsellor might ask are:

Did it help you to sort out your problem?

Has avoiding things helped you to achieve your goals?

Did the situation improve in your absence?

Did you encounter further problems as a result of avoiding the original ones?

Were you happy after avoiding facing up to the problem?

3. The third and fourth points of focus concern the counsellor's assessment of the possible effects of the client's stress on their capacity to use their personal strengths.

How far does this client's current stress and state of mind enable them to use strengths they used in the past?

A client may previously have been quite successful in handling their stress, but this will not serve them if they feel that their mental and physical state is too debilitated for them to be successful now. A counsellor needs to note any ways in which a client's mental energy may be diminished by anxiety or by difficulties in sleeping, for these will then form part of the stress scenario itself.

4. Linked to the third point is the question of how able a person is to propose their own solutions at this particular time. How far are they able to generate ideas about how they might effect change? Would it help to first use physical ways of reducing anxiety such as relaxation or positive imagery? (See Chapter 9.)

Consider personal supports

EMOTIONAL SUPPORT

Emotional well-being is given particular consideration in our approach because emotional pain and pleasure are costs and benefits which are of major significance in the lives of most of us. Sources of emotional support consist of those others with whom people feel able to share aspects of their lives. Such a network may include family members, friends or colleagues at work. Talking to supportive friends can help to put life events into perspective and it may be useful to suggest that clients consider discreetly 'sharing their stress around' and helping them to evolve the skills to do this in a way that will not overwhelm the receiver.

Too often when stressed clients start counselling their sole emotional support is their counsellor. Under stress some people withdraw from supportive relationships and the resulting emotional isolation exacerbates their stress. Gradually building, or re-building emotional support, however limited, is a reminder that in future a problem shared may well be a problem halved and the sharer does not have to be a counsellor.

CONSIDER SPECIALIST SUPPORT

Specialist support may be another form of psychological help, or it may take the form of advice in specific practical areas such as law or finance, or it may combine these as in the case of a service such as Alcoholics Anonymous.

LISTING SUPPORT

Personal support networks act as a buffer against stress (Ganster and Victor, 1988; Gore, 1978). It is fitting for stress counsellors to encourage the making of a list of friends, colleagues or family members whom a client can rely on to help them:

- in a crisis with a work problem; someone who can give constructive feedback
- when they are worried
- when they are under stress; someone who has a calming effect
- when creative ideas are needed.

Two difficulties which counsellors can expect clients to raise about asking others to listen to them when they have a problem are that:

- people will see it as a sign of weakness, or
- people should know when I need help without being asked.

(We cover the skills of helping clients with negative thoughts in Chapter 6 and also later in this chapter.)

Very few people are telepathic: they often do not know we need or want help until we tell them.

Mapping networks of support

Just as we used a mapping process to identify sources of stress (see p. 82), we have also found that visually constructed support networks work for some clients, enabling their various resources to be seen at a glance. Any form of diagram which a client finds convenient can be used for a support map. Palmer and Burton (1996) describe one in the form of a spider diagram with the client at the centre and the network of resources spreading out from them. The strength of support can be differentiated by thicker or thinner lines, or by broken lines, and the accessibility of that support can be indicated by lines which place the people nearer to the client, or further away. In the example in Figure 5.3, the network key includes family (F), social (S), financial (FN), workplace (W) and health (H) resources.

Julian was suffering high levels of stress due to recent redundancies at work. His company was a transport firm which had reduced staffing by 30 per cent in a period of three months.

Some reflective questions a counsellor can ask the client are:

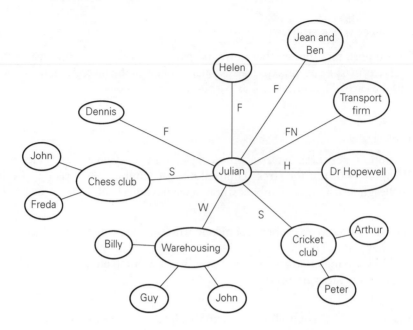

Figure 5.3 *Network support map for Julian*

Where are the gaps in your support map?

Did you anticipate more or less support than you mapped?

What has completing your support map shown you?

Many clients find support mapping an interesting exercise and often they are heartened by the support they have available within their work and social areas. However, others may become demoralized if their support map highlights a lack of support. Therefore counsellors need to be sensitive to the possible issues raised by undertaking this exercise.

A further informative area of reflection can emerge if clients think back to the last time they had a difficulty and to realize who it was within their diagram they received support from and who they did not, and perhaps why this was so.

Explore environmental supports

Environmental support includes any physical factor that contributes to a person's overall quality of life and may be quite critical in enhancing personal effectiveness. Two specific types of environmental support which have been found to be particularly effective are stability zones and rituals (Palmer, 1989)

STABILITY ZONES

Stability zones are those physical areas, belongings or objects which a person may be particularly fond of or accustomed to which help to promote their sense of well-being.

RITUALS

Rituals are enjoyable routines, or more occasional habits which are a positive influence in a person's life. Rituals which are a form of 'obsessive behaviour' are discounted because far from being supportive of well-being they are often responsible for psychological disturbance which may need specific help (see Chapter 7; graded behavioural exposure and response prevention).

Clients can also be helped to bring back into use:

- supports they have found helpful in the past but which have fallen into disuse
- current support which they underuse.

They can also be encouraged to develop new resources.

Reminder lists (see Box 5.1) are a good way of helping clients to record examples of stability zones and rituals. However, they do need to be used with care since clients may need help to deal with the loss of an important stabilizer before looking for suitable replacements.

Box 5.1 *Reminder list for stability zones and routines.*

Reminder list for stability zones

Home	Rooms, rooms with a view, favourite chair, floor cushion, shower
Work	Areas within work place, chair, desk, dining area, rest room area, computer room
Countryside	Favourite walks, landscapes, open spaces, leisure facilities, hills, woods
Town	Shops, restaurant, wine bar, public house
Other	Beach hut, favourite cliff or beach walks, places of worship

Example: Taking a leisurely evening walk in a local park at the end of a busy day, when the rush hour traffic has thinned and the park is really quiet.

Reminder list for rituals/routines

Daily	Morning cup of tea/coffee, glass of fruit juice, breakfast television, newspapers and magazines, walking the dog, watching favourite television programme.
Weekly	Weekend away breaks, Sunday outings, sports activities, visiting favourite restaurant or public house on a Friday evening, going to a religious group, evening classes
Annual	Holidays, anniversaries, Christmas, birthdays, visits to old friends

Example: Regularly spending Wednesday afternoons singing in a local choir.

Typical appraisal questions for step three

Are there other possible ways of reaching your goals?
Have we focused on what you want?
Do you feel clear about the options we have looked at?

STEP FOUR: CONSIDER THE CONSEQUENCES

When clients initially explore alternative ways of making the changes they have identified, it is preferable not to set preconditions or assess the usefulness of the suggested strategies for achieving those changes. Imagination is released to create alternatives and judgement is deferred. Once the options have been explored however, judgement is required to sort out and evaluate each of the possibilities.

Auditing the pros and cons

Assessing the pros and cons of each possible course of problem-solving action involves focusing on the consequences of each of these. This may reveal problems which might otherwise be overlooked. For example, a client may consider acting more assertively at home, which can result in a change in their relationships. In some cases this could increase the risk of personal harm as a result of their partner's reaction.

One helpful method of systematically auditing the pros and cons of different strategies for change is to compile an analysis of the consequences (Palmer and Burton, 1996: 126).

In our example, Christine's goal was to obtain cooperation in sharing household chores from members of her family. The possible options she chose are set out in the left-hand column of Table 5.1.

Table 5.1 *Christine's consequential analysis*

Proposed action	Pros	Cons
Become assertive	Children and partner may start to help with the chores	They could become more intransigent
Get divorced	Resolves the problem	An over-reaction!! It would cause so many additional problems
Hold a family discussion in a calm fashion	If they listen then they might improve their behaviour	Unlikely to take me seriously unless I get angry
Get mother-in-law involved	This will sort out my husband	This could lead to high levels of resentment and future problems! Anyway it won't work with the children after 'granny' has gone home

Table 5.2 shows a simpler, two-column form of consequential analysis by Jane, our deputy head, who believes that she 'must give a perfect presentation to the board

Table 5.2 *Jane's consequential analysis*

Pros	Cons
I will do my best	I'll spend every waking hour thinking about my presentation and, ironically, continue to procrastinate
I will do a good job	Not at this rate. I'm not even sleeping properly now
The head and governors will think really well of me	If I carry on feeling anxious I might do badly and they are less likely to think well of me
At least the house is clean	I am so anxious about performing well, I can't concentrate on the preparation. I find myself wasting time doing the housework

of governors, otherwise things will be awful'. Listing the pros and cons of this type of thinking helps her to see the situation more clearly.

Take precautions against failure

Counsellors encourage clients to consider the consequences for themselves, for their situation and for others in their lives, by asking themselves such questions as:

How will this choice affect the important people in my life?

Are there any disadvantages to this choice? Do I want to accept them?

The process of identifying consequences is a personal one for the client, but the counsellor's additional focus on the wider 'ripple' effects can help clients to take precautions against agreeing to options which sound very desirable, but which are unlikely to be acted upon. Whilst being assertive at home may be the most desirable option, how likely is your client to do this? A client like Christine who wants others' approval is unlikely to be consistently assertive with her family. It may be useful to discuss these issues with the client before she undertakes the assignment. It may be even more preferable to focus on her needs for approval (approval-seeking beliefs), prior to her becoming assertive or attempting to become assertive in her home.

Sometimes the personal costs of a choice weigh heavily against the practical benefits. A client with terminal cancer who abruptly ends his chemotherapy because he cannot cope with the sickness and depression, cannot have second thoughts about it once his health has deteriorated beyond a certain point. Faced with such dilemmas, clients need help to decide whether to (adapted Palmer and Burton 1996):

- reject the choice because of the personal costs
- work on the issue of the personal costs: for example, through emotional problem solving
- risk putting the choice into action in the expectation that the practical benefits will outweigh the personal costs.

If a client considers the third option expedient, the personal issues need to be included as part of the longer term stress management plan.

The balance sheet

An alternative balance sheet method for considering the consequences of choices and the ways of reaching them proposes that clients ask themselves three basic questions. If I choose this course of action:

1. What are the gains and losses for myself?
2. What are the gains and losses for others important to me?
3. What are the gains and losses for my work/social/setting?

Once the gains and losses have been identified they can each be assessed as 'acceptable' or 'not acceptable' and the reasons listed, so that the client's balance sheet includes a statement such as:

> This gain is acceptable because . . . .
> This gain is not acceptable because . . . .
> This loss is acceptable because . . . .
> This loss is not acceptable because . . . .

The above assessments are made for each of the three basic gains and losses questions (adapted Egan, 1998: 344).

Other methods of considering consequences

Pros and cons can also be uncovered through the use of brainstorming (see p. 89) to record the possible results of various courses of action.

Visualization (see p. 80) may also help clients to get a clearer picture of the problems which may emerge from a certain choice. The counsellor can prompt a client to visualize by using a question such as 'What do you see happening if . . .?', which literally helps them to imagine themselves into the future situation.

Typical appraisal questions for step four

> What do you need?
>
> What do you want?
>
> What choices do you have, given the consequences?
>
> What are you willing to pay for the changes you want?

STEP FIVE: MAKE DECISIONS

Step four looked at assessing the consequences, positive and negative, of a range of ways of bringing about the changes a client has chosen to reduce their stress, or deal with a specific problem. They are now in a better position to choose the most appropriate course of action. This is generally a careful balancing act, weighing the pros and cons, or perhaps assessing which chickens will come home to roost if they make a certain choice. However, in some cases the choice is not straightforward. Step five may help a client and counsellor to uncover any additional problems which may be interfering with decision making.

Making a decision plan

Once the available choices and their consequences have been considered there are three stock-taking questions which act as a summary of the work so far. Counsellors can help clients to do this by asking:

1. Can your problem now be resolved?
2. Do we need more information before you make a decision?
3. Which option should you now follow?

If a client answers 'no' to question 1 and 'yes' to question 2, they need to either pose their problem differently so that it can be resolved, or seek more information before they continue. If a client answers 'yes' and 'no' respectively, then it is possible to move on in the decision-making process (Palmer and Burton, 1996).

Decision plans

Decision plans are derived from the work of the psychologist D'Zurilla (1986) who emphasizes that any plan should aim to do the following:

- resolve the problem
- maximize personal and emotional well-being
- minimize time and effort.

TYPES OF PLAN

Plans may be simple or complex. A simple plan focuses on one course of action or decision and is best used when one solution may have positive gains.

D'Zurilla's (1986: 136) view is that a complex plan may involve either:

- following several solutions at the same time, or
- pursuing a series of solutions: A first, and if this does not work, B; then if B does not work, C.

If several problem-solving methods used together is most likely to succeed, whereas one used alone would fail, then the first complex plan option may be considered more helpful. If client and counsellor are unsure whether or not a particular choice will be successful, the second complex plan option enables the client to have other choices readily available as contingencies.

A clear decision plan helps to ensure that clients approach and act upon their stress problem in a systematic rather than a haphazard way. A visual, shareable, step-by-step summary of the activities and behaviours the client will commit themselves to carrying out can be achieved through the processes of externalization, visualization and simplification, which are covered earlier in the chapter.

Problem-facilitating thought forms

At this stage the five-star framework for emotional problem solving may be helpful if the client has a high level of anxiety (see Chapters 2 and 6).

Problem-facilitating thought forms uses Ellis's ABCDE framework as a prompt for clients and help them to reach their goals. The form is usually completed during a counselling session so that its purpose and structure can be explained. However, with experience a client can complete it at home as a homework assignment. (There is a blank form for the use of readers in Appendix 2.)

Figure 5.4 illustrates a form completed by Jane, our deputy head. In this example notice that Jane has now decided to include her self-defeating belief that the 'outcome will be awful', as she had focused on her belief that she would be seen as 'useless' in an earlier counselling session.

1. First Jane chose her presentation to the board of governors as a stressful problem which was affecting her emotional well-being.
   Jane was asked to summarize this situation in column A. Stated problem A: giving a presentation to the board of governors.
2. She was then asked to write her self-defeating and unhelpful feelings and behaviours with which she responded to this problem in column C: emotional/behavioural reaction. Very anxious, procrastination, sleep disturbance, cleaning the house, unable to concentrate.
3. The counsellor helped Jane to do a brief inference chaining in relation to her stated problem in column A (see pp. 119, 123), which resulted in a redefinition of the major concern as being: 'Giving a poor presentation to the board of governors; thus losing her treasured job of deputy head.'
4. It was then suggested that Jane write in column B the thoughts she had which seemed to interfere with her ability to proceed with her presentation. Which included:
   i. 'I've got enough to do already.'
   ii. 'Why are they doing this to me?'
   iii. 'The meeting date is approaching and I haven't done anything yet.'
   iv. 'I must give a perfect presentation otherwise the outcome will be awful.'
   (In general REBT the non-evaluative beliefs such as i, ii and iii, may be included in column B, as well as evaluative beliefs such as iv).
5. With the counsellor's help, Jane then wrote in column D a list of possible ways in which she could challenge the thoughts which prevented her from acting (known as disputing, see Chapter 6):
   i. and ii. 'This is not personal. The school I work in is a high-pressure environment.'
   iii. Stop procrastinating and start the work. Do, don't stew!

Workplace/Other Problem (A)	Thinking Interfering With Problem-Solving (B)	Emotional/Behavioural/Physical Reaction (C)	Thinking Facilitating Problem-Solving (D)	New and Effective Approach to Problem (E)
Giving a presentation to the School Governors I C N H F A E I R N E N N C E *Giving a poor presentation to the governors*	*i* I've got enough to do already *ii* Why are they doing this to me? *iii* The governors' meeting is in 2 weeks and I haven't done anything yet *iv* I must give a perfect presentation otherwise the outcome will be awful	*Very anxious* *Procrastination* *Sleep disturbance* *Cleaning the house when not essential.* *Unable to concentrate*	*i and ii* This is not personal. The school I work in is a high-pressure environment. *iii* Stop procrastinating and start the work. Do, don't stew! *iv Logical:* Just because I want to give a perfect presentation how does it logically follow that I must give a perfect presentation? <u>Empirical:</u> Where is the evidence that my demand must be granted? Am I being realistic. If I don't give a perfect presentation will the outcome really be awful? <u>Pragmatic:</u> Where is it getting me holding on to this way of thinking?	*Although it's obviously preferable to give a perfect presentation, I don't have to do so.* *There is no evidence that I will get what I demand, even if it is preferable and desirable.* *If I don't give a perfect presentation, the outcome may be bad, but hardly awful and devasting.* *If I continue to think this way, I will remain anxious and am even more likely to give a poor presentation.* *If I change my attitude I will feel concerned but not anxious.* *I might even get a better night's sleep.* *Also I'll be able to concentrate and prepare for the presentation. I'll start work on it today.*

Figure 5.4 *Jane's problem-facilitating form*

iv. *Logical* 'Just because I want to give a good presentation how does it logically follow that I must give a good presentation?

Empirical 'Where is the evidence that my demand must be granted?' 'Am I being realistic. If I don't give a good presentation, will the outcome really be awful?'

Pragmatic 'Where is it getting me holding on to this way of thinking?'

6. Column E is for Jane to record her changed and effective approach to her original problem stated in column A. It includes the changes in thinking, the motivating emotions (that is, concern) and the effective behaviours which will help her to free her potential and start work on her presentation.

'Although it's obviously preferable to give a good presentation, I don't have to do so.'

'There is no evidence that I will get what I demand, even if it is preferable and desirable.'

'If I don't perform well, the outcome may be bad, but hardly awful and devastating.'

'If I continue to think this way, I will remain anxious and even more likely to give a poor presentation.'

'If I change my attitude I will feel concerned, but not anxious. Also I'll be able to concentrate and prepare for the presentation. I might even get a better night's sleep. I'll start work on it today.'

Jane's new behaviour is to start organizing her time in order to undertake the work needed for the presentation.

If Jane is to think, feel and behave differently and manage her stress, she needs to understand that her emotional response is largely a result of her way of thinking about the presentation rather than the actual job itself.

REVIEWING PROBLEM-THOUGHT FORM CHANGES

It helps clients if they can review the preparation and the results of their thought form changes with their counsellor, and the following prompts may help them to get started (Palmer and Burton, 1996: 134)

'What did I find surprising?'
'What did I find difficult?'
'What did I find challenging?'
'What did I find most helpful in tackling my problem?'

Those clients who respond to the use of problem-facilitating thought forms may like to use them on a regular basis until gradually they are able to recognize and challenge their thinking, feeling and behaviour almost spontaneously, without need of forms or prompting.

Step five has looked at deciding on ways of resolving stress problems. Both the decision plan and the problem-facilitating thought form are visual aids to assist this process and to bring the client to the point of being able to agree on action.

Typical appraisal questions for step five

There is a continuous evaluation process throughout step five. Some issues of concern for the counsellor are:

How likely is it that the client's decision will achieve the client's goal?

Am I encouraging the client to act on their learning?

Have we spent enough time/too much time on exploring the client's stress and identifying problems and goals?

STEP SIX: AGREE ACTIONS

Steps one to five of the problem-management approach come to naught unless they enable clients to take positive steps to bring about the changes they have chosen.

Making action choices

The criteria for choosing action strategies in many ways parallel those of choosing goals in step two of the problem-management model: specific, realistic, substantial and verifiable, and in keeping with the client's values. These are the points for clients to focus on in their final choice of action strategy. Counsellors will aim to encourage clients to (see: D'Zurilla, 1986; Palmer and Burton, 1996: 136–42):

- describe, step-by-step and in some detail, what they intend to do
- look at achievements as well as behaviour – what clients will achieve as well as what they will do
- look at a realistic goal that will give them a genuine sense of achievement – one that is challenging but not overwhelming
- identify the gains or benefits in their choice
- ensure that they have the resources they need to bring about the change they have chosen.

DESCRIBE SPECIFIC INTENTIONS

It may seem pedantic to pay such attention to detail but the reward from a step-by-step process is the increased likelihood of a positive result. It can also be an enormous boost to a client's confidence to find that he or she has been able to create order out of chaos.

LOOK AT ACHIEVEMENTS

The counsellor can initiate the focus by asking the client to outline the step-by-step details of their plans. They need to know specifically what they are going to do, and to have some plan about the order in which they will do these things and the time scale involved.

Focusing on achievements, like being specific, links clients' goals with their work tasks, which in turn ties in with their real concerns. This not only makes their proposed action to bring about change clear to follow, but also gives them pointers through which to evaluate the results.

LOOK AT REALISTIC GOALS

This point is closely related to the previous one. Clients sometimes choose an achievable task, but not an overwhelming one, like completing a report to a deadline, which helps to build their confidence and thus enables them to reach more demanding targets requiring more of their skills.

IDENTIFY GAINS OR BENEFITS

Different people are motivated by different things – the different strokes for different folks principle. Our experience suggests that people are motivated when they can recognize for themselves the benefits which come from making the changes which will resolve their stress problems. Jane, our deputy head, realizes the gains that changing her self-defeating beliefs will bring in terms of improved work performance and better health, as well as having more time to spend with her family.

ENSURE RESOURCES ARE AVAILABLE

In some respects embarking on a problem-management strategy is like cooking a meal. It is worthwhile to check that the client or chef has the things they need, in terms of ingredients, or resources, to complete the menu they have chosen.

Resources can include:

- personal resources – support and understanding of family, friends or colleagues; perhaps child minding help; who will wash up after this meal?
- physical resources – space and time to carry out planned action; kitchen equipped with oven and cooking utensils; energy and stamina to do the shopping and cook the meal.

Action plans

Once client and counsellor have established that the resources needed are available, the client can move on to action and then to monitoring of action. Some clients respond readily to a detailed step-by-step action plan, others prefer a more free-style day-by-day journal account of their progress. Some cooks stick rigidly to recipes, others rely on 'guesstimating'. Whichever monitoring procedure is chosen it will clearly be most effective if it is chosen by the client, to accommodate both the nature of their problem and their own personal style. The purpose of monitoring is to provide concrete information upon which clients can base a review of their progress. (A blank action plan form is shown in Appendix 4.) A simple way of recording individual tasks or steps is shown in Figure 6.1.

Action-based contracts

Egan (1998: 324) recommends self-contracts as a way of helping clients to commit themselves to what they want, or for helping them to start and sustain problem-managing action he cites the example of a job search agreement developed by Feller (1984).

Feller's Job Search Agreement

Clients are asked to respond 'True' to each of the job-seeking beliefs and behaviours described in the contract. They are then asked to act on these truths. This is a self-contract, one that clients make with themselves, not with their counsellor. Its aim is to help them to persist in their search for work.

I agree that no matter how many times I enter the job market, or the level of skills, experiences or academic successes I have, the following appear TRUE:

1. It takes only one YES to get a job; the number of NOs does not affect my next interview.
2. The open market lists about 20 per cent of the jobs presently open to me.
3. About 80 per cent of the job openings are located by talking to people.
4. The more people who know my skills and know that I'm looking for a job, the more I increase the probability that they'll tell me about a job lead.
5. The more specifically I can tell people about the problems I can solve or outcomes I can attain, rather than describe the jobs I've had, the more jobs they may think I qualify for.

I agree that regardless of how much I need a job, the following appear TRUE:

6. If I cut expenses and do more things for myself, I reduce my money problems.
7. The more I remain positive, the more people will be interested in me and my job skills.
8. If I relax and exercise daily, my attitude and health will appear attractive to potential employers.
9. The more I do positive things and the more I talk with enthusiastic people, the more I will gain the attention of new contacts and potential employers.
10. Even if things don't go as I would like them to, I choose my own thoughts, feelings and behaviours each day.

The psychological principles on which this self-contract is based can be adapted to situations other than that of seeking work.

Mini-review session

Step six usually includes a mini-review session which takes place after clients have had the opportunity to put their plans into action. This gives them the chance to review and evaluate what has happened with the counsellor's support.

When and how a review is undertaken will depend on the proposed problem-management plan. If the client's problem is easy to define and the steps involved in its management are uncomplicated, one review session after a short break may be adequate to monitor the situation and decide what further action needs to be taken, if any.

However, complex problems consisting of a number of steps and at least one goal are likely to require two or more review sessions over a period of time. It is important that client and counsellor are clear about each other's (Palmer and Burton, 1996):

- roles
- expectations
- agreed commitments.

By the end of step six the client should be prepared to set out on a well-defined path to deal with their problem or stressor. Client and counsellor will have worked collaboratively to choose potentially useful methods of reducing stress levels and devised helpful strategies to reach the client's goals. They will have checked that the resources needed for a client to act effectively are available to them.

Typical appraisal questions for step six

Are you clear about the resources you need to help you to act?

Will the rewards you anticipate help you to persevere?

What are your contingency plans?

STEP SEVEN: EVALUATE THE STRATEGY

In the integrative problem-focused approach steps one to six of problem management may be worked through in one counselling session or in several, depending on the client and their situation. What is clear is that before clients can evaluate the effectiveness of their plan they have to go out into the situation which triggers their stress and make changes in their thinking, feeling and behaviour. The review and evaluation of the success of the client's work will therefore necessarily take place in a subsequent counselling session and it may be helpful to set a date for this before the client moves into action.

Both client and counsellor need to be prepared for evaluation sessions which show that clients have succeeded in their plan, have partially achieved what they set out to do, or have not attained their goals at all (Palmer and Burton, 1996). The counsellor's personal aim is to make the evaluation session a positive, 'win–win' situation in which even not succeeding in making changes can be reframed as a useful learning experience for both themselves and their client. Integrative stress counselling is not an approach for pessimistic counsellors.

Placing evaluation as the last step in any helping has its dangers, because, as Egan (1998) emphasizes, if it occurs only at the end, it is too late. He suggests that evaluation is built into counselling in an ongoing way and that client and counsellor regularly ask themselves questions to discover in what ways the sessions are making a substantial contribution to the client's problem management and the development of their opportunities. We have taken a leaf from Egan's book and included typical appraisal questions at the end of each step of the problem-management model. The review which takes place after the client has taken action is a further step in that ongoing evaluation, even though it has a stage of the model to itself.

The review

A counselling session which is set aside for evaluation review will be more helpful if it has some kind of simple agenda to give it structure and to ensure that no important issue is forgotten in the euphoria or disappointment of reporting back. The agenda may be set when the date for the review session itself is decided, or it may be created at the beginning of that session.

The review needs to give an opportunity for the client to say what has happened to them in their own way. Effective evaluation is client-centred and friendly and although of necessity it focuses on client problems, it is not rigidly problem-based. It is necessary to focus on the progress clients have made with their problems, in order to make sure that counselling remains a learning process in which both client and counsellor can learn together about themselves and the process of change.

A skeleton framework for a review agenda (adapted Palmer and Burton, 1996) includes basic items:

- a resumé of the problem and the steps taken to resolve it
- a review of each step of the problem management process
- future action.

Clients will have been asked to monitor their progress as discussed in step six and the counsellor will need to ask them to bring their notes to the review session. They may wish to share their notes with their counsellor, or they may prefer simply to refer to them when they need to. These are the client's notes and although we use the term 'homework' or assignment to refer to the work clients do on their own outside counselling sessions, the results of that work are for them. Although it is often useful, clients are not required to hand them in to the counsellor if they do not wish to and it is important to make that clear.

It is normally beneficial to summarize the exact nature of the problem and this may be presented by the client or the counsellor; it depends on the circumstances. Clients who dread review sessions may need a helping hand to get started and for them a friendly recap from their counsellor may set a welcoming tone to a difficult process. Other clients may have moved so far since their last session that they no longer recognize the counsellor's week-old summary of their situation. For this reason it is important for the counsellor to encourage clients to comment on any issues that they may have perceived or acted on differently. The recap or summary is a means by which client and counsellor can come back into touch with each other and the client's stress scenario after changes have been attempted.

During the review process the client is directly involved in assessing their own progress. The integrative model actively encourages people to take responsibility for themselves and their own stress. Clients are not being examined, although their skills and skills deficits may be assessed. The counsellor's role is to help clients, not to assess them critically.

If the stress management plan has been developed with well-defined goals or specific changes, the review examines whether or not these have been achieved and to what extent.

Criteria for review

There are several ways of reviewing, two of which are to look at the extent to which (Palmer and Burton, 1996):

- the changes or goals chosen by the client have been accomplished
- the stress problem presented by the client has been resolved.

In the evaluation process simplicity scores over complexity. If a client has focused on a number of aspects of a problem which they then list for clarity, a simple scale for each item will show what the client thinks has happened. Such a scale might be:

accomplished   partly accomplished   not yet accomplished

Alternatively, a sliding scale from 0–10, which itemizes the problem and marks the client's assessment of their progress somewhere on a line, may be used.

Accomplished   Not yet accomplished

      10   5   0

or

Resolved   Unresolved

      10   5   0

It is important that the client receives realistic feedback from the counsellor during this process. Often clients who hold rigid perfectionist beliefs use 'all or nothing' thinking and rate a partial accomplishment as totally unachieved.

Action following the review

Action following three possible client evaluation outcomes is briefly considered below (Palmer and Burton, 1996):

- changes or goals substantially accomplished
- changes or goals partly accomplished
- changes or goals not yet accomplished.

CHANGES SUBSTANTIALLY ACCOMPLISHED

When a client achieves what they wanted to accomplish, either wholly or substantially, that particular problem-management process is at an end. However, it is often beneficial to arrange a later review at which client and counsellor will be able to assess the longer term results of the client's action. The time interval before this second review will depend upon several different factors, including the type of problem and whether the change has really had the long-term results envisaged by the client. Therefore, either a pre-arranged appointment can be made or the client contacts the counsellor if the outcome has unforeseen negative consequences.

CHANGES PARTLY ACCOMPLISHED

If a client partially achieves what they wanted it is helpful to discover whether anything seems to be blocking their accomplishment of the goal more fully. Does the client (adapted Palmer and Burton, 1996):

- need to try different solutions
- need more time
- need more resources and support
- have concerns about the consequences of resolving their stress-related problems
- report encountering further difficulties not covered in your previous sessions

If more time, resources or support are needed, a revised or new plan will have to be agreed to accommodate these needs. The revised or new action plan may include different ways of approaching the problem, often evolved from a further brainstorming session.

Sometimes the prospect of the change involved in resolving a stress problem is in itself a difficulty for clients. They may be anxious about being promoted at work as they may get out of their depth. It is important that clients are enabled to voice their own evaluation of their progress and the reasons for the difficulties in making the changes they seek. Sometimes fresh difficulties have arisen for clients since their last counselling session and these may affect their progress towards achieving their original goals.

CHANGES NOT YET ACCOMPLISHED

If in the client's opinion 'little' progress has been made, then any of the problems discussed in the previous section may need to be addressed. It is also worth rechecking whether or not the change which the client has agreed is realistic. If the client has low self-esteem or many skills deficits, then the assignment may have appeared too overwhelming, leading to anxiety and procrastination. When this happens, client and counsellor may need to backtrack and focus on the client's problem–interfering beliefs (see Chapter 6). Then later, the assignment can be divided into a series of smaller, less challenging steps.

The counsellor may wish to return to the CABB assessment. This may indicate that other problems were overlooked, such as not working with catastrophic imagery, or lack of assertion skills. The CABB assessment is a useful *aide-mémoire* which helps to remind the counsellor of the overall picture. We suggest that the counsellor refers to it on a regular basis, revising and updating it as further information becomes available.

We would always recommend that counsellors use supervision to raise problems encountered in work with clients.

Completion of step seven of the problem-management agenda does not necessarily mean the end of problem solving. Clients may need to return to their problem list and deal with other difficulties which they are stressed about, or further problems which may have arisen since the initial list was devised. However, once a client has worked through the skill-sharing process, which is a constant feature of our model, the counsellor's approach and input is likely to change. When clients are themselves familiar with the seven-step process and the other skills we describe, they will be more competent and perhaps more flexible in dealing with their own stress and hopefully will encounter it less frequently. Clients literally become their own 'self counsellor' and the integrative counsellor takes more of a 'back seat' in the remaining sessions.

Box 5.2 shows how the stages of the seven-step problem-focused model may be recorded in their entirety, as the work progresses, so that client and counsellor can have an overview of the whole process. (A blank seven-step form is provided in Appendix 3.)

The reality of integrative problem-focused stress counselling

Planning in reality is not the same as planning in books. Books set out principles, whereas counselling sessions deal with human interaction which is more difficult to convey on the written page. In some cases flexibility – being less specific and rigid in terms of plans, activities and deadlines – can be an encouragement to clients familiar with the integrative problem-focused model to be more self-reliant and pro-active (Egan, 1998).

Our approach offers a fusion of client needs and common sense in its application. Sometimes it helps clients to spell out the action they need to take in specific terms. At other times and with other clients, the art is to help them to outline their action in broad terms and to leave the rest to their own sound judgement.

Typical appraisal questions for step seven

Have the goals the client stated at the beginning been achieved?
Has the problem the client brought to counselling been resolved?
If the client's goals have only partly been achieved, what helpful information has been learned from the work done?

Box 5.2 *Seven-step problem-focused form*

STEP 1: IDENTIFY THE PROBLEM
What is the problem.

Giving a presentation to the School governors (Feeling very anxious, unable to concentrate, disturbed sleep)

STEP 2: SELECT GOALS
Select specific, realistic, substantial and verifiable goal(s)

Reduce anxiety e.g. tension, butterflies, headaches. Stop procrastinating - start preparing for presentation e.g. Initially speak to SMT (Senior Management Team) about topic for 10 minutes.
Give satisfactory presentation to School Governors.

STEP 3: EXPLORE OPTIONS
Write down possible ways of reaching your goals.

Change beliefs and use other coping strategies e.g. relaxation.
Practise speaking to SMT on 'value-added factor'
Go off sick
Get more information on 'value-added factor'
Resign from job

STEP 4: CONSIDER THE CONSEQUENCES
Weight up the pros and cons of the different options/solutions

1. *Change beliefs - this can only help*
2. *Get more information - takes time, but I will feel more confident*
3. *Practise speaking to SMT on 'value-added factor' - relatively easy, if I make a mistake it won't be the 'end of the world'.*
4. *Off sick - I can't avoid the inevitable - I'll have to do it on my return.*
5. *Resign - stupid idea - this won't help me in the long term.*

STEP 5: TAKE DECISIONS
Choose the most feasible solution.

A combination of some of the above - 1, 2 and 3.
Both 4 and 5 will not help me.

STEP 6: AGREE ACTIONS
Develop a step by step action plan.

1. *Change beliefs, coping imagery and relaxation.*
2. *Prepare notes and hand outs.*
3. *Practise speaking to SMT - then*
4. *Modify presentation after receiving feedback.*
5. *Give presentation to School Governors.*

STEP 7: EVALUATE THE STRATEGY
Focus on achievement. Review and revise plan as necessary.

Obtain feedback throughout the process.

CHAPTER 6

Five-Star Framework for Emotional Problem Solving

Intellect is to emotion as our clothes are to our bodies: we could not very well have civilised life without clothes, but we would be in a poor way if we had only clothes without bodies.

Alfred North Whitehead, *Dialogues*: 232

The five-star framework is an account of clothes and bodies: intellect and emotion.

We have suggested in the outline of our integrated model in Chapter 2 that it is naive to imagine that the effective management of stress is just a question of ironing out misunderstandings in thinking. There are times when the consequences of our thinking evoke emotions so powerful that they completely block our capacity to attend to the problems which stress us. We introduced the concept that emotions may have powerful behavioural consequences and that there are positive and negative aspects to emotions. It is at such times that the seven-step model of problem management may be less applicable and the primary focus of counselling needs instead to be directed to working with the emotional block. For this reason we have included the five-star framework for emotional problem solving, based on the view that emotional distress is largely generated by the perceptions, meanings and evaluations we ascribe to life events, rather than by those events themselves. Its essence is distilled by Epictetus, the early Stoic philosopher, thus, 'People are disturbed not by things, but by the views they take of them.'

In the diagrammatic representation of our approach in Figure 2.1 the five-star framework is placed after the CABB assessment profile and alongside the seven-stage problem-management outline. This is done to suggest that it may be used in the early stages of counselling as a way of helping clients to gain some understanding and control over their emotional reactions to stress, where these effectively block them from staying actively focused. It may also be used later in the seven-step model to help with future emotional blocks.

The five-star framework is based on the ABCDE paradigm of Ellis's (1994) Rational Emotive Behaviour Therapy (REBT). Being a victim of powerful emotions is a stress prison from which some clients seek release and we use the hypotheses of

REBT as a way of explaining to clients how we can stress, or distress ourselves, through the beliefs we hold about our lives, how those beliefs can lead us to overly disturb ourselves emotionally and what we can do to change this pattern.

A surprising number of clients have ways of thinking which keep them locked into those problems and situations which generate their stress. As an aid to understanding that it is the way of thinking about the problem, rather than the situation itself which is so self-defeating and stressful, ten of the common beliefs which recognizably get in the way of effective living have been suggested (adapted Ellis and Dryden, 1987):

- I must be liked, loved and approved of
- I must always do everything competently
- I must have what I want and my plans must work out
- I must never be hurt and people who harm me are evil
- I must be anxious and upset about danger
- I must not have problems and if I do there should be quick and easy solutions
- I must not be expected to make demands of myself or exercise self-discipline
- I must not be held responsible for my own misery which is caused by other people and experiences
- What happened to me in the past is responsible for how I act and feel today
- Happiness comes from just enjoying myself, avoiding commitments and being passive.

Ellis contends that when these beliefs become ingrained and absolute, they are 'irrational' and that if any of them are violated in a person's life, she or he tends to think of, and therefore feel, that the experience is awful, terrible or catastrophic. Significantly, catastrophes are things which are out of our control and feeling without control in situations makes a marked contribution to our stress levels. There is support for Ellis's contentions in research which has found that 'irrational' beliefs correlate with a variety of psychological problems which include depression, anxiety in social situations, coronary-prone behaviour and lack of assertion (Daly and Burton, 1983).

On later analysis, Ellis (see 1994) was able to collapse the ten irrational ideas we have just identified into three main headings (Ellis *et al.*, 1997: 8–9).

1. 'I absolutely *must* perform well and/or win the love or approval of significant others or I am an *inadequate, worthless person.*'
2. 'You and other people *must* under all conditions and at all times be nice to me and treat me fairly or else *you are a rotten, horrible person!*'
3. 'Because it is preferable that I experience pleasure rather than pain, conditions under which I live absolutely *must be* comfortable, safe and advantageous or else the world is a *rotten place*, I *can't stand it*, and life is *horrible* and hardly worth living.'

These three irrational beliefs tend to lead to different consequences in people when triggered by external stress.

Number 1 may cause depression, anxiety, guilt and shame, which can lead to substance misuse and social withdrawal.

Number 2 can lead to rage and anger, which can trigger acts of violence or passive–aggressive behaviour.

Number 3 may lead to feelings of hurt and depression and can be associated with substance and alcohol misuse and procrastination.

BASIC THEORY

The five-star framework uses Ellis's primarily cognitively oriented theory of emotions and its ABCDE hypothesis of emotional disturbance and its amelioration (Ellis and Dryden, 1987). In its more elegant form this proposes that:

(A) represents a perceived activating event, experience or situation, actual or inferred, which happened to us in the past, or is occurring in the present, or is anticipated in the future. In the context of stress, (A) is some kind of short-term or chronic stressor or form of adversity confronting the client.

(B) represents the evaluative beliefs we have about the activating event (A) which mediate our view of these events and in terms of the model may be rigid or flexible.

Flexible beliefs or thoughts such as wishes, wants, hopes, preferences, desires are designated rational and helpful in dealing with stressful situations because they are adaptable to life events and keep the person problem-focused.

Rigid beliefs, by definition inflexible and dogmatic, are termed irrational and take the form of absolutes in thinking, such as shoulds, musts, oughts, got to's, have to's, which if not met may lead to the most 'awful' consequences. This way of thinking is usually 'problem interfering' and hinders the person from dealing with a stress problem or situation.

(C) represents those consequences which may be emotional, behavioural or physiological and are determined largely by (B) our evaluative beliefs about the event, not by the situation itself. (In REBT these are termed 'disturbances'.)

In summary:

(A) is an event, situation or experience (external or internal)

(B) is the evaluative belief we hold about that event

(C) is the consequence of that belief

(A) gives rise to (B) which results in (C)

ABC Example 1

(A) Activating event
  - Encountering a woman I really like and want to know better.
  - She may not like me. She may reject me (inference)

(B) Beliefs
  - I must not get rejected (evaluative belief)
  - otherwise I will be worthless and a failure. (evaluative conclusion)
  - It's awful that I don't have a partner. (evaluative conclusion)
  - I can't stand not having a partner. (evaluative conclusion)
  - I absolutely must have a partner. (evaluative belief)

(C) Consequences
  - Depression (emotional)
  - Avoiding women, now and in the future (behavioural)
  - Difficulties with sleeping (physiological)

ABC Example 2

Jane, the deputy head we met previously, wants to give a perfect presentation to the school governors to justify her recent promotion.

Jane's (A) activating event
  - giving a presentation to the governors.

Jane's (B) evaluative beliefs or thoughts about the presentation
  - I must give a perfect presentation (without mistakes, errors or omissions) (evaluative belief)
  - if it is not perfect I will be a complete failure (evaluative conclusion)
  - I couldn't bear to be despised (evaluative conclusion)

Jane's (C) consequences of her beliefs (B)
  - emotional – anxiety, panic, fear
  - biological – stomach upsets, physical feelings of panic
  - behavioural – agitation, inability to concentrate, unnecessarily cleaning the house

The emotional, behavioural and physiological consequences of Jane's persisting problem-interfering beliefs are disturbances which result in her feeling stressed and ill, reduce her ability to perform and block her ability to manage her stress. Consequently Jane cannot get on with her job, prepare her presentation nor focus on ways of relieving her stress.

What to do about it?

Beliefs are not treated as facts, but as assumptions which can be looked at in varying degrees as true or false, logical or illogical and thereby open to challenge and change.

The five-star way of helping Jane to reduce her stress sufficiently to be able to prepare her presentation is to explain that the beliefs she has stated lead to self-defeating emotions and behaviours (she feels upset and she cannot work).

Jane sees the presentation to the governors as the sole cause of her stress. Her counsellor, while understanding that the reality of public speaking does generate anxiety for her, sees her beliefs – that she must do a perfect job, that she will be a complete failure if she does not, and that she could not bear to be despised – as the cause of her stress and explains this to Jane.

The five-star model is used to encourage Jane to weigh the evidence for and against her beliefs with the aim of constructing a different, rational and effective belief system to change the stress situation. Weighing the evidence is achieved when the counsellor examines that evidence with Jane because the consequences of her thinking bring her pain and discomfort (anxiety and panic), divert her to self-defeating behaviour (cleaning the house, when it is already clean) and prevent her from working on her presentation (inability to concentrate).

This introduces the (D) and (E) of the ABCDE paradigm.

(D) represents 'disputing' at a cognitive, emotive, behavioural or imaginal level, those beliefs or ideas which produce disturbance and stress, particularly self-defeating beliefs, and interfere with the ability to focus on the stress problem. The aim of disputing is to achieve (E).

(E) represents a changed effective, efficient and flexible approach to the situation which reverses the client's decline to the consequences at (C). A new and effective, rational outlook. (See Jane's problem-facilitating ABCDE form Figure 5.4 on p. 101)

Box 6.1 offers a brief outline of the language and format involved in disputing five major irrational beliefs.

Box 6.1 *Disputing five major irrational beliefs* (Ellis *et al.*, 1997)

Irrational or self-defeating beliefs are evaluative and consist of a primary 'must' or 'should' followed by four derivative or evaluative conclusions which combine to set the boundaries of what the counsellor examines or disputes with the client.

1. *'Musts'*
   - 'I must perform well.'
   - 'My partner must treat me fairly.'

Demandingness in the form of musts, shoulds, have to's, got to's, oughts are often found at the core of emotional disturbance. However, anxiety-inducing beliefs, such as 'I must succeed', can seldom be disputed with one challenge 'Why must you succeed?', which may invoke the answer 'Because it's what I want'.

Similarly:
   'I must never make a mistake.'
   'Why must you never make a mistake?'
   'Because I'll be pathetic.'

Counsellors will normally need great persistence in applying a range of logical, empirical and pragmatic disputes targeted directly at the self-defeating and problem-interfering beliefs.

Although clients' preferences can be supported there is no evidence to support their 'musts' or 'demands'. It is not life's purpose to provide us with what we want. Just as a demanding client has turned their preferences into musts, they will find it less self-defeating to turn them back into preferences, thus making fewer demands on themselves, others or the universe.

2. *Awfulizing*
   - 'Life is awful.'
   - 'It's terrible to fail.'

Believing that something is awful is a largely destructive way of taking events about which it would be legitimate to say 'that was bad' and instead saying 'that was awful', or 'that was terrible', which makes things appear worse than they really are. This may seem to be semantic nit-picking, but words are powerful and the implication of describing something that was bad as terrible is to turn it into a horror story. It implies that something is 100 per cent bad – or as bad as it could ever be. This can lead to the thought that 'It should not be as bad as this, but because it is so bad I shall never be happy.' It is less self-defeating and stressful to give up the horror and stick with 'it's bad'.

3. *Low frustration tolerance*
   - 'I can't stand the discomfort of this terrible experience.'
   - 'I can't stand this awful feeling of anxiety.'

Life does confront us with stressful circumstances. Yet the logic of the passage of time does suggest that even if the adverse circumstances of the event which activates stress persist, clients can often stand what they think they cannot and can find some degree of happiness. They do, however, make themselves feel worse than they need by holding a basic, self-defeating attitude of 'I can't stand it.'

4. *Damning of self and others*
   - 'I'm worthless.'
   - 'She's a total idiot.'

Although we all may behave in ways which are reprehensible this does not make us totally bad people. Global self-damnation and blame, such as 'I am a total failure', is self-defeating and destructive and can lead clients into emotional difficulties. It is a rational, self-helping alternative to work towards accepting yourself and other people as fallible and the world as a complex place, too complex to be described as wholly bad. The world is not full of evil people, but of fallible human beings.

5. *Always and never-never land thinking*
   - 'Nobody likes me, I will always be rejected.'
   - 'I'm not good enough, I will never succeed.'

This kind of thinking relies on the largely irrational belief that some people are totally unlovable and total failures. It is usually implicit in a primary premise such as 'I must perform well'.

'I'll never get another job.' Never is an overgeneralization. It actually feels very different to think and to say, 'It may be difficult for me to find another job, but if I persist I will increase my chances.'

I'll never . . .' can become a self-fulfilling prophecy, because the person saying it does not try and not trying actually makes the never come true.

The demands of disputing

Disputing absolute beliefs demands persistance and a high frustration tolerance from counsellors, whose faith in the logical and rational needs to be greater than the client's belief in the illogical and irrational. Not all counsellors have, or want, such a faith or persistence. Nevertheless they may well agree with the broad aim of rationality, which is to help people to overcome their problems and achieve their basic goals and purposes, such as to survive and achieve some happiness.

We focus on the irrational beliefs of counsellors towards the end of this chapter – to highlight that we have them and that it is important to deal with them!

THE FIVE-STAR FRAMEWORK IN ACTION

We have suggested that the framework can be used when a problem or stressor triggers a high level of emotional distress, disturbance or avoidance. We have emphasized our view that it is a client's beliefs (B) about stressors at (A) which largely lead to emotional, behavioural and physiological consequences at (C). Through disputing (D) the beliefs which disturb and interfere with problem management through a variety of methods, the client can be helped to internalize a new outlook which reduces their stress and produces a more satisfying and productive life (E).

Difficulties may arise if clients do not accept that their beliefs (B), not the event (A), largely contribute to their stress (C). For example, if a client believes that someone else (A) makes them feel guilty, or angry (C), then they are giving over control of how they feel emotionally and how distressed they become, to that other person. This is called A–C thinking. To give control back to the client, the counsellor can show how their beliefs (B) about the other person (A) largely contribute to their guilt or anger. (This is called B–C thinking.)

DISCRETE STEPS OF THE FIVE-STAR FRAMEWORK IN ACTION
(adapted Palmer, 1997b, c)

In this example we return to Jane our deputy head, who appears throughout the book. However, we focus on different beliefs in this session to help to illustrate the model.

Step one

A problem or stressor is agreed and noted in specific and concrete terms (A). For example, giving a perfect presentation.

Step two

The counsellor asks the client how she or he feels about the problem (C). For example, very anxious.

Step three

The counsellor uses inference chaining to discover which aspect of the problem (A) the client really becomes disturbed about. Often the real underlying fear is not the initial problem which has been presented.

INFERENCE CHAINING

The purpose of inference chaining is to discover the fear which underlies a set of inferences or inter-connected issues about a particular problem. An inference is an interpretation which goes beyond observable reality, but gives meaning to it. Like all interpretations it may be accurate or inaccurate. What chaining can reveal is the particular aspect of an event about which a client is most stressed.

In inference chaining it is temporarily assumed that the client's fears could occur and they are not challenged. Counsellors avoid using A–C language 'she makes you feel angry', and reinforce B–C thinking, 'you feel angry about her behaviour'.

EXAMPLE

Where (C) is anxiety, an inference chain with Jane, our deputy head might start as below.

Co:	What is anxiety-provoking in your mind about not giving a perfect presentation?
Jane:	The governors may laugh.
Co:	Let's assume for the moment that they do laugh, what is anxiety-provoking about that?
	(Counsellor does not challenge her inference and assumes, temporarily that it is true.)
Jane:	I'll be discredited. They might think I'm stupid.
Co:	For the moment let's assume that you are discredited and are seen as stupid, what's anxiety provoking about that?
Jane:	The head might demote me . . . I could lose my promotion. (Client is upset at this point.)
Co:	(Pauses) . . . Mm . . . If the head did demote you and you lost your promotion, what would you be anxious about?
Jane:	Well, I'd have less money and I wouldn't be able to pay the mortgage on my new house. I'd have to sell it.
Co:	Mmm . . . Jane, I'd just like to review what we've covered. You are possibly anxious about a number of issues:
	1. the governors laughing
	2. being discredited and being seen as stupid
	3. you could be demoted
	4. you could lose your new house . . .
	When you are getting anxious which do you think you are most anxious about?
	(Counsellor reviewing inference chain with client.)
Jane:	I very much doubt I'd lose my house, my husband would pay more of the mortgage, but my job as deputy head means so much to me. I wouldn't want to lose that. It's what I've always wanted.
Co:	Are you saying it's not so much the presentation you're anxious about, but losing the deputy head's job which you treasure is the real fear.
	(Counsellor confirming that the Critical A has been found.)
Jane:	Yes, that's it!

> *Co:* Uh-huh . . . That fear is really unpleasant for you, isn't it. We can work on this together and we will see some light at the end of the tunnel.
> (Counsellor acknowledging the power of Jane's feeling and introducing hope for change.)

Step four (a): teaching the B–C connection

Clients vary in their capacity to accept and understand the principles of the B–C connection and there are several standard REBT methods which can be used at this stage, once the problem-interfering beliefs have been elicited. In later counselling sessions, step four (a) is usually unnecessary. One of the ways of teaching this connection is the Money Example (adapted from Dryden, 1990).

> *Co:* I would like to teach you a model which explains how people's thinking generates stress for them. Would you be interested in learning it now?
>
> *Client:* Yes, Okay.
>
> *Co:* This model has four parts. In part one, imagine that you have £10 in cash and the following belief:
> 'I prefer to have a minimum of £11 in cash but it's not essential. It would be bad if I had less than my preferred £11 but it wouldn't be the end of the world.'
> Now, if you really believed this, how would you feel about only having £10, when you prefer, but do not demand that you have a minimum of £11.
>
> *Client:* I'd feel concerned if I only had £10.
>
> *Co:* Right or you'd feel annoyed or disappointed, but you wouldn't feel like killing yourself?
>
> *Client:* Certainly not!
>
> *Co:* Okay . . . Now, in part two of the model you hold a different belief, which is:
> 'I absolutely must have a minimum of £11 in cash at all times. I must! I must! And it would be the end of the world if I had less.'
> Holding this belief you find you have only £10 in cash. How would you feel this time about having £10 when you absolutely insisted that you must have £11?
>
> *Client:* I think I'd feel very anxious.
>
> *Co:* Right. Something important has happened. In both situations you have £10 in cash, but different beliefs lead to different feelings.
> Here is part three of the model. You have the same belief you had in part two:
> 'I absolutely must have a minimum of £11 in cash at all times. I must! I must! And it would be the end of the world if I had less.'
> This time holding this belief you find you have £12 in cash. How would you feel this time about having £12 when you absolutely insist on having a minimum of £11 at all times?
>
> *Client:* I'd feel chuffed, really relieved.
>
> *Co:* Now we come to the fourth and last part of the model. You have £12 in cash and that same belief:
> 'I absolutely must have a minimum of £11 in cash at all times. I must! I must! And it would be the end of the world if I had less.'
> Something could occur to you that you could become anxious about. What do you think it might be?

Client: Well, I believe that I must have a minimum of £11 in cash at all times. I have more than the minimum, yet I'm getting anxious again. Yes. I see it. What if I lose £2? I'm scared I might lose £2. Is that it?

Co: Yes. Or you might spend £2 or you might have it stolen. The point of the model is that practically all people whether rich or poor, black or white, female or male make themselves disturbed when they do not get what they believe they must get. In addition, they are vulnerable to disturbing themselves even when they do have what they believe they must have, because they could always lose it.

Client: I see. So, this means that I will be unhappy by making myself disturbed when I do not get what I believe I must have. It also means that when I do get what I believe I must have, I'm likely to become or remain anxious because I can always lose it.

Co: Right. If people would stick firmly (but not rigidly) to their non-demanding preferences and not turn them into 'musts', they will feel a healthy concern when they don't get what they prefer. They will also be able to take constructive action to change the situation or prevent stress in the future. Does that seem clear?

Client: Yes.

Co: Okay. Well in case I haven't made my point clearly enough can you explain it back to me in your own words.

Dryden (1995) suggests that, when presented correctly, the money example is a powerful way of teaching the ABC model. He also acknowledges that it is difficult to master and that trainees have difficulty in learning it. He deems it important to add a completing rational statement for the client to follow, such as:

'I would prefer to have a minimum of £11 in cash at all times, but it is not essential that I do so. It would be unfortunate to have less than my preferred £11, but it would not be the end of the world.'

In addition, Dryden points to the importance of clarifying client's vague responses to the counsellor's question 'How would you feel?' in the example. If a client answers 'Upset', there is no way of knowing whether this describes a healthy negative feeling such as concern or disappointment, or an unhealthy negative feeling such as anxiety, anger or guilt. To avoid confusion he suggests that counsellors clarify with clients what they mean by 'upset'. This will help them to distinguish healthy from unhealthy emotions and enable the connection to be made between these two kinds of emotion and their accompanying rational and irrational beliefs. Other words or phrases that will need clarifying are 'stressed', 'frustrated' and 'I've lost it'.

Palmer and Dryden (1995: 189) offer an illustration of using an intervention based on the money example with Sue, a client who had become stressed as a result of feeling guilty about not helping a friend in difficulty.

Co: Can you imagine just for the moment that you have this belief that you would prefer or like to have £11 in your pocket but that you don't have to have this amount. Unfortunately there is a hole in your pocket and you've lost £1 and that's left you with only £10. How would you feel?

Sue: It wouldn't concern me too much as I'm used to being like that anyway!

Co: Right. You wouldn't be very stressed about it. You would probably feel some concern. Let's suppose you are now telling yourself that you 'absolutely must have £11 in your pocket' and you still only have £10. How would you feel this time?

Sue: Anxious.

Co: If I said 'here's a pound coin', how would you feel?

Sue: Relieved.

Co: Right. However, with that belief 'I must at all times have £11 in my pocket', you would still be anxious. Why?

Sue: Because I would think that I could lose another £1.

Co: So even when you have what you demand your anxiety could return.

Sue: Yeah.

Step four (b)

When the aspect of (A), the activating event that Sue is really disturbed about, is agreed, the counsellor works with the client to assess the beliefs which disturb her, or interfere with her management of the problem.

Co: Can you see how earlier you were describing how you felt guilty about not helping a friend out and in that situation you were also placing demands on yourself? (Counsellor relating the abstract exercise back to the present.)

Sue: I think that whenever I feel guilty it's because I'm telling myself that I should have done something or shouldn't have done something.

Co: Maybe we could consider in counselling looking at these shoulds and musts.

Sue: Yeah.

Co: However, if you've got a preferable 'should', for example, I preferably should . . . (Sue interrupted at this point.)

Sue: No! No! It's 'I should have done that; it should have been done; it shouldn't have happened, it shouldn't have occurred.'

Co: And that's when you get the guilt or the anxiety? (At this stage to confirm that the client understood the model the counsellor would normally have asked her to explain it in her own words. However . . . she clearly demonstrated her understanding of the model and the counsellor thought that it was unnecessary to check this.)

Sue: Yeah.

Co: To simplify things, we call the activating event 'A'. Thus when you didn't help your friend this was the 'A'. We call your beliefs such as 'I should have helped my friend' the 'B', and the consequences, in this case guilt, the 'C'. If you can remember the sequence as ABC it helps to analyse what is going on in any situation. Therefore it is mainly the 'Bs' and not the 'A' that lead to 'C', the consequences. (The A, B and C were drawn on a whiteboard by the counsellor to demonstrate the sequence.)

Sue: Hmmm. It wasn't just that I should have helped her but the other side of it was that I felt selfish as I wanted to carry on with what I wanted to do. I wanted to have my curry and drink my bottle of wine.

Co: You're right. There are usually a number of thoughts that may be involved with an emotion.

DRAWBACKS

Examples using money are not suitable teaching aids for all clients, some of whom have unfortunate educational, or other associations with 'money work' which may cause them to switch off their brains at this example. There is another example, the Deserted Island Technique (see Chapter 7) which may be used to teach the B–C connection.

RETURN TO JANE

Let's now return to Jane to see how the counsellor elicited her problem-interfering beliefs by using evocative language.

> *Co:*   I want you to really imagine that you've been demoted. You've lost this job that you've always wanted. Remember you've spent years trying to get this deputy head's job and you've lost it. Can you imagine this in your mind's eye?
>
> *Jane:*   (Upset) . . . I can.
>
> *Co:*   Mmm . . . What are you telling yourself at this very moment?
>
> *Jane:*   I must not lose this job.
>
> *Co:*   Ah ha . . . And if you did lose it?
>   (Counsellor assumes the feared event occurs to help to find Jane's derivative beliefs.)
>
> *Jane:*   I just couldn't stand it, life would be so awful.
>
> *Co:*   (Pause) . . . Yeah . . . How would you see yourself as a person?
>
> *Jane:*   A total failure!
>
> *Co:*   Mmm . . . And that really upsets you.

When Jane has had space to express her very real distress and is ready to continue, her self-defeating beliefs are noted down and become the focus for disputation. (It can be helpful to write the problem down either clearly on paper or on a whiteboard, so that she and the counsellor can share exactly what the focus of the session is.) For example:

(A) = losing treasured job
(B) = I must not lose this job, and if I did
     I couldn't stand it
     Life would be so awful
     I would be a total failure
(C) = High anxiety.

Problem-facilitating (ABCDE) forms (Table 6.1) can be used in the counselling session to help client and counsellor to stay problem-focused. Clients can also use these for homework and self-help purposes.

It is worth noting that during this later counselling session, Jane decided that a different inference was more relevant to the one initially agreed (see Chapter 5). This highlights the importance of giving sufficient time to inference chaining and

Table 6.1 *Jane's new problem-facilitating form*

Workplace/other problem (A)	Thinking interfering with problem-solving (B)	Emotional/behavioural/physical reaction (C)	Thinking facilitating problem-solving (D)	New and effective approach to problem (E)
Losing job	If I lost my job I would be a total failure	Anxious Procrastination Unable to concentrate	There is no evidence that if I lost my job therefore I'm a total failure. It's not logical to conclude that if I fail to keep my job, therefore I'm a total failure. If I carry on thinking like this I will remain anxious and more likely to perform badly!	It's almost impossible to become a total failure whatever I do – I may as well get back to work and concentrate on preparing for the presentation – 'Do, don't stew'

also how clients can change their minds over a period of time. Notice that this latest inference has led to different problem interfering beliefs being drawn out.

Step five

The next step in the process is to examine and dispute these beliefs with Jane. A variety of ways can be used to do this and one of the most commonly used methods to help clients to modify or change their beliefs is questioning. In essence, didactic disputing is teaching rational principles by explanation (Dryden, 1995).

Three basic strategies for disputing irrational beliefs which are most effective if used in combination rather than in isolation are logical, empirical and pragmatic questions (Ellis *et al.*, 1997).

1. *Focus on the illogicality of magical thinking.* To believe that because I want something to happen therefore it must happen is to adopt the magical thinking of a small child. What is attractive thinking in a child may be highly stressful in an adult. The purpose is to help the client to understand that the belief makes no logical sense through questions such as 'Does it logically follow that . . .? or 'Where is the logic in . . .?

2. *Focus on the evidence of empiricism.* By using questions which ask clients to support their beliefs with empirical evidence. 'Where is the evidence that you must succeed?' There actually is no law of the universe which says that we must succeed, if there were, we would never fail; we would have to succeed no matter what we did or failed to do. To believe absolutely that you must succeed is inconsistent with reality and generates more stress for you.

3. *Focus on the success of pragmatism.* 'Where is believing that you absolutely must succeed getting you, other than into anxiety and depression?' This is demonstrating to a client that the beliefs do not work, produce stress and poor results and do not help the client to achieve goals.

Palmer and Burton (1996: 80–1) offer some questions qhich are useful when challanging rigid and stress inducing thinking.

Empirical challenge

Is there any evidence that you must?
Is there a law of the universe that states that you must?
If there were a law of the universe that states that you must . . . How do you account for the fact that you didn't do what the law dictated that you do?
Would a scientist think there was any evidence in support of your must?

Logical challenge

Where is the logic that you must?
Does it logically follow that because you want to . . . therefore you must?
Would a philosopher think it was good logic to believe that because you want to . . . therefore you must?

Pragmatic challenge

Where will it get you to believe that you must?
What are the emotional and behavioural consequences of believing that you must?
Is it healthy to believe that you must?
How is believing that you must going to help you to achieve your (long-term/healthy) goals?

RETURN TO JANE

We will now return to the counsellor examining and disputing Jane's problem–interfering beliefs (p. 123).

Counsellor: In this session we now have about twenty minutes left. Which of these four beliefs that we have written down is the one that you are most disturbed about?
Jane: I'm most upset when I think I'm a 'total failure'.
Co: So, in this session we can focus on disputing the belief 'I would be a total failure'. And then in the next session we can return to the other beliefs if you would like that. Is that okay?
Jane: Yeah.
Co: Our job now is to look at your belief and see if it's true. I want to start by asking you a logical question. Is it logical to conclude that if you failed to retain your job, therefore you would be a 'total failure'?
Jane: No, it's not logical, but I still believe I would be a 'total failure'.
Co: How old are you, Jane?

Jane:	I'm 39 next birthday.
Co:	Do you think it's logical to rate yourself as a 'total failure' if over a 38-year period the worst thing you have done is on one occasion to lose your job?
Jane:	I see your point.
Co:	What is my point?
	(Counsellor checking understanding.)
Jane:	Well, I think it is that it's not logical to call myself a 'total failure' after one event.
Co:	Okay. Now I'd like to introduce you to an empirical disputation, which is really a form of reality testing. Where is the evidence that if you lose your job, you will become a 'total failure'?
Jane:	I don't know, but it's what I believe.
Co:	What would you have to do over your 38 years on this planet to be a 'total failure'?
Jane:	Well, I suppose I would have to fail at many things.
Co:	In that case you would be a 'partial failure'. What would you have to do to be a total failure?
Jane:	(laughs) Fail at everything?
Co:	You're right! But that would be difficult. Would a 'total failure' be born? Arrive for her session on time, get out of bed in the morning, pass exams, have children and so on?
Jane:	Okay. Point taken.
Co:	Where is it written that you would be a 'total failure'?
Jane:	In my head? (laughs)
Co:	I would like to suggest that the evidence points to us being able to rate our skills and lack of skills, or skills deficits, aspects of our personality, our abilities, our looks, but we are always too complex to be rated globally as an overall 'total failure'!
Jane:	I've never thought of it like that before.
Co:	Finally I would like to introduce you to pragmatic disputing . . .
Jane:	Oh no! Not another one!
Co:	Just one more. Where is it getting you holding on to the belief 'I would be a "total failure"'?
Jane:	That's easy to answer – I'm so anxious that I can't even prepare for the presentation. In fact, I'm more likely to blow it feeling like this!
Co:	Any thoughts so far about what we have just done?
Jane:	I've never really thought about things this way before. I can now see how the way I think is making me stressed.

The work of this session is recorded in Figure 6.1.

DISPUTING AND CLIENT DISTRESS

It may appear unfeeling to continue to question clients who are clearly upset by their answers and it is important for counsellors to respect and acknowledge their client's distress, without becoming too involved in it. Integrative counsellors are not callous and unfeeling, but their empathy is not easy to translate to the printed page.

This is a teaching approach and its Socratic disputing of beliefs puts the onus on the client to think and answer the questions. Literally the client's brain takes the strain as an alternative to their emotion taking the commotion!

This may lead to cognitive–emotive dissonance as the client thinks about the issues involved in holding onto or modifying their irrational beliefs. As clients work towards change and begin to make progress, they sometimes feel different to the way they felt before. This feeling of difference often does not seem natural and clients may think 'This is not really me' and become fearful about the change. It can be helpful to liken the change in beliefs to suddenly starting to exercise or jog, with a resulting stiffness in previously under-used muscles. As you persist with your exercise, your physique improves and you feel quite at home with the fitter, you. Emotional problem solving is like exercise in the sense that practice improves and perseverance is the key.

In using disputing it is important to give clients sufficient time to think about and then answer the questions. Often clients have not previously considered how their thinking contributes to their distress, or how their thoughts may not be logical, empirical or pragmatic.

Step six

Once the beliefs have been challenged sufficiently for the client to understand the process, counsellor and client develop more helpful, flexible and problem-focused beliefs which offer a different perspective. In Jane's case, her new belief was: 'It's strongly preferable not to lose my job, but if I do, I could stand it. It may be bad, but hardly awful, and it would not prove that I am a failure, only that I failed to keep my job.'

It is crucial for the client to believe that the new rational beliefs make sense to her or him and that there is evidence for them, rather than accept them merely because the counsellor has suggested that they are rational and make sense. One of the most common errors made by counsellors using this method is not regularly obtaining feedback from clients to ensure that they have understood the concepts discussed.

(In actual counselling work we seldom use the words 'irrational' or 'rational' with clients, but prefer to use 'self-defeating' or 'problem-interfering' and self-helping/ problem-focused or problem facilitating.)

Step seven

Usually it is helpful to negotiate a relevant homework assignment so that the client can put her or his new problem-focused beliefs into practice. We remind clients that the most important part of the week is not the one hour they spend in counselling, but the other 167 hours which remain, in which they can apply a new effective approach to dealing with problems.

RETURN TO JANE

We now return to the case study. Jane decided that for a homework assignment she wanted to reinforce the strength of her new problem-focused belief. Obviously the counsellor did not want to encourage her to lose her job by giving a poor presentation to the board of governors, just to prove that she 'could stand it' and that she was not a 'failure'. However, Jane agreed to practise daily using coping imagery in which she imagined losing her job and visualized herself still coping with her life, reminding herself during the exercise: 'Even though I've lost my job, I can stand it. It may be bad, but hardly awful, and it does not prove that I'm a failure, only that I failed to keep my job.'

She agreed to do this assignment for 10 minutes, twice a day – while having a bath before breakfast and after her evening meal. Jane completed an individual assignment record (see Figure 6.1) which ensured that she understood why she was doing the assignment and that she and the counsellor had considered any obstacles which might prevent her from doing the exercise. (See Appendix 5 for copy of blank form.)

We have found from experience that it is important to make sure that the client understands why they are undertaking the particular task, as this helps to increase their willingness to carry it out. In addition, negotiating specific times when clients

Name . . . . _Jane_ . . . . Date . . _28/2/97_ . . . Negotiated with . . . . _Pat_ . . . . .

Agreed assignment:

To practise daily using coping imagery whereby I see myself losing my job but still coping with my life. I will remind myself that 'Even though I've lost my job, I can stand it. It may be bad, but hardly awful, and it does not prove that I'm a failure, only that I failed to keep my job.' I'll do this for 10 minutes twice a day - while having a bath and after my evening meal.

The purpose(s) of the assignment:

To strengthen my belief that I would survive if I lost my job. This will help me to be less anxious when I give a presentation.

What obstacles, if any, stand in the way of your completing this assignment and how can you overcome them?

Obstacle	To be overcome by
1 _May not have time for a bath in the morning before breakfast_	_Set the alarm and get up promptly_
2 _After my meal the telephone may ring_	_Until I've done the exercise I won't answer the phone - I can put the answerphone on_
3 _I may be going out for the evening_	_If this happens, I'll ensure that I'll do the exercise before my evening meal._
4	

Signed . . . . _Jane_ . . . .

Figure 6.1 _Individual assigment record_

will do the exercise usually increases the likelihood of them completing it success-fully, especially if the obstacles have been worked through, because the client is then prepared for them.

HOMEWORK ASSIGNMENTS

There is a range of homework assignments which clients can use to help them to modify their problem-interfering beliefs and work towards increased self acceptance. Some examples are:

- bibliotherapy – reading self-help books such as those by Dryden and Gordon, 1990, 1992, 1993; Ellis and Harper, 1997; Lazarus, *et al.*, 1993; Palmer and Burton, 1996; Palmer and Strickland, 1996.
- listening to recordings of the counselling sessions (Palmer and Dryden, 1995)
- completing problem-facilitating forms (Ellis *et al.*, 1997) (see Appendix 3)
- completing irrational belief and rational belief cost-benefit analysis forms (Palmer and Burton, 1996; Ellis *et al.*, 1997) (see Appendices 6 and 7).

To conclude

The overview of the five-star model for emotional problem solving is now completed. In the next section of this chapter we distinguish between self-esteem and self-acceptance in the five-star framework; describe further ways in which counsellors can dispute and challenge problem-interfering beliefs; and return briefly to the therapeutic working relationship.

SELF-ESTEEM AND SELF-ACCEPTANCE

Unconditional self-acceptance

The concept of unconditional acceptance is probably most associated with the work of Rogers (1957; 1961), but it is also a tenet of the five-star framework that people who hold a rational, flexible, self-helping belief about making a mistake will be able to accept their own fallibility and that of others and of the world without becoming overly distressed if they fail at an endeavour. On the other hand people who believe rigidly that they and others should be infallible, never make significant mistakes because if they do, they are totally worthless people, tend to regard the world as culpable for putting so many difficulties in their way. Such beliefs are more likely to exacerbate stress in such people if they do not achieve their goals. When this happens events which appear innocuous can become scenarios for stress. Our framework uses a number of ways, originating with REBT, of encouraging clients to avoid defining themselves, in the event of failure, with all-encompassing, global ratings such as worthless, incompetent or failure and instead to accept themselves as fallible, complex and changing human beings (Palmer and Dryden, 1995)

Not self-esteem

The concept of unconditional self-acceptance is not the same as self-esteem in the sense that people often believe that it is external factors such as passing exams, having a satisfactory job, being a good parent or grandparent, or being approved of are enhancers of self-esteem. Palmer (1997e: 6) shows that where this philosophy contributes to stress is when a person does not have one of these external factors that is of such personal significance to them. He points out that:

> Considering that all individuals age, are likely to be made redundant, may lose their partner through death or separation, may not be able to purchase or maintain a property, may commit a sin, then holding the philosophy of esteeming oneself upon attributes or external factors, in a modern society may be considered as setting oneself up to fail at some time in the future.

Unconditional self-acceptance is cultivated when clients are encouraged not to give themselves an all-encompassing rating, but to distinguish between different aspects of themselves, the things they do, their thoughts, feelings or behaviour. This is to reduce the risk of them experiencing stressful negative emotions such as depression, anxiety, guilt or shame (Ellis, 1994).

Non-accepting beliefs accrue from childhood when we receive messages which convey that we are 'good' if we do well in exams, or 'stupid' if we make a mistake. If these messages are received and reinforced often enough we may come to believe that we are equivalent to our actions. 'I did a good thing in passing my exams so I'm good' or 'I did a stupid thing, I made a mistake, so I'm stupid'. These non-accepting beliefs are constantly reinforced each time we make a mistake, we remind ourselves that we're 'stupid', worthless or perhaps a hopeless parent. Other people may also reinforce these beliefs for us when we make a mistake and they tell us we are a 'useless worker', or a 'complete write off'.

According to Palmer (1997e), non-accepting beliefs and demanding or 'musturba-tory' beliefs go hand in hand, for example, 'I must perform well, otherwise I am a failure.' It is important to dispute both the 'I must perform well' and the 'otherwise I am a failure' because the two reinforce and sustain each other. For example, a person who really thinks that they will be a failure will usually insist that they 'must' perform well. Disputing the 'I'm a failure' successfully means that the client is less likely to demand that they 'must' perform well.

Encouraging greater self-acceptance

Our approach focuses on helping clients to accept themselves rather than working to improve their self-esteem, which may lead to them creating stress for themselves when they do not succeed as well as they would like, or when they receive the disapproval of other people. We include several interventions, in addition to the disputing form of questions already described. These are designed to help clients to increase their self-acceptance and thereby reduce their stress and are adapted from Palmer (1997e).

BOWL OF FRUIT ANALOGY

A well-known intervention which temporarily moves the attention of the client away from their present-ing problem.

> *Co:* I want to make sure I've understood you correctly. You're saying that if you fail to reach your deadline, in your eyes you are a 'total failure' and 'a waste of space'.
>
> *Client:* Yes, a total failure and a waste of space.
>
> *Co:* We'll come back to this in a minute, but can we first look at an analogy that may help you to see the situation differently. Is that OK?
>
> *Client:* That's fine.
>
> *Co:* Imagine for a moment that you have a bowl of fruit in front of you. What are your favourite fruits?
>
> *Client:* Bananas, apples, oranges, perhaps grapes.
>
> *Co:* In your mind's eye, really imagine the bananas . . . apples . . . oranges . . . and grapes . . . in the fruit bowl. Can you see them?
>
> *Client:* Yes, easily.
>
> *Co:* Now look at the grapes. Imagine finding one bad grape in the bowl. What would you do?
>
> *Client:* I'd throw the grape away of course.
>
> *Co:* Isn't it interesting. If you have a bowl of fruit with just one bad grape, you would throw away the bad grape and keep the rest of the fruit. Yet if you fail to reach a deadline, you consider yourself 'a total failure and a waste of space' and effectively would throw yourself away! Do you agree that you are more complex than a bowl of fruit?'
>
> *Client:* Of course!
>
> *Co:* Then something doesn't quite add up.
>
> *Client:* I see what you're saying, it doesn't add up.
>
> *Co:* Do you think it would be useful if we continue examining your belief, 'I'm a total failure and a waste of space'?

This technique can also be used in assessment. If a client says that they would throw out the entire bowl of fruit on finding one bad grape, this would suggest an extreme case of 'all or nothing' thinking and in our experience such a client may require more help than is usual.

SERIOUSLY, BUT NOT TOO SERIOUSLY

It is a firm tenet of REBT to use humour in a sensitive way to both dispute irrational beliefs and reinforce rational self-helping beliefs and to help clients (with a sense of humour) to see that their problems may be exaggerations and have a funny side.

RATIONAL AND IRRATIONAL TENNIS

Dryden (1994: 119) communicates the principle of self-acceptance through the example of 'rational and irrational tennis'.

- Irrational tennis: 'I hit a bad shot, therefore I am a bad person – I hit a good shot therefore I am a good person.'
- Rational tennis: 'I hit a bad shot, therefore I am a fallible person – I hit a good shot therefore I am a fallible person.'

IN EXTREMIS – A GLASS OF WATER

Dryden (1994: 119) is also responsible for describing the therapist who throws a glass of water over himself (or possibly herself?) and then asks the client, 'Was that a silly thing to do?' To which the client frequently replies, 'Yes' or even 'Extremely'. The therapist then asks, 'Does that therefore make me a silly person?' To which, hopefully, the client responds, 'No'!

Counsellors who are unwilling to soak themselves could try asking the client, 'If I threw a glass of water over myself would that be a silly thing to do?' Less dramatic but perhaps indicative of a drier sense of humour!

THE GREEN FROG

Clients often believe that they do not have the skills to change their all-encompassing, damning self-rating and the green frog can be a helpful reminder that they do already possess some of these skills, without realizing it. This is a technique which can also be used in group work (see Palmer, 1997e: 14).

Co: So you are saying that if your boss thinks you are stupid for making mistakes, he must be right?

Client: Yes.

Co: If I said, 'You are a green frog', would you believe it?

Client: (laughing) Of course not!

Co: OK. Let's extend the argument. What if all eight of us in this room looked at you and said, 'You really are a green frog.' Would you believe it?

Client: Of course not!

Co: What happens if you went to a show and a whole theatre full of people, perhaps 500, all turned to you and sang, 'Jane is a green frog, do da, do da, Jane is a green frog, do da, do da day.' Would you believe it?

Client: (laughing) I might start to doubt myself!

Co: If you then went and looked in a mirror and just saw yourself as you are now, what then?

Client: Assuming I didn't look the same as a green frog, I would think that everybody else had lost their minds! (giggles)

Co: What if I, or all of us in the group said, 'You've made one mistake, therefore you are stupid', would you believe us?

Client: Probably.

Co: Isn't this interesting. When 500 people in a theatre say you are a 'green frog', you retain great powers of discrimination. Yet after making a mistake, if you mind-read your boss, or we tell you that you are stupid, you lose all your powers of discrimination, and agree with our crazy thinking.

Client: I haven't thought of it like that before.

Co: All I'm suggesting is that you could also choose to use your mental powers of discrimination in situations where you make mistakes and upset yourself.

BIG I, LITTLE I

A technique which specifically targets self-acceptance is one devised by Lazarus (1977), described by Ellis and associates (1997: 112) and adapted by Palmer (1997: 15–17).

The counsellor draws a 'big I' on a whiteboard or a sheet of paper (see Figure 6.2).

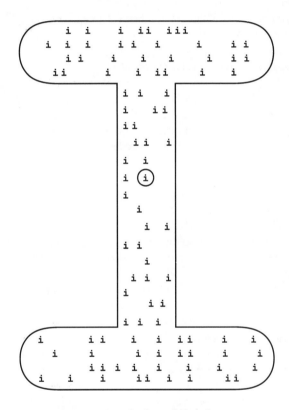

Figure 6.2   *The big I/little I diagram*

Co: Now this big I represents you, your totality, and we're going to fill it up in a minute with little 'i's which stand for various things about you, such as the way you smile, the kind of TV programme you like, and so on.

Client: I get you.

Co: OK. Now let's fill in this big I with a few things about you. What would your family or friends say were some of your good points?

Client: Oh, well, I've got a sense of humour, and let me see, I am kind-hearted, good to my children, I keep the house clean, I see that they're all looked after properly . . . will that do?

(As the client was speaking the therapist drew small 'i's inside the big I to represent the different aspects the client mentioned.)

Co:	Each of these little 'i's stands for some aspect of you; this one (pointing to a little 'i') stands for your good sense of humour, this other one stands for your kind-heartedness, and these other little 'i's represent all those other good points you mentioned you had.
Client:	I understand.
Co:	Now, these are some of the positive things. I imagine your friends and family may know you reasonably well.
Client:	Yes, they do.
Co:	What negative things would they say about you?
Client:	I easily get angry, I drive too fast . . . and I'm too trusting.
Co:	(Writing more little 'i's inside the big I) . . . gets angry, drives too fast, too trusting. Now what about any neutral or indifferent things about you?
Client:	Well, my dress sense isn't too bad; I can do alterations to the children's clothes and my house decorating ability is about average.
Co:	(Adding more little 'i's to represent the client's neutral points.) If we spent all day on this and considered all the things you have done, including every thought or idea you've had since you were born, how many little 'i's do you think we would have?
Client:	Loads! We'd easily fill up the big I.
Co:	Yes, millions of different aspects of yourself, good, bad and neutral. Now let's return to your problem. When you fail at something, like picking your ex-boyfriend and then finding you have made a bad choice (counsellor now circles one little 'i' to denote this), you say, 'Because I picked this partner and I made a poor choice yet again, that proves I'm a total failure, I'm weak and an inadequate person.' Bearing in mind what we've been discussing in the last five minutes, are you actually being accurate?
Client:	Well, I did make a big mistake when I picked him, and that's the fourth time I've been dumped after picking the wrong chap! Once again I failed to pick somebody who was right for me.
Co:	(Pointing to the little 'i' she had circled inside the big I.) Agreed; you did fail to pick the right person. But how does that – this little 'i' – make *you* (drawing a circle round the entire big I) a total failure, and a weak and inadequate person?
Client:	I suppose it doesn't.
Co:	Granted that you may have some skills lacking when it comes to choosing the right partner and you may sometimes act in a weak and inadequate way, but as we can see from the diagram, this doesn't make you a total failure. When would we have all the facts in so we could really decide if you were a total failure and a weak and inadequate person?
Client:	. . . When I die I suppose!
Co:	You're absolutely right. On your deathbed, when you could have your own day of judgement. You could open up the big book (therapist opens up her hands as if

opening up a large book) and count up the number of times you had been a failure in your entire life. 'Yes, I was a failure on 23rd February 1978; in 1983 I got a low mark in that exam; on four occasions I showed poor decision-making skills when I picked the wrong partners; my children weren't happy every day of their childhood; in 1985 I acted weakly; I lost my job, twice!'

Client: (laughing) Stop! Don't go on. It's ridiculous – to be a total failure I would have to be a failure all of my life which is blatantly absurd.

Co: Could you summarize what point you think I'm attempting to make?

Client: I'm too complex to be rated as a total failure although you can rate the things I do such as acting weakly or picking the wrong partner four times.

Co: You're right, you can rate your traits, deeds, appearance, actions, skills or skills deficits, but you are too complex to rate your entire self. To be fair to yourself, the only time you may wish to rate yourself globally, is when you have all the facts in, on your deathbed. And even then if we discover that you have failed at some or even many things in your life, it would still be an impossible task to rate yourself as a total failure! In fact one of the aspects of being human is dying, and I can guarantee that you won't fail at that!

Client: (laughs) You're not joking.

As Palmer emphasizes, the counsellor has to adapt the model to the particular problem which the client brings. The Socratic questions usually actively involve clients and then provide a wealth of ammunition to dispute their non-accepting and self-damning beliefs.

A major benefit of visual interventions is that, unlike dialogue, they are often easier for clients to recall when they become stressed about an event. Clients will reveal that they saw a 'big I, little i' diagram in their mind when trying to counter negative thoughts such as, 'Because I've failed my exam, I'm a total failure.'

Challenging exaggerations

We include a list of questions that may help the counsellor to challenge the exaggerations of clients (Palmer and Burton, 1996: 81–2).

In all these examples, the way in which the response is framed by the counsellor depends on the dynamics of the session and the situation of the individual client. The timing and the language are crucial.

- What makes that awful/devastating?
- Is it really that awful?
- Can you think of anything worse?
- Is it really as bad as your finger dropping off?
- I can see that it was very bad but how does that make it awful?
- When you say that you can't stand it, what do you picture happening to you?
- Surely you are living evidence that you have stood it for x years? Of course you may have stood it miserably.
- Just because you made a mistake, how does it logically follow that you are totally worthless/useless?

Counsellor-related irrational beliefs

Ellis (1983) suggests (and we concur) that counsellors fall victim to disabling irrational beliefs about their work, namely:

- I have to be successful with all my clients virtually all the time.
- I must be an outstanding counsellor, clearly better than other counsellors that I know or hear about
- I have to be greatly respected and loved by all my clients.
- Since I am doing my best and working so hard as a counsellor, my clients should be equally hard working and responsible, should listen to me carefully and should always push themselves to change.
- Because I am a person in my own right, I must be able to enjoy myself during therapy sessions and to use these sessions to solve my personal problems as much as to help my clients with their difficulties.

Palmer (1995a: 148) points out how these irrational beliefs can generate counsellor stress and reduce counsellor effectiveness. He uses the example of the irrational belief, 'I must be an outstanding counsellor', and suggests that counsellors dispute with themselves thus:

Logical: Although it may be preferable to be an outstanding counsellor, how does it logically follow that I *must be one*?
Answer: It does not logically follow.

Empirical: There is plenty of evidence that I strongly desire to be an outstanding counsellor, but where is the evidence that I must be an outstanding one? Or – where is it written that I must be an outstanding counsellor?
Answer: There is no evidence anywhere, nor is it written anywhere (apart from inside my own head) that I must be an outstanding counsellor.

Pragmatic: If I carry on holding on to this belief that I must be an outstanding counsellor, where is it going to get me?
Answer Whether my clients improve or do not improve, either way I will remain anxious and, paradoxically, my anxiety will reduce my effectiveness. This is exactly what I do not want.

Palmer (1995a: 148) further recommends that when counsellors have disputed their irrational beliefs with themselves, they are in a position to develop a more helpful coping statement such as: 'Although it is strongly preferable and desirable to be an outstanding counsellor, I don't have to be one. I'll just do my best whenever I can.'

To conclude

Although so far this chapter has focused on assessing and challenging clients' evaluative beliefs, in general, and counsellors also disputing thinking errors and inferences. Within the integrative approach the counsellor may become aware of a problem-interfering belief while working through the seven-step problem-solving model. It is feasible to challenge these beliefs as they arise within the seven steps, without going through the entire five-star framework.

In the next two sections we look at how to challenge thinking errors and inferences.

APPROACHES FOR CHALLENGING THINKING ERRORS AND INFERENCES

Challenging thinking errors

The term 'cognitive distortions' is familiarly used in cognitive therapies to describe those aspects of our thinking, whether they be rigid and inflexible patterns or those errors or illogical thoughts, which lead us to distress ourselves (Beck *et al.*, 1979). A list of common 'thinking errors' (sometimes known as thinking skills deficits) is given in chapter 2 in our outline of the model. Clients can use such a list, with its examples, as a way of checking to see if they recognize any of their own thought patterns.

Another example of a self-audit of thinking patterns is given in Box 6.2.

Box 6.2 *Self-audit of thinking patterns*

Thinking pattern

Jumping to conclusions: typically a conclusion which reflects poorly on myself.
Example: What's the point of applying for any more jobs? I've already been rejected by five employers.
Your personal example:
Your rating

Mind reading: reasoning from actions to thoughts, usually to my disadvantage.
Example: He's looking angry, it must be something I said.
Your personal example:
Your rating

All or nothing thinking: thinking in extreme terms.
Example: I must do each job extremely well, or I am a total failure.
Your personal example:
Your rating

Personalizing: taking things personally that have little to do with me; blaming myself for things that are not my responsibility.
Example: My students have not passed all their exams, I've only myself to blame.
Your personal example:
Your rating

Perfectionism: expecting myself or others to be perfect; condemning myself for not fully achieving an impossible goal.
Example: My children should always get good marks.
Your personal example:
Your rating

Minimizing: concentrating on my weaknesses and neglecting my strengths; using a double standard.
Example: Although I scored three goals, they were all pathetic.
Your personal example:
Your rating

Discounting the positive: paying attention only to negative or critical aspects; suspicious of positive feedback or events.
Example: My tutor said my essay was good but that's because she didn't have time to read it properly.
Your personal example:
Your rating

Fortune-telling: over-estimating the chances of disaster; predicting the outcome instead of experimenting with it.
Example: The weather is bound to be awful on our holiday.
Your personal example:
Your rating

Emotional reasoning: assuming my feelings about things are the way they really are; 'I don't feel like it now, I'll do it later', procrastination.
Example: She made me angry, so she must have treated me badly.
Your personal example:
Your rating

Labelling: totally condemning myself (or another) on the basis of a single event.
Example: Failing my driving test proves I'm stupid and a complete failure.
Your personal example:
Your rating

Adapted from Palmer and Burton (1996: 60–5, 83) who recommend the following rating scale:

1. I think like this very frequently.
2. I think like this quite frequently.
3. I think like this occasionally.
4. I never think like this.

Further ways in which clients can help themselves to correct their thinking errors, or untwist their thinking, are provided in Box 6.3.

Box 6.3   *I want to correct my thinking errors*

It is helpful if client and counsellor work through the examples together until the client feels practised enough to use the techniques themselves.

1. *Identify the distortions*   Monitor your negative thoughts and write down any that you recognize as distorted. If you recognize that a thought pattern is a thinking error, that will help you to see stress problems realistically.

2. *Examine the evidence*   Rather than automatically believing that your thinking error is true, ask yourself, 'What is the actual evidence for the way I am thinking?' If a person believes that their partner never helps around the house, they can make a list of the things that the partner does contribute.

3. *The double standard pattern*   Do you condemn yourself harshly for certain actions? How would you treat a work colleague or friend in the same situation? Would you condemn your friend? If not what is so special about you that you deserve harsh treatment whereas you would spare your work colleague or friend such complete condemnation?

4. *The experiment*   Try an experiment to test the validity of your thinking error thought. If you avoid small crowded rooms and believe you could not stand being in one for more than 30 seconds, try to stay in one for 90 seconds.

5. *Thinking grey*   Do you think of problems in all or nothing terms; for example, if you make a mistake are you a total failure? Instead, try assessing all the different aspects of the situation on a 0–100 success scale.

6. *Do a survey*   Ask your friends and colleagues whether or not they agree with your thinking errors and general beliefs. If you feel anxious about taking a driving test, do your friends think this is unnatural? Will they see you as a total failure if the driving test is not passed?

7. *Definition of terms*   Do you use emotive, all-embracing terms such as 'stupid', 'fool', 'idiot', 'loser' to describe yourself or others? What exactly is the definition of a 'fool'? Would a complete fool ever manage to get up in the morning? Is it just a description of one aspect of a person's behaviour? Can one aspect of a person's behaviour make them a complete 'fool'? Would a complete fool ever manage to turn up for a counselling session?

8. *Watch your semantics*   Substitute extreme and emotive language with beliefs that are less evocative. 'I must give a perfect presentation' could become 'It's strongly preferable to give a good presentation but I don't have to.'

9. *Reattribute*   Instead of blaming yourself or others for a particular problem, think about all the different factors which may have contributed to it. Then focus on solving the problem rather than feeling angry or guilty about it.

10. *Do a cost-benefit analysis*   Make a list of the pros and cons of having a particular feeling or 'thinking error'. What are the pros and cons for you of becoming angry in long traffic queues, of thinking that you are a total failure or of avoiding friends?

Adapted Palmer and Dryden (1995: 50–1).

Box 6.4 *Questions to challenge my negative thinking*

What is the evidence for my belief?
Am I jumping to conclusions?
What alternatives are there to my belief?
Am I assuming my view of things is the only one possible?
What is the effect of thinking the way I do?
What are the advantages and disadvantages of thinking this way?
Am I asking questions that have no answers?
What thinking errors am I making?
Am I thinking in all-or-nothing terms?
Am I using 'ultimatum' words in my thinking?
Am I totally condemning myself (or another) on the basis of a single event?
Am I concentrating on my weaknesses and neglecting my strengths?
Am I blaming myself for something which is not really my fault?
Am I taking things personally which have little or nothing to do with me?
Am I expecting myself to be perfect?
Am I using a double standard?
Am I only paying attention to the negative side of things?
Am I over-estimating the chances of disaster?
Am I exaggerating the importance of events?
Am I fretting about how things should be, instead of accepting and dealing with them as they are?
Am I assuming I cannot do anything to alter my situation?
Is the outcome really going to be catastrophic?
Am I predicting the outcome instead of experimenting with it?

Source: Palmer and Dryden (1995: 52); adapted Fennell (1989: 225)

Some questions which can be used instead of the self-audit of thinking patterns as a help to clients in challenging their negative thinking are also listed in Box 6.4.

Challenging inferences

We all can, and do, draw accurate or inaccurate inferences about other people's thoughts or about what is happening in a situation. When the conclusions we reach are negative we can distress ourselves emotionally. Because jumping to the wrong conclusions is a universal human practice, challenging inferences will, at some time help most clients (and counsellors).

Inferences tend to develop, in much the same way as the old-fashioned party game of consequences, as Malcom shows us.

Malcolm's friend did not telephone last night and she always rings on a Wednesday. Malcolm's initial inference was:

My friend has snubbed me.

This escalated into:

She must be annoyed with me.
She doesn't like me.

Martin's conclusion was:

It is terrible that she doesn't like me.

The consequences of the inferences were:

Martin avoided his friend and became lonely and depressed.

An integrative counsellor (or an enlightened friend) can help Martin to consider other inferences which may be more accurate: Martin's friend may have been suddenly called away, or may have been upset by something in her life and usually avoids people when she feels like that; also the friend's behaviour may not be the result of being annoyed with Martin, nor of disliking him (see also Box 6.4).

ADDITIONAL ASSESSMENT SKILLS

In this section we introduce a number of assessment skills which complement those already included in the several stages of the integrative approach.

Identifying thoughts and feelings in assessment

Although the verbal dialogue of many current assessment processes can be very helpful, there are some clients who are not immediately in touch with certain events or fears which stress them. Given open-ended counselling time, such clients may gradually recall such events, but when they come for help with their stress, they usually do not want to remain in a distressed state for an unlimited period. The technique of evocative imagery will enable certain clients to recall vividly a situation that they are not immediately in touch with. This approach often reveals the underlying cause of stress as the following example illustrates.

EVOCATIVE IMAGERY

The client, Marjorie was terrified that her mother might die at any time, which led her to be very compliant in their relationship. 'The counsellor used evocative imagery to bring the future event into the present' (adapted Dryden, 1990: 49–50).

> *Counsellor:* So you feel you just can't speak up to her. Because if you did, what might happen?
>
> *Marjorie:* Well, she might have a fit.
>
> *Counsellor:* And what might happen if she did?
>
> *Marjorie:* She might have a heart attack and die.
>
> *Counsellor:* Well, we know she is a fit woman, but let's go along with your fear for the moment, OK?
>
> *Marjorie:* Yes, yes.
>
> *Counsellor:* What if she did die?
>
> *Marjorie:* I just can't think. . . . I . . . I'm sorry.
>
> *Counsellor:* That's all right. I know this is difficult, but I really think it would be helpful if we could get to the bottom of things. Shall we go on? (Client nods. Counsellor continues watchfully.) Look Marjorie, I want you to imagine that your mother

has just died this morning . . . Can you imagine that? (Client nods and begins
to shake.) . . . What are you experiencing now, Marjorie?

Marjorie: When you said my mother was dead I began to feel all alone . . . like there was
no one to care for me . . . no one I could turn to . . .

Counsellor: Mmm . . . and if there is no one who cares for you, no one you can turn to . . .?

Marjorie: Oh, God! I know I couldn't cope on my own.

The imagery has evoked one of Marjorie's deepest fears, one which is central to her
stress and her life. Encouraging clients to imagine vividly something they have been
avoiding often leads to the underlying cause of the anxiety. 'The use of evocative
imagery can help them to focus on a problem which is central to their stress', so that
in Marjorie's case, rather than her mother being the focus of her attention, she can
be helped to cope with her own loneliness.

Feeling identification

In common with many humanistic approaches, the integrative way of working is
most helpful if client and counsellor have a mutual and fairly specific understanding
of the different emotions which a client may experience. A client who says 'I feel
stressed' can be helped to focus more clearly on the elements of the feeling through
the enquiry 'Do you mean anxious stressed; angry stressed; depressed stressed;
guilty stressed; tense stressed?' etc. However, a client may say they feel tense when
they are in fact experiencing the physical symptoms of anxiety or anger.

In most cases exploration of the thoughts attached to the emotions may be a guide
to how the client feels and offer greater insight into the nature of the client's stress.

Sometimes a person may experience a number of emotions simultaneously, such
as guilt about being depressed, anxiety about being anxious, and these may need to
be explored so that the emotion which the client finds most unhelpful is dealt with
first. The counsellor may need to help the client to tease out the order of the events
and the emotions which led up to those feelings which the client is finally
experiencing. In the area of feeling things are not always what they seem and mis-
reading emotions, our own, or those of others, can contribute to stress.

Two further ways of increasing understanding of a client's stress during assessment are tracking and bridging.

TRACKING

Although the assessment profile is described under the CABB outline, of course the
client does not actually experience cognitions, affect, biology and behaviour in that
order in a stress situation. Moreover, the order in which the client's thoughts,
feelings, physical sensations and behaviour are experienced will affect the way in
which they are helped. Tracking is the term given to a close following of the
interaction between the different modes of assessment and the sequence in which
they occur in any specific situation.

In tracking, the Behaviour mode of CABB is designated 'Beh'. To distinguish it
from Biology – 'Bio'.

We offer an example of tracking adapted from Palmer (1996: 54) of a client, whom we have called Michael, who became stressed in enclosed situations (such as a lift). The first recognition that Michael had was the bodily sensation of a rapid heart beat, quickly followed by the thoughts, 'I'm going to panic. It will be awful. I can't stand it.' Michael then had the image of himself collapsing in front of a group of people, who all looked at him, to his total shame. His behavioural reaction was to escape from the situation by, for example, getting out of the lift. Thus Michael's stress started with a bodily sensation (Bio) followed quickly by thoughts (C) an image of his collapse (C), feelings of anxiety and shame (A) and an escape from the situation (Beh). By tracking the sequence Bio – C – C – A – Beh, the counsellor was able to offer Michael some alternatives. It was suggested that if the situation happened again, he would relax momentarily (Bio), while at the same time saying to himself, 'It's only my heart beating faster. It feels bad but it's not awful. It's not the end of the world. I can stand it.' (C). If Michael still had an image (C) of himself collapsing, he would replace it with a relaxing and pleasant image previously chosen, which would help to reduce his feelings of anxiety and shame (A). Michael was advised not to leave the situation because this would not help him to overcome his problem (Beh).

Thus Michael's sequence of therapeutic strategies followed the sequence of his modes of experiencing the stress problem: Bio – C – C – A – Beh.

The order of occurrence or 'firing order' of the CABB modes is matched with a sequence of interventions to reduce Martin's stress.

BRIDGING

Some clients have a preferred mode (in terms of the CABB profile) of experiencing the world and of communicating that experience. Many counsellors will be familiar with clients who when asked how they feel (Affect) about a situation respond by giving a clear description of what happened (C), rather than of how they felt. Such clients may or may not be avoiding the area of feelings and they can be unaware that they have evaded the enquiry. Because affect is not their preferred mode, they do not hear the significance which the counsellor places on their feelings.

Bridging happens when a counsellor starts with the client's preferred mode and takes an indirect route through the other profile areas, until they and the client arrive together at the client's least preferred mode.

An example of bridging is described by Palmer and Dryden (1995: 37).

Counsellor: When you heard the news, how did you feel about it?

Jan: I remember the telephone ringing. I answered it and it was James. He told me how it happened. Jill had run out of school and straight out into the road and there just wasn't enough time for the car to stop. Fortunately, the ambulance came quickly and she was rushed off to hospital. I left for the hospital immediately. When I arrived my daughter was there too . . . (The story continued.)

Counsellor: Jan, as you describe what happened, you looked very tense . . . I wonder if you have any sensations in your body at the moment?

Jan: Funnily enough, I do! I have a vague headache. It's at the back of my head.

Counsellor: If you don't mind, I would like you just to concentrate on your headache for the moment. (Pause) How does it feel now?

Jan: It feels much worse. I feel that it's going to explode.

Counsellor: Mmm . . . do you recall having this sort of headache before?

Jan: Yes. (pause) In fact I've had it since James told me the news.

Counsellor: How's your headache now?

Jan: It's getting worse.

Counsellor: Are you feeling any emotion at the moment?

Jan: (pause) I'm sad about what happened. (cries)

Counsellor: . . . It may be helpful if we explore your sadness.

Comment

The counsellor allowed the client to tell her 'story' as she saw it without interruption. Bridging started when the counsellor asked the client if she was feeling any sensations. This helped to shift the client away from the cognitive modality.

Palmer goes on to show how exploring the (bodily) sensations (Bio), allowed Jan and the counsellor to 'bridge' into feelings (A) without directly challenging the client. This is called a 'through the back door' way of reaching an important area which Jan had difficulty in accessing by focusing on a mode which is less threatening to her.

Bridging is helpful for clients who are unable to respond to the specific invitation to 'get in touch with their feelings' or other modes. Without realizing it, intuitive counsellors may already use this technique. However, our description hopefully helps to formalize the interaction and make it more accessible to less experienced counsellors.

THE FIVE-STAR FRAMEWORK AND THE THERAPEUTIC WORKING RELATIONSHIP

Lazarus's (1993) concept of the counsellor as authentic chameleon described in chapter 5 is particularly relevant in helping clients to work with those emotional blocks which both cause and prevent them from dealing with their stress. Because the content is both cognitive and emotional and the counsellor's stance is understanding, active–directive (teaching) and empathic, in that sequence, we need to return briefly to the therapeutic working relationship.

The three core conditions remain central within the counselling–teaching relationship (Rogers 1961, 1980).

Ellis and associates (1997) point out that counsellors strive to accept their clients as fallible human beings who make mistakes, sometimes frequently! ('Screw up' seems to be the favourite REBT term for this.) Regardless of how badly clients act towards the counsellor or towards others, they are never intrinsically 'good' or 'bad' people. While counsellors draw client's attention to aspects of their negative behaviour which do not seem to be helping them, they especially avoid denigrating their clients for their self-defeating behaviour. Counsellors, in attempting to accept themselves as fallible people, provide an instructive role model for clients and work towards a therapeutic relationship in which both counsellor and client can accept mutual fallibility.

There is emphasis in the five-star framework on differentiating between emotions which have positive effects and those which have negative ones. Nevertheless it is equally important to emphasize that not all negative emotions are unhealthy and self-defeating.

Genuineness is allied to openness and counsellors will share personal information about themselves, if asked, unless they have good reason to think that clients might misuse such information (Ellis *et al.*, 1997).

Empathy is seen as both communicating an understanding of how clients feel (affective empathy) and showing them that the counsellor understands how they are thinking, thus seeing the philosophies which lie behind and give rise to their feelings (philosophic empathy).

> The preferred therapeutic relationship is one in which clients see themselves as equal and active collaborators with their therapist in seeking to bring about fundamental change into their stress-filled lives, and where both participants see themselves as equal in their humanity, although unequal at the outset in therapeutic expertise and problem solving skills.
>
> (Ellis *et al.*, 1997: 32)

SUMMARY

In countering the specific beliefs, philosophies and attitudes with which clients create stress for themselves, disputing teaches them how to do the following:

- Disputing absolute musts: 'Why must I always succeed and experience no unfortunate hassles?' Answer: 'I never have to succeed, though I would very much prefer to do so. I really have to experience many unfortunate hassles because that is the nature of normal living. It's too bad – but hardly awful or terrible.'
- Disputing I-can't-stand-it-itis: 'Where is the evidence that I can't stand these stressors that are now occurring?' Answer: 'Only in my nutty head! I won't die of them and can be quite happy in spite of them. They're not horrible, but only bearably painful.'
- Disputing feelings of worthlessness: 'Is it true that I am an inadequate, worthless person if I do not handle stressful conditions well and even make them worse?' Answer: 'No, I am a person who may well be acting inadequately at this time in this respect, but I am never a totally worthless (or good) person, just a fallible human who is doing my best to cope with difficult conditions.'

(Abrams and Ellis, 1996: 68)

The purpose of the five-star framework is to help people to make their thinking more effective and less disturbing; to show clients how to discover good things in some of the bad things that happen to them and how to face the challenge of not upsetting themselves when they are under unusual stress. It is used to reduce the emotional temperature, and to work out with clients self-statements which are rational and coping to replace some of those which have in the past disturbed them. It is a philosophical thought process which clients can use in accepting some of their worst stresses while refusing to upset themselves. 'Yes I am under great stress just now and there is little I can do to relieve some of it, but I don't have to have a stress-free life and I can lead a reasonably happy life even if my difficulties continue.'

A caveat

It is clear to the authors that challenging clients' self-defeating thinking can be very beneficial for them. However, the importance of empathy in the process is crucial if counsellors are not to fall into the trap of supposing that clients are thinking what the REBT theory says they are thinking, without actually checking it out. Earning the right to challenge the way clients think demands that counsellors first understand what and how they think (Egan, 1990: 199).

All counselling approaches contain dangers for the unwary practitioner. Just as over-passivity can lead counsellors to be unhelpful, users of this more active approach are asked to be alert to the danger of pushing their own set of values in the process and in so doing, over-riding the values of their clients. Disputation theory can tempt counsellors with latent (or obvious) control needs into a strident bossiness, and those with skin-deep respect into blatantly rude, self-indulgent behaviour under the camouflage of challenge. Within the therapeutic relationship, counsellors are often perceived by their clients as powerful people and the five-star framework is powerful medicine; small doses are efficacious, over-prescription can be iatrogenic and damage health.

CHAPTER 7
Additional Stress Counselling Techniques

Perhaps there will always be a place for psychological technicians who can render the intolerable somehow survivable.

Brian Thorne (1997: 165)

In this chapter we include techniques that we have found particularly useful in integrative stress counselling and stress management. The chapter is divided into four sections consisting of the main modalities: Cognitive, Affective, Biological/ health-related, Behavioural. The techniques and interventions are suitable for a wide range of stress-related problems and disorders.

Some of the techniques such as implosion, rational-emotive imagery and behavioural/imaginal exposure can lead to high levels of anxiety in many people. If clients have the conditions below, extreme care should be taken when using these types of techniques:

- asthma attacks triggered by stress/anxiety
- seizures triggered by stress/anxiety
- heart condition or other related medical conditions
- depression with suicidal ideation
- hysteria
- pregnant women
- severe psychiatric disorders.

In these cases alternative techniques that do not necessarily trigger high levels of anxiety such as relaxation or coping imagery, should be considered as more appropriate. It is recommended that counsellors liaise with a client's general practitioner with regard to the above conditions or with biological/health-related interventions.

Surprisingly, even innocuous techniques such as relaxation may be contraindicated in certain circumstances; for example, with clients who suffer from narcolepsy. In addition, some clients who perceive a state of relaxation as 'losing control' may feel anxious as they start to relax. Also, simple health-related interventions such as cutting salt out of a diet may seem quite safe. Yet, with clients who already have low blood pressure, in some cases a further reduction in blood pressure by reducing their salt intake can lead to permanent damage to the optic nerve. Readers are referred to Palmer and Dryden (1995) for a complete account of the indications and contra-indications of the most commonly used stress counselling techniques. We recommend counsellors ensure that they receive regular supervision from an experienced supervisor qualified in cognitive behavioural methods and stress management techniques.

COGNITIVE/IMAGERY TECHNIQUES

Some cognitive and imagery techniques and interventions have been described in the previous chapters. This section includes additional techniques that we have found useful in stress counselling and management.

Anti-future shock imagery

This technique was developed by Lazarus (1984) to help clients deal with future life events and changes. Common examples are death of parents, redundancy, children leaving home and retirement. In this technique clients are asked to visualize themselves coping with different aspects of the future feared event or change. For example, Sara was concerned how she and her partner were going to care for their elderly parents if, or more likely when, they were to fall ill. Before the exercise was attempted, Sara discussed with the counsellor possible ways of dealing with the problem should it arise. This included brainstorming possible coping strategies that she and her partner could use. Then the counsellor asked Sara to visualize coping with the feared event. This procedure helped Sara to de-awfulize the predicted stress scenario and also realize that the potential difficult period would not last forever. Sara decided that she could use this method with other concerns too without having external assistance.

This technique is particularly helpful with future events unforeseen by the client that the counsellor believes may need to be faced. It is also indicated as a relapse prevention technique used in the later stages of counselling as it primes clients to cope with future unexpected problems.

Associated imagery

This technique was developed to help clients to explore negative emotions and sensations of which the origin is unknown (see Lazarus, 1984: 18). The technique will be described in a slightly modified format.

The client is asked to close their eyes and then focus on the negative emotion or sensation. For example, if the client feels guilty, then they are directed to make themselves feel more guilty. They are then instructed to focus on any image that enters their mind. Later, they are then directed to concentrate on any new image that also occurs. If no new image occurs then the client is asked to just concentrate on the original image in as much detail as possible, as if they were looking through a zoom lens. The image can be observed from different angles. If another image then occurs the client can start to concentrate on that instead. As different images are tracked, the client can return to some of the earlier ones to notice whether they evoke new images, emotions or insights.

This procedure may help the client to understand the meaning or origin of the negative emotion, sensation or image. After the procedure has been completed, the counsellor discusses the possible meanings with the client. The technique is contra-indicated for clients who would feel overwhelmed by focusing on their negative emotions.

Audioloop recorded tapes

This technique forms part of a behavioural exposure programme (see p. 183). It is used with clients who are suffering from obsessive ruminations (thoughts). The client is asked to record, in his or her own voice, the rumination on to a loop tape, that is, an audio cassette tape that after a set period of time starts back at the beginning again. The client is instructed to listen to the tape as soon as the rumination recurs and is also asked to listen regularly to the tape as a homework assignment. The client is also instructed to refrain from performing any rituals, such as washing hands, if this is the normal method of coping with the rumination. Generally, with regular use, the client becomes less anxious about the particular rumination. If the client is experiencing suicidal ideation the method may be contra-indicated as it may trigger high levels of anxiety.

Aversive imagery

It is possible to link an unpleasant image together with a stimulus that triggers an undesirable response (Cautela, 1967). By this action it is possible that the undesirable response will not occur. For example, if a client on a stop smoking programme is offered a cigarette by a friend and then immediately visualizes tar accumulating in his or her lungs, it may reduce the likelihood of the cigarette being accepted. The counsellor needs to train the client in the session to visualize the negative image as vividly as possible. The counsellor negotiates with the client the most suitable image that may help to reduce the undesired behaviour.

If the client becomes used to the negative image by visualizing the image for a prolonged period, then his or her abhorrence may subside. Therefore, we recommend that clients are instructed not to use the visualization for longer than five minutes at a time. Although this technique can be beneficial for clients wishing to reduce or stop behaviour they do not want, with some individuals care is needed to avoid triggering extreme levels of anxiety. With clients who suffer from blood, injury or other medical phobias, care should be taken to avoid using images that remind them of these specific fears as they may faint when applying the technique.

Bibliotherapy and bibliotraining

In the field of stress counselling and stress management, bibliotherapy/bibliotraining is probably one of the most important forms of intervention. It consists of the client using relevant self-help books, manuals, leaflets, audio-tapes, videos and CD-ROMs at the counsellor's suggestion. This can help clients to understand the nature of their particular problem and, subsequently, how to deal with it. The counsellor suggests that the client reads relevant literature as a homework assignment. We have successfully used bibliotherapy on a variety of topics including anxiety and stress management, anger management, assertion and communication skills, asthma, back-ache, chronic fatigue syndrome, depression, exercise, irritable bowel syndrome, massage, nutrition, obsessive–compulsive disorder, overcoming guilt and sulking, problem-solving, public speaking, relaxation, safer sex, self-hypnosis, smoking cessation, and weight control.

The counsellor will need to go through any issues or misunderstandings that may arise from the homework assignment in the following training or counselling session. The beauty of this technique is that it can be easily adapted to the client's situation and abilities. For example, clients with reading difficulties can use audio-tapes or videos instead. Bibliotherapy can also be used in family or group settings. In our experience videos are a powerful method of learning.

We recommend that stress counsellors maintain a library of health-related materials and also low-cost audio-tapes and videos that clients can either purchase or borrow.

Correcting misconceptions

Clients may hold misconceptions regarding many aspects of life as well as health-related issues. It is important for counsellors to provide, wherever possible, correct information about any subject that the client does not understand if it will help them. Bibliotherapy in the form of books, manuals and educational leaflets may prove useful. It is recommended that the counsellors have a range of material covering a variety of subjects, for example, diet, exercise, stress, religion and so on. If misconceptions are expressed by the client during counselling, the counsellor needs to explain his or her understanding of the subject in a straightforward but non-patronizing way. In some circumstances information should be conveyed with great sensitivity as clients may have held misconceptions on particular issues for many years. It is not always apparent that a client may have a misconception about a particular issue. Palmer and Dryden (1995: 58) recommend that a counsellor can ask him or herself 'Would I be as anxious (or depressed) as my client if I understood all the facts?' If the answer is 'no', then this may be a rough guide that the client is holding a misconception. In many cases the client may also hold self-defeating or dysfunctional beliefs about a problem which also contribute to his or her levels of distress.

Although in many cases the misconception may have increased a client's anxiety, on some issues it may have helped to lower anxiety; for example, ignoring the serious nature of an illness (Palmer and Dryden, 1995).

Coping imagery

Coping imagery is used with clients who need to cope with specific situations with which they have had or anticipate having difficulty (see Palmer and Dryden, 1995).

It has been used for many different situations, for example, driving tests, public speaking, being assertive, etc. Initially, the counsellor discusses with the client what they both believe would be the most suitable behaviour that could be used in a specific situation. Once agreed, the client closes his or her eyes and imagines coping with the situation, from the beginning to the end of the event. The client's worst fears, such as making a mistake, are incorporated into the coping imagery with the client visualizing him/herself recovering and dealing with the difficulty as it arises. The client would regularly repeat the exercise as a homework assignment. If the counsellor talks the client through the visualization in the training session it can be tape recorded. The client could listen to the recording for the homework assignment. The imagery has to be realistic and within the experience of the client, therefore total mastery imagery whereby they perform perfectly is avoided.

De-awfulizing

In our experience when clients are distressed or anxious about difficult forthcoming events such as giving wedding speeches or sitting exams, they often predict that the outcome may be 'awful', 'terrible' or 'horrible'. They may use other words or phrases which essentially convey the same message: the outcome should or should not happen and if it does, it will be awful. De-awfulizing is a technique to demonstrate to clients that although bad things may happen, they are seldom (if ever) awful, that is, worse than bad. By using a continuum of badness scale from 1 to 99.9 the counsellor asks the client to state how bad the situation will be. It is usually advantageous to use either a whiteboard or a large sheet of paper for this exercise to plot the relative scores (see Figure 7.1).

A typical transcript of a counselling session where the counsellor is de-awfulizing a client's fears about not reaching an important deadline follows.

Counsellor: Ken, remember the last time when you were really stressed about your problem, on a scale of 1 to 99.9, where 99.9 is really bad, how bad is it not achieving this important deadline? (Counsellor asks the client to remember when he was last disturbed about the problem to evoke hot cognitions and emotions in the counselling session.)

Client: Off the end scale. 110! (humorously). It's really awful!

Counsellor: (laughs) Obviously, on a scale of 1 to 99.9 you cannot go any higher than 99.9.

Client: Okay. It feels so bad that it must be at 99.9.
(Counsellor draws lines on the badness scale to represent not reaching deadline.)

Counsellor: You realize that logically at that moment in time when you are really stressed you believe that nothing worse could actually happen to you as you have scored 99.9?

Client: Well, I suppose so.

Counsellor: Just think for the moment. Could anything worse happen?

Client: If I didn't reach the deadline and I lost my job, that would be worse.

Counsellor: Let's suppose that did happen. On a scale of 1 to 99.9 how bad would that be?

Client: Off the end scale again! 110.

Counsellor: Ah, but Ken . . .

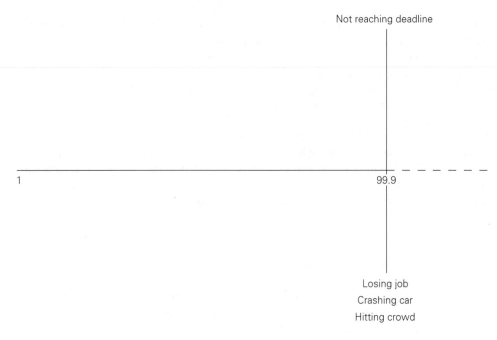

Figure 7.1 *Ken's badness scale*

Client: I know what you're going to say: you can't go higher than 99.9. Losing my job must also be 99.9. (Counsellor adds this score to the diagram.)

Counsellor: You're catching on fast. Let's assume that you didn't reach the deadline and you lose your job. As you drive home from work what else could happen that would be worse?

Client: I could crash the car and get hurt.

Counsellor: How bad would that be?

Client: 99.9! (Counsellor adds this score to the diagram.)

Counsellor: As you crashed the car, you may have driven into a crowd of people waiting at a bus stop. How bad would that be?

Client: Really awful. 200.

Counsellor: On a scale of 1 to 99.9 it can only be a maxiumum of 99.9. (Counsellor adds this score to the diagram.)

Client: Logically you're right.

Counsellor: Notice how everything you are scoring is at the high end of the scale. According to the way you rate things crashing the car into a crowd of people is as bad as not reaching a deadline. Have you any thoughts about this?

Client: It's ludicrous. Obviously that can't be true. I need to re-score the whole lot.

Counsellor: Okay. Let's start. If we leave crashing the car into a group of people at 99.9, then how would you now score crashing the car and hurting yourself?

Client: About 90. (Counsellor adds this to new score to the diagram; see Figure 7.2.)

Counsellor: What about losing your job?

Client: By comparison, it can only be about 50.

Counsellor: And not reaching your deadline?

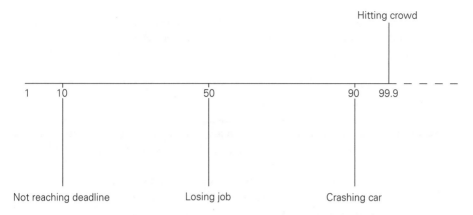

Figure 7.2 *Ken's re-calibrated badness scale*

Client: Well, put like this, it can only be about 10.

Counsellor: What do you think was the point of this exercise? (Counsellor checking that the client has understood this difficult concept.)

Client: When I'm telling myself things such as not reaching deadlines is really awful, I make myself stressed and blow everything up out of proportion. In reality, it may feel bad but it's hardly awful, off the end scale.

Counsellor: Correct. In fact when you become stressed does it actually help you to remain problem-focused and goal-orientated? (Counsellor hoping to demonstrate the benefits of de-awfulizing possible events.)

Client: No way. I find I can't concentrate and I spend more time talking to colleagues, smoking and drinking coffee.

De-awfulizing is a technique that helps clients to step back from future or current stress scenarios thereby allowing them to keep the situation or the possible negative outcome in proportion. This can also be beneficial as the individual is more likely to remain problem- or task-focused and not waste valuable time being anxious, procrastinating and exhibiting displacement behaviour such as cleaning desks, attempting to finish unimportant work or washing the car. This technique is frequently used to help de-awfulize presentations, exams, job interviews, deadlines and other events clients become anxious about. Although it can be applied to personally very significant issues, such as loss of a partner through separation or bereavement, it should be used with great care and sensitivity otherwise the therapeutic relationship is likely to suffer leading to attrition (that is, premature termination of counselling).

Deserted Island technique

Sometimes clients do not see why it may be beneficial to modify self-defeating or problem-interfering cognitions. One of the authors (see Palmer, 1993a) has developed the 'Deserted Island' technique to demonstrate to clients that holding on to self-defeating beliefs, and not necessarily the activating event, can lead to a heightened emotional disturbance or unhelpful emotions such as anxiety, damning anger or depression instead of more problem-focused emotions such as concern, non-damning annoyance or sadness. This is a variation of the money model illustrated in Chapter 6.

Palmer (1993a) described a typical transcript of a counselling session using the Deserted Island technique as below.

Counsellor:	Let's say, for example, you've been left on a deserted island. You have all your needs such as accommodation and food met, but one thing you don't have on the island is any friends. Imagine being on the island and you hold the belief: 'I really would prefer to have a friend with me on the island but I don't have to have one.' How would you emotionally feel about your situation?
Client:	I would be concerned I didn't have anybody to share it with.
Counsellor:	Now, let's say that you're still on the island but this time your belief is: 'I must, I must, I really must have a friend on the island.' How would you feel this time?
Client:	Pretty anxious!
Counsellor:	Let's just stay with this for a moment. Just imagine that an aeroplane flies over and a friend of yours jumps out and parachutes slowly towards the deserted island. Now imagine that you are still holding the beliefs: 'I must, I must, I really must have a friend on the island.' How do you feel now?
Client:	Very relieved.
Counsellor:	After a period of time, let's imagine that you are still holding the belief: 'I must, I must, I really must have a friend on the island.' Don't forget, you've still got your friend on the island with you. Can you foresee anything that could happen that you could become upset about again?
Client:	The friend could be taken away.
Counsellor:	So even though you have your friend on the island, after a period of time your anxiety might return, especially if you feared that your friend could be taken away.
Cient:	Yeah.
Counsellor:	I wonder what your behaviour would be like?
Client:	Knowing me I'd be all clingy just in case he was going to leave.
Counsellor:	Would that help your relationship?
Client:	I doubt it. He's more likely to want to leave if he had the chance!
Counsellor:	Let's change it slightly again. You're still on the island and your friend is there and this time you're holding the belief: 'I really would prefer to have a friend with me on the island but I don't have to have one.' Would you feel anxious this time?
Client:	No. I'd feel much better.
Counsellor:	Why? (Counsellor checking out whether the client has understood the model.)
Client:	Because I was not insisting that I must have a friend with me.
Counsellor:	Can you see that in each example I've described similar situations? The only difference has been your beliefs and the different beliefs evoked different emotions and possibly different behaviours too. The 'must' belief led to you feeling 'pretty anxious', while the preference belief led you to feeling just 'concerned'.
Client:	Yeah.

In our experience with the Deserted Island technique most clients are able to see how rigid, absolutist and dogmatic beliefs consisting of musts, shoulds, have to's, got to's and oughts lead to a greater emotional disturbance than more flexible, non-absolutist and realistic beliefs consisting of preferences, wishes and desires. The technique also highlights how the beliefs largely contribute to a person's level of distress and not necessarily the situation itself. If there is any doubt, it is a good idea to ask the client to explain what the example demonstrated.

With new clients, the technique would be taught after inference chaining thereby ensuring that the client has understood why the counsellor will devote much time and energy to disputing or challenging self-defeating beliefs. Once the counsellor has ensured that the client has understood the model the next step is to assess the client's self-defeating beliefs. A typical transcript of the assessment procedure is as follows.

Counsellor: You agreed that the Deserted Island model demonstrated how the demands such as the musts and the shoulds led to high levels of stress. Now, if we return to your problem of giving a presentation to your managers, what do you think you are telling yourself to add pressure to an already difficult situation? (Counsellor eliciting evaluative self-defeating and problem-interfering beliefs.)

Client: I must perform well.

Counsellor: And if you don't perform well, what would be the outcome? (Counsellor attempting to elicit an evaluative conclusion.)

Client: It would be awful; absolutely terrible!

Counsellor: Could you still accept yourself as a person? (Counsellor assessing whether the client would self-down.)

Client: No. I would be a total failure?

Counsellor: As long as you tell yourself (counsellor writes the following three beliefs on a whiteboard):

I must perform well, and if I don't
it would be awful, absolutely terrible
and I would be a total failure

How will you feel? (Counsellor confirming the emotional disturbance.)

Client: Very anxious.

Counsellor: Will that help your performance? (Counsellor illustrating the benefits of changing the self-defeating beliefs.)

Client: No. I get so anxious I can't think or speak properly.

Counsellor: Do you think it would be useful to examine these (counsellor pointing to whiteboard) problem-interfering beliefs or thoughts and perhaps modify them to problem-facilitating beliefs to help you reduce your anxiety, remain problem-focused and perhaps perform better?

Client: Sounds a great idea to me.

Once the evaluative problem-interfering beliefs have been elicited then the counsellor gets explicit agreement from the client to examine them further. Finally the counsellor challenges the beliefs and with the client develops more self-helping and problem-focused beliefs.

Image reduction

If a client is anxious about a particular thing, for example, a spider, then in his mind's eye, if he visualizes it and then reduces it down in size, this may help him to put it into perspective. This may allow the client to feel in control of the situation and reduce apprehension (McMullin, 1986).

Implosion

With this technique the client is exposed to their most feared situation in fantasy until their anxiety subsides (see Kirchner and Hogan, 1966). However, this can be a very distressing experience for the client and the anxiety does not always subside (habituate) quickly. In fact if the procedure is prematurely terminated the client can be left even more fearful of the feared situation. It is important that the procedure is adequately explained to the client and their explicit consent is obtained.

Implosion has also been used with clients who have persistent nightmares (see Marks, 1987). Different variations of the technique have been used with clients suffering from post-traumatic stress disorder (for example, Muss, 1991). Essentially, the clients are directed to run the whole traumatic event through in their mind's eye from the beginning to the end (and sometimes backwards too). The client repeats this exercise until their anxiety subsides. This may take up to a couple of hours. (It is recommended that counsellors should receive relevant training if they wish to use these techniques due to the high level of distress they can trigger in clients.)

This technique may be contra-indicated for clients with a history of cardiac complaints or for pregnant women. It is not recommended for use with clients who suffer from asthma attacks when very anxious or clients with severe depression or suicidal ideation. In these cases graded behavioural/imaginal exposure, relaxation techniques or medication may be possible alternatives.

Imaginal exposure

This important technique is basically the same as graded behavioural exposure (see p. 183). The main difference is that the prolonged exposure to a feared situation is undertaken in fantasy until the anxiety subsides. The technique is ideal for clients who want to overcome their anxiety about specific situations but are either not prepared to start using real-life exposure or are unable to have regular exposure to the feared experience. A hierarchy of fears is noted and the client initially chooses to visualize a fear that triggers a bearable level of anxiety. Once the anxiety has subsided, the client then visualizes another feared situation further up on his hierarchy of fears.

Imaginal exposure usually forms part of an entire graded exposure programme and is included in the hierarchy of fears (see Table. 7.1). It is especially useful when the exposure programme is difficult for the client to undertake. For example, a fear of flying in planes, or a fear of travelling in trains that stop for periods in tunnels. The client undertakes the imaginal exposure in the therapy session and is also set the exercise as a homework assignment. As with graded exposure, a diary is kept to monitor progress (see p. 185).

Table 7.1 *Hierarchy of fears for a combined imaginal and behavioural exposure programme*

Rank	Subjective units of distress	Event
1	10.0	Aeroplane taking off
2	9.5	Aeroplane landing
3	9.0	Flying on aeroplane in turbulence
4	8.5	Imagining aeroplane taking off
5	8.0	Imagining aeroplane landing
6	7.5	Imagining aeroplane in turbulence
7	7.0	Imagining self vomiting on aeroplane
8	6.0	Aeroplane cruising
9	5.5	Imagining aeroplane cruising
10	5.0	Aeroplane taxiing
11	4.0	Imagining aeroplane taxiing
12	3.5	Waiting for delayed aeroplane

Positive imagery

In this technique clients visualize any scene, real or imaginary, that they find positive or pleasant. It is import to discuss with clients exactly what they find pleasant about their scenes. When the technique is initially carried out, the counsellor can help reinforce the visualization by asking clients to focus on different aspects of it. Clients are encouraged to use this technique regularly as it can help to reduce or inhibit anxiety and lower tension levels. As it is a good cognitive distraction technique it is particularly useful in pain management. Some of our clients have also found this technique helpful to manage mild depression or boredom.

Rational–emotive imagery

In rational–emotive imagery (Ellis, 1979 version), the client is instructed to visualize a scene that he or she finds upsetting or disturbing; for example, being ignored at a party. The client is then asked to try and change the emotion that they are experiencing to a more helpful emotion, for example, anxiety to concern. Once this is achieved the counsellor discusses with the client how the change was achieved. It is preferable for the client to make the change by disputing any self-defeating beliefs they may hold about the event (see Chapter 6). The counsellor may need to demonstrate to the client how this can be done. Rational–emotive imagery is initially undertaken during the counselling or training session and is then set as a homework assignment. The technique gives the client a method of controlling how they feel about disturbing situations.

Maultsby (1975) developed an alternative version of rational–emotive imagery in which the client is also instructed to picture the situation, but this time they repeat very forcefully to themselves (either out loud or internally depending upon the situation) a self-helping belief. This helps the client to experience a less disabling emotion (for example, concern instead of anxiety, sadness instead of depression).

The technique helps to prepare clients for difficult situations or it can be used to help them deal with how they behaved in an earlier situation. In the latter case the client's goal may be to feel remorse instead of guilt or regret instead of shame.

Step-up technique

This technique is used if a client is anxious about a probable event occurring in the future, such as attending a job interview or reaching a deadline, and the underlying cause of the client's anxiety is unclear. This technique may help the client determine the cause of their anticipatory anxiety (see Lazarus, 1984: 25). The client is instructed to imagine the feared situation unfolding. Often this will be sufficient for the client to grasp the underlying cause of the anxiety. However, in some cases it is worthwhile asking the client to 'step-up' the scene by visualizing the very worst possible outcome. Then, usually with helpful suggestions from the counsellor on how to deal with the situation, the client is asked to visualize using the coping strategies. Often the client realizes the very worst outcome is unlikely to occur and if it did happen then it is still survivable.

Time-projection imagery

Time-projection imagery guides a client backwards or forwards in time to relive past events or to see that a present negative event has been overcome sometime in the future (Lazarus, 1989); for example, a client may be depressed about the end of a relationship. The client is asked to imagine themselves 6 months in the future and to describe what they are doing. This exercise is repeated for 1 year, 2 years and possibly 5 years into the future. It is likely that the present loss will become less important in the future and this technique demonstrates to the client that they will be able to survive the current situation. In this example, if the client was not able to see a positive future then the counsellor could ask the client to imagine meeting new people, undertaking favourite pastimes etc. This procedure usually helps to lift the client's mood and instil a sense of hope. 'Time tripping' backwards in time can allow the client to confront abusers from childhood in imagination or relive past events and put them into perspective. (See Postscript, p. 194.)

Thought stopping

There are a variety of techniques that can be used to help clients stop or control thoughts or images that they feel anxious about. Thought stopping is usually applied if the client experiences difficulty in using habituation training where the client is encouraged to focus on the disturbing thought or image and not avoid it until the anxiety subsides (see implosion or audioloop taping). In the counselling session a client is asked to think about the obsessive thought or image (Salkovskis and Kirk, 1989). Once the client has invoked it the counsellor then makes a loud noise such as clapping their hands or shouting 'STOP', and also directs the client to perform the same action. Assuming that this procedure helps to stop the unwanted thought, the technique is repeated at a reduced volume until the client is able to stop the thought without having to make an external noise at all. This procedure is practised in the counselling session a number of times before the client undertakes the exercise as a homework assignment.

Other methods of thought stopping include the client imagining a road 'Stop' sign, or a red traffic light or a relaxing scene (see Lazarus, 1989). One useful technique involves the client wearing an elastic band around their wrist and snapping it when the thought occurs. The pain distracts the client from the negative train of thought or disturbing image.

AFFECTIVE TECHNIQUES

The techniques and interventions used in problem-focused stress counselling and stress management in the Affective modality tend to incorporate the techniques drawn from the other modalities. For example, cognitive disputation of clients' self-defeating beliefs is likely to ameliorate the strength of their negative emotions. Therefore the range of techniques in this section is rather limited but for convenience they can be found elsewhere in the other three sections.

Anger management

This is the management of inappropriate anger that a client may exhibit. Anger management may involve techniques that help to dispute the client's unhelpful beliefs, challenging faulty inferences, positive self-statements, coping imagery, relaxation and breathing exercises, assertion training, communication skills, and social skills training. As the exact anger management programme depends upon the individual, additional techniques may be necessary. For example, if a high level of anger was due to previous experiences in childhood, then the empty chair technique may prove helpful (see p. 160). Anger could be a symptom of post-traumatic stress disorder. If it is, then the client may need to re-experience the event using imagery techniques such as implosion (see p. 156).

Anxiety and stress management

This is the management of an unhealthy level of anxiety or stress. The interventions usually include techniques drawn from all of the different modalities. In addition, in stress management skills, time management may also need to be learnt by the client.

If a client states that they are 'stressed', it is clinically helpful to enquire the exact nature of the 'stress' as this may be an indicator of which intervention to apply. If the client is unsure of how they feel emotionally the therapist can ask, 'Do you mean angry stressed, depressed stressed, anxious stressed, tense stressed (and so on)?' Client assessment is a crucial link in choosing the most appropriate technique or intervention for a specific stress-related problem. For example, commonly used relaxation techniques may not be effective with all clients suffering from anxiety as they may not help them deal with their stress-evoking self-defeating cognitions and negative images.

Empty chair

This well-known technique can be used when a client has unfinished business with another person. (The person may be dead or alive.) It is useful when clients are feeling emotionally blocked about a past event or series of events. It can also be used with current situations where the client is unable to behave in a desirable manner; for example, acting assertively with their manager. In the session, the client sits opposite an empty chair. The client is then asked to imagine that the person they want to talk to is sitting in the empty chair. The client is then asked to imagine telling the person what they feel and think about the particular person or problem. Then the client can sit in the empty chair and role play the other person. The client is asked to respond in the manner that the other person would normally use. The conversation can go back and forth until a resolution is achieved. The client can re-live a previous childhood experience or talk to different aspects of themselves such as the 'hard man' versus the 'caring man', the 'good mother' versus the 'loving partner'. Care needs to be taken when using this technique as it is not always possible to predict the outcome. Extreme care should be taken if used with clients with suicidal ideation (thoughts) as the technique may exacerbate their condition.

Focusing

In a quiet, relaxed state, the client examines spontaneous feelings and thoughts until one of them comes into full conscious awareness (adapted Gendlin, 1981). The client then focuses totally on it and notices if any new insights can be gleaned from the feelings, images or sensations they have experienced. This technique sometimes allows the client to bypass blocks that may have occurred by concentrating on only one modality at a time with a specific problem. However, the outcome is not predictable and the exercise can sometimes trigger upsetting memories or ideas.

Letter writing

Often clients are unable to express how they feel about a particular person or situation. If clients are emotionally blocked, then asking them to write a letter to the person, with a caveat that they do not send it, usually helps them to start expressing how they feel. This is of particular use in cases of complicated grief or abuse. Clients may present with a lack of affect or sometimes depression and the process of writing the letter or series of letters tends to help them feel their repressed emotions such as anger. As these emotions arise the counsellor can deal with them in the counselling session.

BIOLOGICAL/HEALTH-RELATED INTERVENTIONS

Interventions in this modality help to improve a person's overall physical health which may also have a positive affect on their psychological well-being. Relaxation and hypnosis techniques reduce sympathetic nervous activity thereby increasing the restorative powers of the parasympathetic nervous system which conserves energy, aids relaxation and digestion (see Chapter 1). This also decreases levels of cortisol and enables the immune system to work at maximum efficiency to combat infection and illness.

If clients wish to control their weight, avoid binge eating/drinking, or stop smoking they may benefit from using a number of behavioural interventions or techniques such as cue exposure, response cost/penalty, self-monitoring/recording, and/or stimulus control. These interventions are described in the last part of this chapter. However, they may also need to use cognitive techniques such as powerful coping statements to control any discomfort or anxiety that they may encounter when they change their diet, reduce caffeine intake, or stop smoking/drinking/bingeing. We would recommend that the counsellor develop a CABB profile for a client wishing to deal with these particular problems.

Finally, to help clients improve their diet or start to exercise we suggest that the counsellor have a range of bibliotherapy such as books, leaflets or handouts on these particular topics. Also it may be advisable for the clients to see their general practitioner for a medical check-up to ensure that they are able to commence a programme.

Biofeedback

Biofeedback is a method of monitoring and giving feedback to a client on certain physiological functions such as blood pressure, heart rate, skin temperature, and sweating. Biofeedback can help a client to gain control over the so-called 'automatic' functions. Feedback to the client is usually visual or auditory, although any of the five senses can be used. Low-cost biofeedback equipment is now available. The most commonly used is the galvanic skin response instrument, which monitors the change in skin conductivity, and the biodot, which monitors the change in skin temperature. These instruments give clients feedback on whether other techniques such as relaxation exercises are actually working. Generally, as individuals relax their skin conductivity decreases (due to less sweating) and their surface body temperature increases (due to vasodilation of the blood capillaries). Biofeedback training has been used successfully to help people to control anxiety, colitis, hyperarousal disorders, insomnia, irritable bowel syndrome, migraine, pain, Raynaud's disease or syndrome, and tension headache.

Diagnostic trance

This is a technique taken from hypnosis. Clients are asked to make themselves comfortable and close their eyes. Then they are directed to attend to any unpleasant sensations they may be experiencing. They are asked to describe any thoughts, images or different memories that may occur. By focusing on a negative memory for a sufficient length of time, the client can come to terms with the events. (Similar to focusing, p. 160.)

Exercise

Regular exercise has many benefits. It can improve self-esteem, self-image and general mental health. Vigorous exercise has been shown to improve depression, although over-exercise can increase cortisol levels, reduce the effectiveness of the immune system and increase anxiety and irritability. Regular exercise can also help people to control their weight if it is incorporated into a controlled programme. We suggest integrative stress counsellors wishing to help clients include exercise in their counselling programme obtain relevant information on this subject or attend relevant training courses. Another option is to refer the client to a suitably qualified practitioner or consultant who specializes in this field of work.

We reiterate, if clients are over 35, overweight, have chest pains, have a cardiac condition or have a family history of heart disease, are recovering from illness, pregnant, suffer from asthma, high blood pressure, diabetes or bronchitis, they should initially consult their medical practitioner.

Hypnosis

Often clients have a strong belief that hypnosis will help them handle difficult situations, relieve stress or overcome somatic problems. We have found that hypnosis can be particuarly successful with these clients (see also Lazarus, 1973). As there is a tendency for hypnosis to be used by stress counsellors to reduce the physical effects of stress; we consider it a biological intervention although it can include a wide range of techniques such as cognitive restructuring, imaginal exposure and coping imagery.

We will now cover the various stages of hypnosis before we come to the hypnosis script.

PREPARATION AND PRELIMINARY INDUCTION

At the preparation stage, the counsellor ensures that the client is put at ease. This may involve answering any questions that the client may have about hypnosis. The following are the usual questions that may be encountered:

- What is hypnosis?
- How will I know if I've been hypnotized?
- Will you take control of my mind?
- What will you be doing?
- What happens if I don't come out of hypnosis?
- Will I tell you all my secrets?

It is important to explain that hypnosis can be considered as a form of relaxation where the mind may be receptive to positive self-helping and problem-facilitating suggestions. Hypnosis will only occur if clients want it to happen. They will be in total control and if they want to wake up they will be able to even if anything untoward such as a heart attack is experienced by their counsellor. If there is a fire they will not ignore it. They will not reveal any secrets if they do not want to.

To reduce anxiety, it is a good policy to describe briefly to the client the different stages of hypnosis so that they will know what to expect. At the preliminary induction stage, the client can be warned that it is quite normal during hypnosis to feel tingling, warm or heavy feelings in their hands and limbs. It is recommended that the client either lies on a couch or is seated in a comfortable chair with a headrest. The room should be at a reasonable temperature as some individuals feel cold during hypnosis. The room preferably needs to be located in a quiet part of the building and decorated in relaxing colours. It is usually more comfortable to clients if they remove their glasses or contact lenses. To avoid cramp, hands, fingers or legs should not be crossed.

The preliminary induction part of the hypnosis script is designed to encourage a state of hypnoidal relaxation. The method described is just one of the many different induction techniques that counsellors can use. Unlike the more traditional methods, the counsellor does not 'will' the client to close their eyes as this can be counter-productive in some cases.

DEEPENING

The deepening stage of hypnosis is designed to deepen the client's state of relaxation. In traditional hypnosis, this may be done by arm-heaviness or arm-levitation techniques. We have found it more advantageous to use less directive techniques. The method described later in the hypnosis script uses a counting and breathing technique. This method can generally be used in most cases except where clients experience breathing difficulties, which may occur if they suffer from asthma or a smoker's cough.

Imagery can also be used very successfully as a deepening technique. However, this method would need to be discussed with the client beforehand to elicit a suitable relaxing scene. Imagery that involves the client imagining going down something such as a country lane, a hill, a lift, flight of stairs, or a beach is ideal. Avoid imagery that may trigger anxiety as this will not help the relaxation process; for example, instructing a client who is phobic of open spaces to imagine walking down a field. With clients who have not been hypnotized previously it is sometimes helpful to include an additional imagery deepening stage as well as the counting and breathing method.

An example of the use of imagery is included in this section. It assumes that the counsellor has previously elicited from the client a suitable relaxing scene that they can imagine, preferably from their own experience. The counsellor gently emphasizes the trigger words 'DOWN' and 'NOW' as this seems to induce a deeper state of relaxation in most individuals.

OPTIONAL IMAGERY DEEPENER

(Palmer, 1993b: 28–31)

I want you now to imagine that you are at the top of the hill that you described to me earlier

PAUSE
Just look at the view. Notice the colours of the plants in the fields

PAUSE
As you look down the hill you can see the cows in the meadow at the bottom of the hill

PAUSE

You can feel the warmth of the sun on your face

PAUSE

In a few moments time

PAUSE

But not quite yet

PAUSE

You are going to take three steps DOWN the hill, one at a time

PAUSE

And by the time you take the third step you will be at the bottom of the hill in the meadow

PAUSE

And every time you take one step DOWN the hill you will feel more and more relaxed than you do NOW

PAUSE

In a few moments time, you are going to take your first step DOWN the hill, but not quite yet, and when you do, you are going to feel so very relaxed

PAUSE

Take your first step DOWN the hill NOW

PAUSE

NOW you are feeling more relaxed than you did a few seconds ago, a few minutes ago, a few days ago, even a few weeks ago

PAUSE

NOW that you are one third of the way DOWN the hill, notice how your view has changed

PAUSE

Take your time and just look at the view that you know so well. And as you look around, notice how very relaxed you are now feeling

PAUSE

Can you see that you are now closer to the bottom of the hill. Your view of the meadow has improved

PAUSE

In a few moments time, I'm going to ask you to take your second step DOWN the hill, and when you take that step you are going to feel even more relaxed than you do NOW

PAUSE

Take your second step DOWN the hill NOW

PAUSE

NOW you feel even more relaxed than you did a few moments ago, a few minutes ago, much more relaxed than you did a few hours ago

PAUSE

Your view has altered again as you approach the bottom of the hill. The meadow looks much closer. If you look back up the hill, notice how far away the top of the hill now seems

PAUSE

Look in the fields at the plants and the cows. Notice the smells of the flowers in the hedgerow.

PAUSE

You are feeling so very relaxed now, it feels that you are really there in your favourite countryside walk

PAUSE

In a few moments time, but not quite yet, you take your last step DOWN the hill, and when you do, you will feel so very relaxed when you arrive in the meadow

PAUSE

Take your last step DOWN the hill NOW

PAUSE

NOW you are feeling so very, very relaxed. More relaxed than you felt a few moments ago, a few minutes ago, much more relaxed than you felt a few hours ago

(At this point, continue with the ego-strengthening script.)

EGO STRENGTHENING

At this stage the therapist makes positive suggestions targeted at the client's general mental and physical condition. It can be altered to take into account any general condition from which the client may be suffering. This script emphasizes improvement in the affective, behavioural and cognitive modalities. Key words are repeated and stressed to reiterate the positive effects of hypnosis outside the therapeutic hour. This may have a beneficial post-hypnotic effect which is an important component of hypnosis. Coping imagery and self-helping coping statements can be included to enable the client to deal with difficult situations such as giving presentations, being assertive with a significant other, or phobias. Each relevant self-defeating belief that the client holds can be reframed. The 'pauses' help to underscore the ego-strengthening suggestions and enhance their effect.

SYMPTOM REMOVAL

This stage is not always necessary. If it is left out, then the termination script can be inserted at this point. Symptom removal is targeted at specific symptoms that the client may be suffering from such as allergies, anxiety, asthma, habits (e.g., overeating, smoking), headaches, insomnia, migraine, pain, panic attacks, phobias, ticks, skin disorders, and speech disorders, etc. The hypnosis script described is to help with the alleviation of migraine and tension headaches. Hartland (1987) can be consulted for other examples of symptom removal scripts.

It is important to ensure that the client does not have an underlying organic condition if treatment is directed towards symptom removal. An appropriate referral to a medical practitioner may be necessary.

TERMINATION

The termination stage is the last part of the hypnosis procedure. It reminds clients that they are in full control of their body and mind. The termination is undertaken even if clients open their eyes. In these cases clients are asked to close their eyes and the termination stage is completed.

DEBRIEF

Once the client has opened their eyes then the counsellor asks how they felt during hypnosis and if there were any problems. The counsellor can answer any queries that may have arisen during the session. It is a good idea to ask whether they would like any part of the script altered especially if imagery has been used. As counselling progresses the client may only need a short induction and deepening phase.

Hypnosis script

PRELIMINARY INDUCTION

(Adapted Palmer, 1993b: 33–6)

Can you make yourself as comfortable as possible in your chair

PAUSE
And if you would just like to close your eyes

PAUSE
If you would like to listen to the noises outside the room

PAUSE
And now listen to the noises inside the room

PAUSE
These noises will come and go probably throughout this session and you can choose to let them just drift over your mind and choose to ignore them if you so wish

PAUSE
You will probably notice how these noises and the sound of my voice will become softer and louder and softer again during this session. This is quite normal and will indicate that you are in a state of hypnosis

PAUSE
Let your whole body go limp and slack

PAUSE
Now keeping your eyelids closed and without moving your head, I would like you to look upwards, keep your eyes closed, just look upwards

PAUSE
Notice the feeling of tiredness, sleepiness

PAUSE
And relaxation

PAUSE
In your eye muscles

PAUSE
And when your eyes feel so tired, so very, very, tired, just let your eyes drop back DOWN

PAUSE
Notice the feeling of tiredness, sleepiness and relaxation in your eyes

PAUSE
Let this travel DOWN your face to your jaw

PAUSE
Now just relax your jaw

PAUSE
If your teeth are clenched, then unclench them

PAUSE
Now relax your tongue. If it's touching the roof of your mouth then just let it fall down

PAUSE
Let the feeling of relaxation slowly travel up over your face to your forehead

PAUSE
To the top of your head

PAUSE
To the back of your head

LONG PAUSE
Then slowly DOWN through the neck muscles

PAUSE
and DOWN to your shoulders

LONG PAUSE
Now concentrate on relaxing your shoulders, just let them drop DOWN

PAUSE
Now let that feeling of relaxation in your shoulders slowly travel DOWN your right arm, DOWN through the muscles, DOWN through your elbow, DOWN through your wrist, DOWN to your hand, right DOWN to your finger tips

LONG PAUSE
Now let that feeling of relaxation in your shoulders slowly travel DOWN your left arm, DOWN through the muscles, DOWN through your elbow, DOWN through your wrist, DOWN to your hand, right DOWN to your finger tips

LONG PAUSE
And let that feeling of relaxation in your shoulders slowly travel DOWN your chest right DOWN to your stomach

PAUSE

Notice that every time you breathe out, you feel more and more relaxed

PAUSE

Let that feeling of relaxation and tiredness travel DOWN from your shoulders DOWN your back, right DOWN through your back muscles

LONG PAUSE

Right DOWN your right leg, DOWN through the muscles, DOWN through your knee, DOWN through your ankle

PAUSE

To your foot, right DOWN to your toes

LONG PAUSE

Let the feeling of relaxation and tiredness now travel DOWN your left leg

PAUSE

DOWN through the muscles, DOWN through your knee, DOWN through your ankle

PAUSE

To your foot, right DOWN to your toes

LONG PAUSE

I'll give you a few moments now

PAUSE

To allow you to focus on any part of your body that you would like to relax even further

15-SECOND PAUSE OR LONGER IF NECESSARY

DEEPENING

(Adapted Palmer, 1993b: 36–8)
(Insert optional imagery deepener if preferred)

I want you now to concentrate on your breathing

PAUSE

Notice how every time you breathe out, you feel more, and more, relaxed

PAUSE

With each breath you take you feel so relaxed, so very, very relaxed

PAUSE

Breathe in slowly through your nose and slowly out through your mouth

PAUSE

With each breath you take

PAUSE

Every time you take a new breath of air

PAUSE
You are becoming more and more relaxed

PAUSE
Gradually you are drifting away as you become more, and more, relaxed

PAUSE
On every out-breath you are becoming more, and more, sleepy

PAUSE
More and more deeply relaxed

PAUSE
Notice how, as you relax, you are breathing more, and more, slowly

PAUSE
And more, and more, steadily, as you become more, and more, deeply, very deeply, relaxed

PAUSE
You are drifting DOWN into a deep state of relaxation

PAUSE
Your whole body is becoming more, and more, relaxed, every time, you breathe out

PAUSE
I'm slowly going to count to five, and as I do, you will feel even more relaxed than you do now

PAUSE
ONE

PAUSE
NOW you are feeling more and more relaxed than you did a few minutes ago. More and more relaxed than you did a few seconds ago

PAUSE
TWO

PAUSE
Notice how you are feeling so relaxed, that you are finding it so difficult to concentrate on my voice all the time

PAUSE
THREE

PAUSE
NOW every time I say a number, every time you breathe out, you feel more and more deeply, very, very deeply relaxed. An overwhelming feeling of tiredness and relaxation is descending upon you as you listen to my voice

PAUSE
FOUR

PAUSE

You are feeling even more relaxed NOW than you did a few minutes, a few seconds ago. In a moment when I say the number five, but not quite yet, you are going to feel so very deeply relaxed . . .

PAUSE

FIVE

PAUSE

NOW you feel even more relaxed than you did a moment ago, more relaxed than a few seconds ago, much more relaxed than you did a few minutes ago, and very much more relaxed than you did a few hours ago.

PAUSE

EGO STRENGTHENING

(Adapted Palmer, 1993b: 38–41)

You are now so relaxed, so very relaxed, that you are becoming very aware of what I am saying to you

PAUSE

You are so aware that your mind is open to any positive suggestions I may make for your benefit

PAUSE

You are feeling so relaxed that when I make positive suggestions about your health, you will accept these suggestions, and gradually over a period of time you will feel better and better, even though you will not be here with me

PAUSE

My suggestions will just drift over your mind and you will be able to remember all the relevant ones that will influence your feelings

PAUSE

Your thoughts

PAUSE

And your behaviour

PAUSE

As you feel more and more deeply relaxed during this session, you will find new energy to help you cope with any problems you may have had recently

PAUSE

New energy to lessen any fatigue

PAUSE

New energy to help you concentrate on your goals

PAUSE

A new strength of mind and body to deal with internal and external pressures

PAUSE

Gradually, you will become absorbed in life again, looking forward to every day

PAUSE

And as every day goes by, you will become more relaxed, and much calmer than you have been for some time

PAUSE

And each day, you will feel far less tense, and far less concerned with unimportant matters

PAUSE

And as this happens, your confidence will grow as your old fears become a distant memory

PAUSE

Week by week, day by day, hour by hour, minute by minute, second by second, your independence will grow

PAUSE

Any anxiety or depression or guilt or stress will fade away as you learn to cope with life

(NB. Target relevant emotion or physical state according to the client's presenting problem.)

PAUSE

You will be able to stand difficult situations much more easily

PAUSE

You will no longer hear yourself saying 'I can't stand it', but instead you will realistically say to yourself, 'It's unpleasant but I CAN STAND IT'

PAUSE

As you learn that you can stand situations, you will procrastinate less often and you will be able to start and continue your tasks more easily

PAUSE

You will question whether things are really awful. They may be bad but are they really awful?

PAUSE

As you realize that you can stand situations, and that things are seldom awful, you will be able to face your fears much more easily

PAUSE

If you fail at a task, you will not condemn yourself as a failure or stupid

PAUSE

All it means is that you did not achieve your target

PAUSE

No more, no less

PAUSE

You will learn to accept yourself more for the person you are and not just for your achievements

PAUSE

Your internal demands, many of those unnecessary, inflexible musts and shoulds

PAUSE

Will change to preferences and coulds and subsequently your anxieties will lessen

(NB. Target relevant emotion according to the client's presenting problem.)

PAUSE

Gradually, as time goes by, you will feel better and better and your life will improve

PAUSE

And your recent worries will be a thing of the past

PAUSE

And you will be able to put them behind you

PAUSE

AN EXAMPLE OF SYMPTOM REMOVAL

(Adapted Palmer, 1993b: 42–3)

Day by day, week by week, month by month

PAUSE

As you become much more relaxed

PAUSE

And far less tense

PAUSE

Gradually, the tension in your shoulders

PAUSE

And in your neck will fade

PAUSE

You will stand and sit in a very relaxed manner

PAUSE

And as you do, you will feel so comfortable that any pain will become a distant memory

PAUSE

If you concentrate now on your face

PAUSE

On your head

PAUSE

And on your neck, notice how, as you relax even further

PAUSE

Gradually your head and face, are starting to feel warm

PAUSE

As this feeling of warmth increases, you are starting to feel even more relaxed than you did a few minutes ago

PAUSE
And day by day

PAUSE
As you feel less tense, in your body and mind, this state of relaxation will help to prevent headaches occurring

PAUSE
And as the pain is normally related to stress and tension

PAUSE
Day by day, as you become more relaxed

PAUSE
And less tense, the pain will diminish

PAUSE
And if you ever feel the headache returning

PAUSE
You will be able to sit down, relax your shoulders

PAUSE
Relax your neck muscles

PAUSE
Relax your face and head

PAUSE
And the pain will just drift away

PAUSE

TERMINATION

(Adapted Palmer, 1993b: 43–4)

In a few moments' time, but not quite yet, I am going to count to three, and when I do, you will open your eyes and wake up, and feel relaxed and refreshed

PAUSE
You will be able to remember or forget whatever you want to of this hypnosis session

And you will be in full control of your body and mind

PAUSE
And wake up today on (insert here: day, time, location)

PAUSE
As I count to three, you will wake up

PAUSE (NB. Counsellor starts to speak louder with each subsequent number)
One

PAUSE

TWO

PAUSE

THREE

PAUSE

Open your eyes in your own time

Presupposing that the client wants to use hypnosis, it is indicated for a wide range of psychosomatic and stress-related disorders, including anxiety, asthma, allergies, behavioural problems (e.g. smoking, ticks, over-eating and weight control), blushing, common and classic migraine, depression, hypertension, insomnia, irritable bowel syndrome, pain, phobias, physical tension, skin disorders, (e.g. eczema), stress, speech disorders, (e.g. stammering) and tension headache (Hartland, 1987). To reiterate, before hypnosis is used to alleviate a physical condition, we would strongly recommend that the client receives a medical check-up to ensure the problem is not of an organic nature requiring a medical intervention.

Massage

Many individuals find massage relaxing. However, it is strongly advisable for counsellors not to blur therapeutic boundaries. Therefore if a client believes that massage may help them relax, a suitable referral to a qualified masseur or aromatherapist may be necessary. The counsellor can still remain the primary therapist dealing with the other interventions.

Multimodal relaxation method

This technique was developed by Palmer (1993b) to be used in one-to-one counselling or in group settings. It offers the client a range of different modality interventions thereby allowing the individual to discover the best technique that induces a state of relaxation. In our experience some clients prefer imagery exercises whereas others prefer cognitive distractions such as repeating a mantra. After trying the method, clients can then use biofeedback instruments to determine which particular modality intervention is most beneficial. As the medical condition of group members may be unknown muscular contraction techniques are not included as they may raise blood pressure. Deep breathing is also avoided as this can trigger panic attacks in anxious individuals (Palmer, 1992).

Clients are encouraged to choose their own image or picture to avoid the counsellor or trainer inadvertently suggesting unsuitable guided images which may trigger elevated levels of anxiety or panic attacks. For example, asking a person to imagine lying on a beach may appear totally innocuous and safe. However, if that individual had experienced an unpleasant or frightening incident on a beach then this image is likely to trigger anxiety.

If the session is tape recorded, the client can use the multimodal relaxation method outside the session. The end of the script can be altered to help clients fall asleep if they are suffering from insomnia or disturbed sleep patterns. If the method is being used in one-to-one counselling then the counsellor can inquire beforehand what image the client would like inserted into the script.

The method has been designed to last about 8 to 12 minutes so that busy individuals are able to fit it in easily to their daily routine. Depending upon the setting, it can be lengthened if required. Clients are usually encouraged to undertake the exercise while sitting in a chair so that they can transfer the skill to other situations such as the workplace or while sitting or even standing on a train. With practice, most clients will not need to close their eyes.

With regular practice clients will usually be able to use the method as a rapid relaxation technique, which is particularly helpful during or prior to stressful events. In fact, this is one goal of conditioned relaxation training whereby clients learn to relax in response to a specific self-produced cue. Some may find that by breathing slowly and saying in their mind the number 'one' or 'relax' on their out breath they can quickly relax whereas others may need to be able to focus on an image.

Assuming that the counsellor has answered any queries and has prepared the clients(s) for the exercise (see hypnosis) then the script is as follows:

MULTIMODAL RELAXATION METHOD

(Palmer, 1993b: 17–23)

If you could make yourself as comfortable as possible on your chair

PAUSE
And if you would just like to close your eyes

PAUSE
As you do this exercise, if you feel any odd feelings such as tingling sensations, light headedness, or whatever, then this is quite normal. If you open your eyes then these feelings will go away. If you carry on with the relaxation exercise usually the feelings will disappear anyway

PAUSE
If you would like to listen to the noises outside the room first of all

LONG PAUSE
And now listen to any noises inside the room

PAUSE
You may be aware of yourself breathing

PAUSE
These noises will come and go probably throughout this session and you can choose to let them just drift over your mind and choose to ignore them if you so wish

PAUSE
Now keeping your eyelids closed and without moving your head, I would like you to look upwards, keep your eyes closed, just look upwards

LONG PAUSE (NB. If participants wear contact lenses then they can remove them before the exercise or not look upwards)

Notice the feeling of tiredness

PAUSE
And relaxation

PAUSE
In your eye muscles

PAUSE
Now let your eyes drop back down

PAUSE
Notice the tiredness and the relaxation in those muscles of your eyes

PAUSE
Let the feeling now travel down your face to your jaw, just relax your jaw

LONG PAUSE
Now relax your tongue

PAUSE
Let the feeling of relaxation slowly travel up over your face to the top of your head

PAUSE
To the back of your head

LONG PAUSE
Then slowly down through the neck muscles

PAUSE
And down to your shoulders

LONG PAUSE
Now concentrate on relaxing your shoulders, just let them drop down

PAUSE
Now let that feeling of relaxation now in your shoulders slowly travel down your right arm, down through the muscles, down through your elbow, down through your wrist, to your hand, right down to your finger tips

LONG PAUSE
Let the feeling of relaxation now in your shoulders slowly travel down your left arm, down through your muscles, down through your elbow, through your wrist, down to your hand, right down to your finger tips

LONG PAUSE
And let that feeling of relaxation now in your shoulders slowly travel down your chest right down to your stomach

PAUSE
Just concentrate now on your breathing

PAUSE
Notice that every time as you breathe out you feel more

PAUSE
And more relaxed

LONG PAUSE
Let that feeling of relaxation travel down from your shoulders right down your back muscles

LONG PAUSE
Right down your right leg, down through the muscles, down through your knee, down through your ankle

PAUSE
To your foot, right down to your toes

LONG PAUSE
Let the feeling of relaxation now travel down your left leg

PAUSE
Down through the muscles, down through your knee, down through your ankle, and foot, and right down to your toes

LONG PAUSE
I'll give you a few moments now

PAUSE
To allow you to concentrate on any part of your body that you would like to relax even further

15-SECOND PAUSE
I want you to concentrate on your breathing again

PAUSE
Notice as you breathe out

PAUSE
On each out-breath you feel more and more relaxed

LONG PAUSE
I would like you in your mind to say the number one

PAUSE (NB. Option: if the number one evokes an emotion then participants are asked to choose another number of their choice)

And say it every time you breathe out

LONG PAUSE
This will help you to push away any unwanted thoughts you may have

PAUSE
Each time you breathe out just say the number in your mind

30-SECOND PAUSE (NB. Option: up to 20 minutes pause here if an extended session is required. If extended then regular input from the trainer is needed to remind the participants to repeat the mantra 'one' or whatever number they have chosen)

I want you now to stop saying the number one and instead picture your favourite relaxing place

PAUSE
I want you to concentrate

PAUSE
On your favourite relaxing place

LONG PAUSE
Try and see it in your mind's eye

LONG PAUSE
Look at the colours

PAUSE
Perhaps concentrate on one of the colours now

PAUSE
Maybe one of your favourite colours if it's there

LONG PAUSE
Now concentrate on any sounds or noises or the silence in your favourite relaxing place

LONG PAUSE
Now concentrate on any smells or aromas in your favourite relaxing place

LONG PAUSE
Now just imagine touching something in your favourite relaxing place

LONG PAUSE
Just imagine how it feels

LONG PAUSE
I want you now to concentrate on your breathing again

PAUSE
Notice once again that every time you breathe out

PAUSE
You feel more

PAUSE
And more relaxed

LONG PAUSE
Whenever you want to in the future you will be able to remember your favourite relaxing place or the breathing exercise and it will help you to relax quickly

LONG PAUSE
In a few moments time, but not quite yet, I'm going to count to three

PAUSE
And you will be able to open your eyes in your own time

PAUSE (NB. Option: go off to sleep if you so wish)

One

PAUSE

TWO

PAUSE

THREE

PAUSE

Open your eyes in your own time (optional)

Key: PAUSE is about 1–3 seconds in length
LONG PAUSE is about 5–15 seconds in length

NB. Lengths vary depending upon the time allocated to the relaxation exercise.

The multimodal relaxation method is particularly indicated for clients with anxiety, classic and common migraine, colitis, essential hypertension, high blood pressure, hyperarousal disorders (e.g. Post Traumatic Stress Disorder), insomnia, irritable bowel syndrome, mixed tension–vascular heachache, physical tension, psychosomatic disorders, tension headache, and Type A behaviour. It can also help clients to control their general irritability if they are on a stop smoking programme (Palmer and Dryden, 1995). To facilitate and monitor progress we have found it helpful if the client completes a Relaxation Diary (Appendix 8, Palmer, 1993b: 52) after undertaking relaxation exercises. The client can bring the diary to the next counselling session and share his or her progress or any difficulties encountered with the stress counsellor.

Progressive relaxation

Jacobson (1938) developed 'progressive relaxation', which consisted of teaching clients to tense different groups of muscles for approximately 6 seconds and then to relax them for a longer period. Although this relaxation technique was a great breakthrough in its day, the entire procedure took many training sessions and was very time-consuming. Later, Wolpe and Lazarus (1966) refined and shortened the process. The exercise is in four sections: relaxation of arms; facial area with neck, shoulders and upper back; chest, stomach and lower back; hips, thighs and calves followed by complete body relaxation. As the technique is repetitive and due to space constraints, we will describe a part of the relaxation of the arms.

Settle back as comfortably as you can. Let yourself relax to the best of your ability . . . Now, as you relax like that, clench your right fist, just clench your fist tighter and tighter, and study the tension as you do so. Keep it clenched and feel the tension in your right fist, hand forearm . . . and now relax. Let the fingers of your right hand become loose, and observe the contrast in your feelings . . . Now let yourself go and try to become more relaxed all over . . . once more, clench your right fist really tight . . . hold it, and notice the tension again . . . now let go, relax; your fingers straighten out, and you notice the difference once more . . . (and so on).

This procedure is continued for the entire arm and takes about five minutes to complete. Other parts of the body are relaxed in a similar process. With some clients the relaxed state can be induced more speedily and many of the instructions can be omitted. The technique is particularly useful for physically tense clients. It is indicated for clients suffering from anxiety (specific or generalized), asthma, convulsive tic, depression, oesophageal spasm, high blood pressure, hypertension, insomnia, pain (chronic), phobias, spasmodic dysmenorrhoea, tension headache, and tinnitus (see McGuigan, 1993). As this technique could temporarily raise blood pressure, care should be taken with clients with cardiac disorders or glaucoma.

Nutrition

Poor or inadequate diet can lead to a variety of illnesses, which include digestive disorders, obesity and coronary heart disease. High intakes of sugar, alcohol, salt and saturated fats are considered unhealthy. Caffeine enhances the sympathetic nervous system and high levels can cause nervousness, insomnia, palpitations, feelings of anxiety, muscle tremors, restlessness, jitteriness and shakiness. Caffeine withdrawal symptoms include headaches, migraines, palpitations and shakiness. In our experience withdrawal symptoms often occur at weekends when people may drink less coffee than they would normally consume at work. Similarly to exercise interventions, we would recommend that counsellors have information available to educate their clients on healthy eating. Bibliotherapy in the form of books, videos, handouts and leaflets are normally ideal for education purposes.

When clients wish to start a weight control programme we have found undertaking a CABB profile useful as it will often highlight other areas that may need attention. A completed CABB is illustrated in Table 7.2.

Relaxation response

The relaxation response is a Westernized verion of meditation. Benson (1976) removed any cultural influence and replaced the mantra with the number 'one'. One of the main advantages of this technique is that the repitition of the number 'one' helps clients to ignore any negative or distracting thoughts that they may have as they relax. Palmer and Dryden (adapted 1995: 133) modified the original text:

1. Find a comfortable position and sit quietly.
2. Close your eyes.
3. Relax your muscles, starting at your face and progress down to your toes.
4. Now concentrate on your breathing. Breathe naturally through your nose. In your mind say the number 'one' as you breathe out.
5. If negative or distracting thoughts occur, let them just pass over your mind and return to repeating the number 'one'. Do not try to force relaxation. Just let it occur in its own time.
6. Continue this exercise for a further 10–20 minutes.
7. When you finish, keep your eyes closed for a couple of minutes and sit quietly.

Table 7.2 *CABB for weight control programme*

Modality	Problem	Proposed programme
Cognitive	I must eat what I want	Dispute self-defeating beliefs
	I can't stand not eating what I want to eat	Develop powerful coping statements
	If I eat too much then I've completely blown my diet.	
	What's the point of continuing?	Highlight 'all and never' thinking
	I'm a pig when I binge	Focus on self-acceptance training
	Poor self-image	Coping imagery
Affect	Mild depression	Dispute self-defeating thinking
	Discomfort anxiety	Relaxation or self-hypnosis to help cope with discomfort anxiety
	Shame	Discuss shame attacking exercise
Biological	Four stone overweight	Provide information about diet and blood pressure
	Raised blood pressure	
	Pain in knees	Refer to medical practitioner
	Unhealthy diet	
	Lack of exercise	Exercise programme subject to blood pressure and painful knees being dealt with – liaise with medical practitioner
Behaviour	Binge eats when anxious or depressed	Examine beliefs and apply stimulus control
	Does not eat breakfast and eats chocolate later in the day	Explain benefits of eating breakfast
		Monitor food intake by daily completion of diary

Carrington (1993: 150–1) has suggested a number of primary indications for modern forms of meditation:

- abuse of 'soft' drugs, alcohol or tobacco
- blocks to productivity or creativity
- chronic fatigue states
- chronic low-grade depressions
- difficulties with self-assertion
- subacute reaction depressions
- excessive self-blame
- hypersomnias
- irritability, low-frustration tolerance
- inadequate contact with affective life
- pathological bereavement reactions, separation anxiety
- poorly developed psychological differentiation
- strong submissive trends
- shifting emphasis from client's reliance on counsellor to reliance on self (particularly useful when terminating counselling).

Carrington (1993) warns that some individuals may not be able to tolerate the usual 20-minutes sessions and in these cases, the meditation time needs to be reduced.

BEHAVIOURAL INTERVENTIONS

Behavioural guidance

Behavioural guidance is the explanation to a client of a therapeutic programme or intervention. Usually helped if specific examples are given, for example, how to undertake a behavioural exposure programme.

Contracting

In contracting, the client contracts or makes a formal agreement with a significant other, such as a partner or friend, to make a specific positive behavioural change that they both desire (Marks, 1986). It is crucial that the target behaviours are not complex, are easy to repeat and are viewed as positive by both parties; for example, stop smoking, stop moaning, or cessation of eating unhealthy foods. We have found it useful for both parties to write down the agreed behaviours in terms that are clear and specific. The counsellor should encourage both parties to work together as a team and to remind each other of the benefits of change.

Cue exposure

The client is exposed to the cue or 'temptation' to enable the learning of ways of coping with the resultant impulsive urges. For example, a binge eater may sit in front of a plate of favourite food such as biscuits resisting the urge to eat them. A distraction technique may be taught. Eventually the urge subsides. Whenever possible, the technique should first be used in a counselling session enabling the counsellor to help the client develop coping strategies to deal with the cue. It is useful for the client in the session to rate on a scale of 0–10 the strength of their urge. In the previous example the coping strategies could include aversive imagery, coping statements and relaxation techniques. Extreme care needs to be taken with clients coming off drugs because they will be tempted to lapse when alone.

Fixed-role therapy

This intervention is based on the work of Kelly (1955). The counsellor negotiates with the client that they will perform a specific set of behaviours which they do not usually exhibit. This would be performed for an agreed number of days, for example, 7–14 days. The new behaviours would need to be relevant to the social context of the client. For example, a client, Sue, who wished to become more assertive at work took on a new set of behaviours in certain reasonably safe situations. She monitored how she felt and how others reacted to her. In the next counselling session Sue and her counsellor reviewed the progress and modified certain behaviours which had proved unhelpful.

The behaviours chosen would not normally be too challenging for the client as this could lead to the client not undertaking the exercise and subsequently in some cases reduce self-esteem. For some clients the reduction of specific behaviours, for example, aggressive behaviour, may be part of the intervention. We have found it helpful if the clients know a person who acts in the way that they are going to experiment with as they can imagine what the person may do in similar circumstances.

This technique has proved to be a very beneficial exercise with Type A individuals who wish to talk, eat, and walk more slowly and be less hostile at work. Many clients start to learn that including new behaviours and attitudes in their repertoire is not as difficult as they first imagined. It is important that the counsellor ensures that the client has practised various coping strategies to deal with other people's reactions to the client's new behaviours, especially if the client is going to apply assertion skills with significant others, such as their work colleagues or members of their family.

Flooding

Flooding is prolonged exposure to the most feared thing or situation. This is continued until the client's anxiety finally subsides. Due to the high levels of anxiety usually triggered by this technique it is important to ensure that the client's explicit consent has been received and that they have a clear understanding of the procedures involved. Similar to implosion, the client needs to understand the rationale for using the technique and that premature termination of the exposure to the feared situation or whatever, can in some cases lead subsequently to even higher levels of anxiety.

This technique is contra-indicated with clients with heart disease or other related medical disorders and those who would be easily overwhelmed by high levels of anxiety (see general comments under Implosion, p. 156).

Graded behavioural exposure

This is one of the main behavioural techniques used to reduce anxiety. Exposure to the feared situation (fantasy or live) is graded into discrete steps. A hierarchy of fears is drawn up and the client is initially exposed to the situation that they are least anxious about. The client indicates on a 0–10 scale their level of anxiety where the highest score represents panic and 0 represents no anxiety. Once the first step has been coped with and the client's anxiety has reduced to acceptable levels then the client faces up to a situation higher up the hierarchy. The hierarchy of feared situations below illustrates an individual who becomes anxious when speaking publicly. The client would first be exposed to a situation that they felt was not overwhelming. Often it is not the lowest item on the list. In the case illustrated the client may also need to learn additional skills, for example, how to use an overhead projector.

Hierarchy of feared situations

MOST FEARED SITUATION: 10   Speaking publicly at a conference
9.5 Being interviewed on the radio
9.0 Presentation to Board of Directors
8.0 Speaking publicly to 25 staff
7.0 Speaking informally to 25 friends
6.5 Speaking to 12 staff
5.0 Speaking to 6 staff
4.5 Speaking to 10 friends
4.0 Presentation to 3 staff
LEAST FEARED SITUATION: 2.0 Talking 'one to one'

It is helpful if the client monitors how anxious they feel during exposure. Over a period of time this will clearly highlight any improvement the client may be making. Once again the scale of 0–8 or 0–10 is used where 0 represents no anxiety and 10 represents very anxious or panic. The monitoring is usually recorded in a homework diary (see Table 7.3, Palmer, 1991a; and Appendix 9). The goals for the week are negotiated with the therapist. The client includes comments on the exposure and notes any coping strategy used. In some cases, the assistance of an aide, such as a friend or work colleague, may be beneficial. However, the aide needs to be instructed not to reassure the client during exposure otherwise the effectiveness of the programme will be reduced.

Habit control

These are interventions designed to reduce or stop undesired habits such as bed-wetting, cramps, nail biting, stuttering, tics, etc. For example, clients who bite their nails would be asked to clench their fists or grasp an object when they had the urge to bite. Clients with tics would be directed to perform an opposite action just prior and after a tic occurring. Often, the counsellor has to be creative in designing an intervention to help the client control the habit. Additional techniques or interventions may be necessary; for example, biofeedback monitors are very useful in helping clients who bed-wet.

Interpersonal skills

Many clients come to counselling because they are distressed by and are encountering difficulties in their relationships. Experience suggests that much client stress in this area of their lives is occasioned by them not having had the positive opportunities and/or modelling to learn social and interpersonal skills. This does not appear to be in the nature of a national psychological inadequacy or virtue, depending on which way it is seen. There is a place for the traditional 'stiff-upper-lip', but we believe that the cost of sustaining it, in personal terms, is cumulative and far outweighs its national value.

Although counsellors are, hopefully, models for interpersonal skills through their

Table 7.3 *Homework diary for a blood/injury/medical phobia*

Week commencing: 23–30/11
Goals for the week

1. Watch video (aneurism)
2. Read – medical text book
3. Pictures of childbirth
4. Visualization – blood donor, smear

Name ....

| | Session | | Goal | | **0** no anxiety | **2** slight anxiety | **4** definite anxiety | **6** marked anxiety | **8** panic |
| | Began | Ended | no. | | | Anxiety | | Comments | |
Date				Task performed	Before	During	After	incl. coping tactics	
23/11	18.30	19.30	1	Watched video	3	6–3	3		
25/11	10.30	11.45	2	Read new sections from textbooks	3	3–4	2	Less anxious than previously when reading new sections	
26/11	11.00	12.00	4	Visualization – blood donation and smear	4	4–3	3		
29/11	9.30	10.30	4	Watched video of TV programme on transplants	1	4/3	2	Repeated unpleasant sections	

Source: Palmer (1991a)

relationship building work with clients, the problem-focused approach sees a need for a more active teaching role for counsellors in all its stages. The area of interpersonal skills is no exception. In this section we discuss basic assertiveness skills training.

Assertiveness

Assertiveness training has been described as a 'system of techniques taught to enable people to ask for what they want, complain appropriately, give positive feedback to others, stand up for themselves and, when necessary, defend themselves' (Feltham and Dryden, 1993: 12). Thus assertion is a form of skills training which helps people to change their thinking and make themselves less vulnerable to emotional distress, by giving them more control over their own lives. Anne Dickson (1982) sees it as 'the art of clear, honest, direct communication . . . which helps you to kick the need for approval . . . make your own decisions . . . evaluate your behaviour in the light of other's criticisms rather than denying it defensively, or being demolished by it.'

ASSERTIVE BELIEFS

We have seen in Chapter 6 that there can be a correlation between what a person believes and their levels of stress. Clients can be helped to believe more assertively, as an integral part of behaving more assertively and having a greater self-belief. By discussing assertiveness skills work, counsellors offer the opportunity to understand the framework which permits assertiveness and reduces guilt, while also giving broad social and ethical guidelines for respecting other people.

Stress can result in a reduction in self-confidence, which impedes our capacity to speak up for ourselves. Non-assertiveness can lead people into further distress because they do not get their needs met, often lack respect from others and feel bad about themselves, all of which reduce self-confidence further. Discussing assertive beliefs can help clients to regain self-confidence, reminding them of the rights they have as individuals when interacting with other people, who also have rights (see Box 7.1).

Just as there are self-defeating beliefs which negatively affect our problem solving, there are also self-defeating beliefs about assertion we can use to prevent ourselves from becoming more assertive. Box 7.2 lists some of these. It is useful sharing this list with clients who wish to become assertive to discover whether they share any of the beliefs. If they do, then the counsellor will probably need to take a pragmatic approach and discuss with the client how holding these beliefs will interfere with their acquisition and application of assertiveness skills. This will help to troubleshoot difficulties that are likely to occur later in training.

ASSERTION, AGGRESSION AND PASSIVITY

Clients embarking on assertion skills training need help in distinguishing between assertion and the non-assertive approaches of aggression and passivity.

A useful illustration of the differences may be found in the area of decision making, in which:

Box 7.1 *Assertive beliefs*

Assertive beliefs which I can use to reduce my stress.

I believe I can increase my assertiveness and reduce my stress by:

- sometimes saying 'no'
- recognizing my own needs as important
- making mistakes without feeling ashamed
- taking responsibility for my own actions
- acknowledging when I do not understand something
- setting and following my own priorities
- asking for what I want and need
- being me and respecting myself
- choosing to be assertive or unassertive without feeling guilty
- expressing my feelings in a way that respects those of others.

Box 7.2 *Self-defeating assertive beliefs*

Self-defeating assertive beliefs which I can use to stress myself:

1. It is uncaring to be assertive.
2. It is part of my role as a
   (father/mother/nurse/teacher/doctor/counsellor, etc.) to meet everyone else's needs.
3. My definition of a team is a group who do as I say.
4. I have no right to change my mind, neither has anyone else.
5. When something goes wrong somebody must always be to blame.
6. I must be liked by everyone and they must all approve of what I do.
7. There's nothing I can do about shortage of staff or money for resources.
8. If someone turns down my request it is because they do not like me.
9. It would be a disaster if someone turned down my request, so I will not take the risk of asking. I will just hope that somehow I will get what I want or need.
10. I have no right to express my opinion, my (parents/teachers/manager/boss/spouse/best friend/counsellor)'s decision is final and I must do what they say without question.
11. I ought to be tough at all times and never show any vulnerability.
12. I must keep the peace at all costs.

Source: adapted from Bond (1986: 10)

- being assertive means deciding for yourself and allowing and enabling other people to decide for themselves
- being aggressive means deciding for yourself, not allowing others to decide for themselves and often deciding for them
- being passive means allowing others to decide for you.

Bond (1986: 100) also includes the non-assertive approach of manipulation which she describes as: 'being manipulative means making decisions for yourself and other people, while giving the impression that you are allowing them to think for themselves.'

ASSERTIVE, AGGRESSIVE AND PASSIVE BEHAVIOUR

Palmer (1990b) lists examples of assertive, aggressive and passive behaviour which may be used to help clients to understand their component parts (see Box 7.3). It is normally a good idea to ascertain which behaviours and phases are generally used by the client in specific situations or with particular people. Useful assessment questions are (see adapted Palmer and Dryden, 1995: 139):

- Are you able to express positive feelings?
- Are you able to express negative feelings?
- Can you refuse requests and invitations?
- Can you express personal opinions?
- Are you able to express justified anger or annoyance?
- Are there any particular situations in which you experience problems with asserting yourself (for example, home, extended family, neighbours, work, shops, visitors to the home, pubs, restaurants, church, dealing with professionals/service trades etc.)?

If clients have a number of areas in which being assertive is a problem, they can set out these by ranking each area in order of importance for them. This can be done on a whiteboard, or it can be done more formally on an Assertiveness Problem Hierarchy Form (APH) (see Appendix 10). Figure 7.3 is a completed APH (Palmer, 1997a).

Name: Marie
Date: 27 June 1996

1 Difficulty in complaining with any services, e.g. motor trade
2 Dealing with situations where I feel vulnerable
3 Feeling unnecessarily guilty if I upset friends and family
4 Dealing with demanding students
5 Dealing with patronizing callers on the telephone
6 Saying 'no' to my children
7 Being too obliging with friends
8 Being too obliging with work colleagues
9
10

Continue if necessary.

Figure 7.3 *Assertiveness problem hierarchy form*

Although the client chooses which problem to attempt first, it is wise not to start on the most difficult one in the early stages of assertiveness training. Nothing succeeds like success and it builds up confidence if a client starts to practise some of the skills in less threatening situations. However, at this stage it is worthwhile discussing in some depth with the client the exact nature of assertive, aggressive and passive behaviours. Box 7.3 contains material that can be used as a handout to clients to help this process (adapted Palmer, 1990b).

The counseller can then discuss useful assertiveness skills. Box 7.4 contains material for a handout showing some of the main skills. A good place to start practising is during the counselling session whereby the counsellor can demonstrate the appropriate behaviours and skills (see Modelling). Then during role play the counsellor can act the part of significant others while the client practises assertiveness skills. Usually the counsellor will need to swop roles with the client to demonstrate how to use assertiveness skills with difficult significant others in the client's life. Bibliotherapy such as self-help books and training videos can be very beneficial in helping clients to understand the relevant skills necessary to become assertive. As the client becomes more assertive in a range of different situations or with particular people, the APH may need to be revised and new goals negotiated.

To help evaluate progress we recommend that clients complete an assertiveness behaviour diary in between counselling sessions (see Appendix 11) this method of recording will help to monitor difficulties that may arise in the application of specific assertiveness skills as well as focusing on success. Figure 7.4 is a completed diary.

Clients need to be advised when not to use assertiveness skills. For example, when an employer may use it as an excuse to dismiss them or with people that may resort to the use of violence (see Palmer and Dryden, 1995). Clients should be reminded that possessing assertiveness skills does not necessarily mean that they have to use them in all situations.

Modelling

This technique is useful in both individual and group counselling settings. Prior to a client undertaking a task or exercise, the counsellor models or demonstrates, step by step, the desired behaviour. In our experience, it is helpful if the counsellor emulates the client by demonstrating the particular skill at an acceptable standard and not in a 'perfect' manner. The client can practise the behaviour, such as assertion skills, in the session with the counsellor giving encouraging and constructive feedback. The client can then apply the skill in real-life as a homework assignment and report back on progress in the following session. One of the most important mottoes for counsellors to remember when negotiating homework assignments with clients is 'challenging but not overwhelming'.

Psychodrama

Psychodrama is a form of group therapy which allows a single group member, known as the protagonist, to act out a past, present or future problem with the aid of a therapist, known as a director, using other group members to play the parts of significant others in the story. Normally there is more than one scene, with the scenes being used to explore the problem, create insight into it and heal past hurts, and create realistic aspirations and strategies for future behaviour. Important elements include spontaneity, role reversal, catharsis and role

Box 7.3 *Assertive, aggressive and passive behaviour*

Assertive

Behaviour
  Relaxed
  Smiles when pleased
  Good eye contact
  No slouching/fidgeting
  Collaborative
  Not hostile

Words/phrases used
  'I' statements: I think, I fear, I want
  Open questions: what do you want/think; how do you feel
  Cooperative: let's, we could

Aggressive

Behaviour
  Points finger
  Leans forward
  Firm, sharp, sarcastic voice
  Thumps fist(s)
  Loud/shouts
  Violates rights of others
  Dominating

Words/phrases used
  You'd better
  Your fault
  You're joking
  Don't be an idiot
  Don't be stupid
  You must, should, ought

Passive/non-assertive

Behaviour
  Shrugs
  Hunched shoulders
  Hand wringing
  Shifts body weight
  Downcast eyes
  Steps backwards
  Whining, giggly, quiet voice

Words/phrases used
  Maybe
  Just
  Perhaps
  I wonder if you could
  I'm hopeless
  I can't
  I mean
  Never mind
  It's not important
  Well, uh

---

play. Other group members benefit through participation in the protagonist's drama and through sharing their feelings afterwards. (Gale, 1990: 98)

Although this approach may be beneficial in group settings, we would recommend that counsellors receive adequate training before attempting its use.

Box 7.4 *Assertiveness skills*

Broken record: expressing your viewpoint in a calm manner, ignoring irrelevant arguments, manipulative traps and provocation.

For example:
 Awkward customer: 'I want a refund. I know my rights.'
 You: 'Unfortunately the product is damaged, so I am unable to give you a refund or an exchange.'
 Awkward customer: 'Call yourself a manager? You wouldn't use it in this state, would you?'
 You: 'As you didn't purchase it from us damaged, I'm not in a position to help you.'

Fogging: This helps you to distinguish real points that may need dealing with from irrelevant criticism. By only acknowledging your actual mistakes you maintain your self-respect.

For example:
 Your boss: 'You never hand your work in on time and it puts a strain on all of us in this office.'
 You: 'In the past six months, I've missed two deadlines, and I take full responsibility for that.'

Negative enquiry: this encourages the other person to give you constructive feedback instead of unhelpful criticism.

For example:
 Critic: 'You are a hopeless mother!'
 You: 'In what way do you find me hopeless?'

Workable compromise: Offer the other person a compromise in such a way that your self-respect is not affected.

For example:
 Your boss: 'I really must have those papers by tomorrow morning. Can you finish them tonight?'
 You: 'I've already arranged to go to the cinema tonight. But I could come in earlier tomorrow morning and have the papers ready for you by 10am. Is that okay?'

Source: adapted Palmer and Strickland, 1996: 28–9

Response cost or penalty

This is a form of self-control and aversion training. It involves the client agreeing to a forfeit or penalty if she or he does not undertake a particular action (Marks, 1986). For example, clients who wish to maintain a healthy diet agree to donate a sum of money to their least favourite charity if they eat snacks. This technique is usually

Name:	Helen				
Date	Describe situation	Person/people involved	Assertiveness skills used	Evaluation of skills	Areas for improvement
21/3/97	Boss was unreasonable and over-reacted about me not reaching a deadline. He suggested that I never handed my work in on time.	Boss	Fogging	My boss realized, very quickly that I had only missed two deadlines in the past six months, for which I accepted full responsibility.	To begin with, I was flustered. It took a moment or two before I had calmed down sufficiently to use my assertion skills. I need more practice.

Figure 7.4 *Assertiveness behaviour diary*

applied when homework assignments have been negotiated and the client needs additional encouragement to either decrease or increase the frequency of a specific behaviour.

Response prevention

This intervention is used with clients suffering from obsessive–compulsive disorders (see p. 149) (Salkovskis and Kirk, 1989). It involves the client being exposed to ritual-evoking cues or thoughts and resisting the urge to perform rituals. After a period of time, the anxiety habituates in a similar manner to a graded exposure programme for sufferers of phobias. Homework diaries are used to monitor progress. In the early stages of counselling, the client is asked to prolong the time before performing the ritual and also to reduce the number of times the ritual is performed. For example, if when anxious the client touches an object 20 times then the therapist encourages the client to only touch it 15 times. If clients are initially asked to stop touching the object completely, they are likely to find this extremely difficult and may terminate therapy.

Self-monitoring and recording

Clients often find self-monitoring and recording their progress very helpful. Homework diaries and daily logs (see appendices) are particularly useful. Clients who wish to reduce their weight find monitoring and recording of their calorific intake beneficial.

Stimulus control

A client may wish to reduce specific behaviours such as smoking or eating certain foods. Stimulus control involves changing the environment so that the client does not have easy access to the stimulus. For example, a client on a weight control programme would remove unsuitable food from the kitchen and home. In addition, the client would only eat in a specific room, while sitting at a particular chair to discourage eating between meals.

Shame attacking

Clients who experience debilitating shame in specific situations are encouraged to carry out a 'shameful' act while disputing their shame-creating beliefs (Dryden, 1987). For example, taking a toy dog on a lead for a walk. The client needs to be cognitively prepared before undertaking this kind of exercise to remind them that 'They may believe I'm an idiot for acting in this way but I'm just a person who acted idiotically and not a total idiot. I can still accept myself.' Coping statements like these can be written on a small card and read by the client while undertaking the exercise. This technique encourages self-acceptance.

Symptom prescription (paradoxical intention)

This is a form of paradoxical intention where the client is asked to increase or decrease the performance of a certain undesired behaviour (see Frankl, 1960). For example, a client who has a ritual of touching a door handle 25 times could be asked to touch it 50 times instead. A client who blushes at social gatherings would be asked to intentionally blush in these situations. This intervention needs to be used with care as the client may misinterpret the intentions of the counsellor and the technique is likely to lead to high levels of anxiety in most clients. It is not recommended if the therapeutic alliance is poor. Due to the possible difficulties encountered with symptom prescription, including unpredictable outcomes, we suggest that this technique is only used when other standard procedures have failed to work.

Time management

Managing time at home and at work can help to reduce stress. Often clients may blame their employers for giving them too much work to do in a limited time. However, in many cases, on closer investigation a behavioural analysis reveals that the client is procrastinating and possibly avoiding dealing with the main priorities. In cases of severe occupational stress a complete CABB assessment may be necessary to uncover the underlying cause of the problem. An example is given in Table 7.4 to illustrate this point.

In many cases the client may have previously attended time management training seminars. However, successful behavioural change such as keeping to priority lists, saying 'no', etc. requires a shift in the person's attitudes and problem-interfering beliefs that are beyond simplistic training programmes. We would recommend that counsellors have suitable bibliotherapy such as books and handouts on time management (see Clarke and Palmer, 1994a, b) to aid the behavioural training component of stress counselling.

Table 7.4 *CABB to help time management problem*

Modality	Problem	Proposed programme
Cognitive	I must perform well otherwise I am a total failure	Dispute self-defeating beliefs (ABCDE model)
	I can't stand failure	Rational–emotive and coping imagery
	It would be awful to fail	De-awfulize failing
	Other people must approve me	Self-acceptance training
Affect	Anxiety about failing	Examine beliefs
	Depression/shame about failure	
Biological	Smokes 15 cigarettes a day	Stop smoking programme. Relaxation to help with discomfort anxiety
	Unhealthy diet	Discuss benefits of healthy diet
	High caffeine intake	Reduce coffee consumption
Behaviour	'Headless chicken' when under pressure	Behavioural programme
	Procrastinates due to fear of failure	Examine problem interfering beliefs
	Can't say 'no' to others' requests	Assertiveness training and focus on disputing approval seeking beliefs

POSTSCRIPT: MOTIVATING CLIENTS

Double imagery procedure

One of the authors (SP) and a colleague (M. Neenan) have developed a variation of time projection imagery to help motivate and encourage reluctant clients to face up to and deal with their problems. Initially, clients are asked to visualize their future based on avoiding their problem(s), including all the associated disadvantages (inaction imagery). Then they are asked to contrast this picture with another view of their future based on tackling their problem(s) including the associated advantages (action imagery). The procedure is also known as Inaction versus Action Imagery. This method may be contraindicated with clients experiencing suicidal ideation.

CHAPTER 8

Understanding Occupational and Organizational Stress

O, how full of briers is this working day world.

William Shakespeare *As You Like It*

In our experience, counsellors helping clients suffering from occupational stress can be more effective if they have a basic understanding of organizational stressors that may lead to distress. In this chapter we will cover a number of the key issues involved.

SYMPTOMS AND COMMON FACTORS

Statistics suggest that stress has become one of the major causes of absenteeism in the workplace. Prolonged stress has a negative effect on employees' health and well-being (see Chapter 1). The main symptoms of organizational stress are reduced efficiency, high absenteeism, high staff turnover, low morale, increased health care claims, increased industrial accidents, industrial relations difficulties, poor quality control, poor job performance, staff burnout and suicide. Even though each occupation has its own potential stressors, there are some common factors (adapted Cooper *et al.*, 1988):

- home/work interface
- internal demands (i.e., irrational beliefs)
- factors intrinsic to the job
- organizational structure and climate
- career development
- role in the organization
- relationships at work.

Figure 8.1 illustrates the relationship between the common factors, the individual, the home/work interface, internal demands and the symptoms. These issues will not

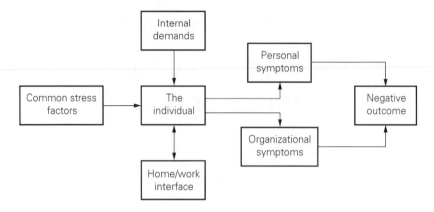

Figure 8.1 *The relationship between stress factors, the individual and the symptoms*

be considered along with the interventions that an integrative stress counsellor or trainer could use to deal with these problems. Possible organizational interventions will also be covered.

HOME/WORK INTERFACE

Often problems at work can affect an employee's homelife and vice versa. A common example would be an employee who is having to work long hours to complete her work. This may negatively impact upon her relationship with her spouse and children. Similarly, if an employee is going through a relationship breakdown then it is very likely that he will not be able to concentrate fully on his work. Figure 8.2 illustrates this negative stress cycle (Palmer, 1996a: 546).

This could subsequently lead to disciplinary action by management if performance is reduced. However, if the true cause of the problem is recognized by management then the employee could be offered counselling (see Allison *et al.*, 1989). Large organizations may be able to afford to employ a counsellor, whereas smaller organizations may need to either use an external counsellor or employ an Employee Assistance Programme.

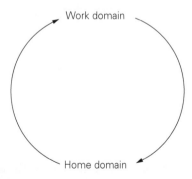

Figure 8.2 *The negative stress cycle*

INTERNAL DEMANDS

Employees may distress themselves by holding absolutist and dogmatic demands and self-defeating attitudes about themselves, others and the world. These beliefs affect their appraisal of workplace problems. We have found that often it is not the external stressor such as meeting a deadline that is the real problem, but the individual's belief that, 'I must reach the deadline', which is largely triggering the stress response. Palmer (adapted, 1993c) found a number of internal demands or problem-interfering beliefs that can be the major contributory factor to occupational stress:

- I/others must perform well at all times otherwise it would be awful.
- I/others must always reach deadlines.
- I/others must be perfect.
- The organization must treat me fairly at all times.
- I should get what I want otherwise I can't stand it.
- Significant others must appreciate my work otherwise I am worthless.

The integrative stress counsellor can use interventions described in the previous chapters to help distressed employees change their problem-interfering beliefs and attitudes to problem-facilitating beliefs and more helpful attitudes. So often inflexible, perfectionist beliefs are one of the major contributory factors to occupational stress.

FACTORS INTRINSIC TO THE JOB

Although many differing stressors intrinsic to the job can cause stress, some of the more common environmental workplace stressors are:

- air pollution
- fibres/dust
- dust
- humidity
- lighting
- nicotine
- noise
- noxious chemicals
- 'sick building' syndrome
- static electricity
- uncomfortable chairs/work stations
- VDU screen glare.

These stressors can be responsible for a wide range of different physical ailments including allergic reactions, backache, chest infections, deafness, eye strain, headache, neckache and skin rashes. An employee's general morale and work productivity can also be affected. Counsellors should assess whether environmental stressors are a factor that may be directly causing the client's physical symptoms of stress. When in doubt, the counsellor can undertake a behavioural analysis to ascertain exactly what the client was doing before the stress-related symptoms developed. Palmer (see Ellis *et al.*, 1997: 142–3) described a counsellor attempting to discover the cause of a client's recurrent neckache:

Counsellor: Does there appear to be any pattern to when your neckache occurs?

Client: No. It seems to come and go.

Counsellor: It may be helpful if we look at a specific example to help us ascertain the possible causes of your neckache. Think back to the last time you had neckache. Can you remember? (The counsellor wishes to examine a specific example to assess whether the neckaches do occur at random.)

Client: Yes. It was last Monday and I was at work. I had it by late afternoon.

Counsellor: Were you doing anything different to usual that day. (The counsellor is checking whether he did anything different from his usual routine that may be the cause of the neckaches.)

Client: No. It was a typical Monday. You know, the usual thing; plenty of telephone calls and arranging meetings for the week.

Counsellor: Tell me exactly what you did once you arrived at work.

Client: I sat down and opened my mail. I had a fair amount to deal with being a typical Monday. I then listened to my answerphone and collected my faxes from John's office. Then it was my coffee break.

Counsellor: Then . . .

Client: It was about 11.00 am. I spent the rest of the morning on the telephone. I had a quick lunch as I was so busy. Then I spent until my afternoon coffee break talking to customers on the telephone about difficulties they had encountered with the new computer program.

Counsellor: So when did you first notice that your neck was aching?

Client: Hmmm. By the time I was having my afternoon break. Thinking about it, I reckon that I generally get my neckache at the beginning of the week.

Counsellor: And Monday usually involves a day on the telephone.

Client: Yes.

Counsellor: How exactly do you hold your telephone handset? (In the counsellor's experience, some individuals may give themselves either tension neckaches or headaches because of the way they hold a telephone handset.)

Client: Like this. Between my ear and shoulder. (Client shows the counsellor how he usually holds the handset between his ear and shoulder.)

Counsellor: Hmm. I suspect that you may find that the cause of your neckache is spending the day on the telephone and holding the handset in such an awkward position. To see if my hypothesis is correct, I suggest that next Monday when you are at work you sit upright in your chair, keeping your neck upright without using your shoulders to conveniently position your handset. Perhaps try and stagger your calls during the day, giving yourself short breaks. What do you think?

Client: I must admit, it does make sense. In fact, it is usually days I'm in the office when I get neckache and not when I'm out on the road visiting customers.

With this client a counsellor could have assumed that the cause of the neckache was due to excessive work overload if he or she had not undertaken a systematic problem-focused behavioural analysis. It is recommended that integrative stress counsellors use hypothesis testing to ensure that they have found the major cause of the problem, especially if ergonomics are involved, that is, the relationship between employees and their environment, in particular the equipment and machines they utilize (see Ellis *et al.*, 1997). In some circumstances referral to other health professionals such as physiotherapists may be necessary.

Further stressful factors intrinsic to a job include:

- boring repetitive tasks
- dangerous work
- deadlines
- excessive travel
- isolated working conditions
- long hours
- shift work
- work underload/overload
- work too difficult for the employee.

These stressors can be discussed with a client in counselling or with employees during stress-management workshops. Research has found that some occupations are more stressful than others. For example, advertising, building, dentistry, journalism, mining, the police force, the prison service, are more stressful than accountancy, biochemistry, geology, insurance, the Church, nature conservancy, and horticulture (Sloane and Cooper, 1986).

ORGANIZATIONAL STRUCTURE AND CLIMATE

Frequently it is found that the organizational structure and climate in a company may limit the autonomy of the employee. Employees may perceive, quite correctly, that they have little influence or control over their workload. Research indicates that this can contribute to reduced self-esteem, apathy, job dissatisfaction, resentment and a loss of identity. This can lead to increased rates of absenteeism. Integrative stress counsellors and trainers can help employees to examine and challenge self-defeating and unhelpful beliefs they may hold that contribute to a low self-esteem and self-worth thereby improving self-acceptance (see Chapters 6 and 7). Companies wishing to ameliorate these problems can increase participation in decision making and team work to help overcome an actual or perceived lack of control. In recent years we have noted an increasing trend for organizations to encourage all staff, including temporary workers, to become actively involved in decision making. This philosophy has become a part of the management ethos and has been stated in the relevant staff manuals or documents. Where appropriate, trade unions can be involved in planning job rotation and employees could elect their own supervisors. This can help to increase job morale and commitment to the work (see Ellis *et al.*, 1997; Palmer, 1996a).

In the last decade many organizations have either made or are considering making redundancies (lay-offs). Not surprisingly, staff facing this threat can suffer from increased levels of stress. At the organizational level, possibly the only way to help deal with this problem is to ensure that the senior management are seen to communicate promptly on all related issues. Integrative problem-focused stress counsellors can focus on two levels with clients working under these conditions. First, the counsellor would target the client's problem-interfering beliefs and attitudes relating to the current or feared problem for disputation. This is important if the employee is finding that their anxiety or depression about the situation is preventing them from making urgent decisions about possible career moves. Second, practical problem solving would be focused on helping the person to change or improve the situation or prepare for the worst scenario. For example, dealing assertively with the management regarding communication breakdown, job seeking and up-dating the client's resumé or CV. If the counsellor does not possess the necessary skills, a judicious referral to a careers adviser may be necessary. Some organizations employ outplacement companies to offer staff a range of services to help them deal with redundancy. Others employ stress management trainers to run workshops, courses and seminars. However, these courses are not always received well by participants as they may view this action as the company abdicating responsibility for largely causing their stress. Companies sometimes run seminars on 'Coping with retirement' or 'Coping with redundancy', which may be helpful for some staff.

In the last decade we have seen organizations 'downsize', 'rightsize' or 'de-layer', in other words reduce staffing levels thereby increasing the workload for the so-called 'survivors'. This, plus the increased use of technology and job relocations are changes that contribute to stress in employees. Although retraining, outplacement counselling, time and change management seminars or workshops may help to reduce the negative effects of these types of change, unfortunately, increased workloads have proved very difficult for many employees to manage. In addition, with the introduction of information technology, word processors and computers, staff are expected to be more productive than their counterparts from two decades ago.

Racism, sexism and ageism can also be pervasive in some organizations. Management can draw up a set policy and procedure to deal with these issues if and when they arise. Management should be seen to be proactive and in some cases awareness programmes may be necessary.

CAREER DEVELOPMENT

Career development is an important part of work life for many people. Sadly, promotion prospects can become progressively limited at higher management levels of a company. Ambitious employees may only improve their chances of promotion by applying for jobs outside their organization. Often older employees have to receive training to enable them to use new technology. Employees can become anxious and stressed about these and other challenges such as learning new management skills. Research has also found that older employees are likely to fear demotion, obsolescence, redundancy, lack of job security and forced early retirement. Not surprisingly, these issues can often lead to reduced self-esteem and self-worth. They can suffer anxiety about what may occur and experience depression if it does happen. Counsellors and trainers can examine these issues in counselling and on relevant workshops. Often it is helpful to focus on any self-defeating beliefs or images that the person may hold which triggers or exacerbates anxiety or depression in addition to teaching suitable coping strategies. In many instances outplacement counselling can enable the individual to find suitable employment elsewhere.

ROLE IN THE ORGANIZATION

Depending upon the person–job fit, different roles in an organization can lead to varying amounts of stress. In many instances, employees who are responsible for subordinates are more likely to suffer from coronary heart disease and other stress-related illnesses than those who are responsible for machinery. There are a number of different role demands that can contribute to stress, such as ambiguity, conflict, definition, expectations, incompatibility, overload and underload. Often employees do not recognize these external sources of their stress and therefore are unable to manage to change it. Counsellors can help the employee to explore their role in the organization and discover any stress-inducing role demands. Stress mapping is a technique that is useful for this exercise (see Chapter 5). We have found three major demands that commonly cause stress: role ambiguity; role conflict; role overload. We will briefly cover these three demands.

Role ambiguity occurs when employees are unsure about the role expectations that are required of them. Ross and Altmaier (1994: 36) highlight an example of role ambiguity:

Manager: Well, Dave, you've been with us for two months. How have things been going?

Trainee: I must admit that while I'm glad to be here, I am feeling overwhelmed.

Manager: I'm sorry to hear that, Dave. This is all news to me. What exactly is causing your problem?

Trainee: Well, it's just that there is so much to learn, I don't know how to keep up.

Manager: But Dave, we sent you to several training seminars and we haven't even given you any project assignments – you've only been asked to read the training manuals.

Trainee: I know you've been very generous with the time you've allowed for training and I'm really not having a problem with the technical part of the job. I think I'm more worried about the other part of the job. I'm trying to figure out how I'm supposed to act, whom I'm supposed to meet and which things I should be doing to avoid overstepping my role as a rookie.

To avoid role ambiguity, management need to ensure that their staff are made explicitly aware of what they are supposed to do and to whom they should report. In Dave's case the manager could have explained some of the informal organizational rules and also helped him to identify key people that he should meet within the first few months of joining the company. Managers need to offer new staff relevant job training and orientation (Ross and Altmaier, 1994).

Role conflict involves different role expectations made by the following groups on the employee:

- superiors
- superiors' superior
- peers
- clients
- subordinates
- subordinates' subordinates

Role conflict occurs when compliance with one set of role pressures makes compliance with another set of role pressures difficult or impossible (see Ross and Altmaier, 1994).

With the recent re-structuring of numerous organizations many employees have become stressed about role overload as they experience difficulty coping with the amount of work. Qualitative role overload occurs when the employee does not possess adequate skills to do a specific job. Quantitative role overload occurs when the employee has insufficient time to complete the work. In both cases management will usually need to intervene directly to resolve difficulties of overload. However, employees may also need to consider if they are responsible for accepting too much work, especially if they hold approval-seeking beliefs.

Counsellors and trainers can help employees to recognize the specific role demands that may be contributing to their occupational stress and to develop strategies to attempt to overcome them. In many cases, employees need to use assertion and communication skills to discuss their specific role demand problems with their managers. However, discussion does not always lead to successful resolution of the problems and counsellors need to judge the likely impact of such interventions used with specific people. Counsellors also need to assess whether the employee has any self-defeating beliefs about role demands such as 'I must not lose control, otherwise it would be awful', which is often present with clients who are stressed about role overload, role conflict and role ambiguity. Unhelpful beliefs involving low self-esteem and low frustration tolerance may also be present (Ellis *et al.*, 1997).

RELATIONSHIPS AT WORK

Interpersonal relationships at work can be a major source of stress. Interpersonal stressors include abrasive personalities, leadership style, peer/group pressures, social density and social incongruence (Quick and Quick, 1984). Managers, supervisors and other staff who act aggressively often benefit from receiving assertion skills training. Troublesome passive–aggressive behaviours include:

- sulking
- pointing finger
- inappropriate anger/hostility
- aggressive body posture
- angry intonation
- verbal put-downs, e.g. 'come on', 'you'd better', 'you should', 'you must', 'you ought'.

Staff who behave in a hostile or bullying manner invariably cause interpersonal difficulties, such as resentment and/or fear, in the workplace. Often these individuals are Type A (i.e., ambitious, aggressive, pressured by time constraints, talk/walk/eat quickly) and they inadvertently increase their chances of dying early from coronary heart disease (see Friedman and Ulmer, 1985). In our clinical experience with very Type A people short stress-management courses are usually insufficient to help them modify their behaviour, as extremely low self-esteem and low-frustration tolerance are normally present. In-depth counselling or psychotherapy may be necessary. However, when Type A individuals have suffered from a heart attack they are more likely to change their hostile behaviour if they are informed that the behaviour may have been partially responsible for their condition.

Although relationships between co-workers can provide a social support structure which helps to buffer individuals from stress (Cowen, 1982), they can also be negative due to competition, rivalry, and 'office politics'. Social support networks are sometimes created when organizations offer their employees social and sports facilities (Cox et al., 1988). We have often found that clients who do not share their problems with their co-workers or others suffer from higher levels of stress than those workers who discuss their problems with each other. Facilitators can encourage employees to share their work problems with each other during stress management workshops. Often, this helps employees put work events into perspective. Role play exercises where employees can learn assertion techniques to deal with difficult co-workers or customers can be beneficial.

MANAGING WORKPLACE STRESS

External counsellors may not be in an ideal position to influence the managing of workplace stress at the organizational level although in-house counsellors and Employee Assistance Programmes may be able to recognize key stressors and suggest policy changes. However, this may raise issues of breach of confidentiality. The individual methods for reducing or managing workplace stress have focused on interventions at three different levels (see Quick and Quick, 1984):

- Primary prevention (stressor-directed)
- Secondary prevention (response-directed)
- Tertiary prevention (symptom-directed).

The counsellor may be able to help employees with individual-focused interventions either during counselling or at workshops. At the primary level the employee can attempt to manage their personal perceptions of stressors by reappraising situations more realistically, disputing cognitive distortions and changing internal demands, reducing Type A behaviour, etc. The employee can manage the personal work environment by using assertion and communication skills, time management, social support, task variation, overload/underload avoidance, etc. Lifestyle management can also be beneficial such as suitable diet and exercise, maintaining a balance, appropriate leisure time use, etc.

At the secondary prevention level, the employee can endeavour to modify the ways in which they respond to stressors by using relaxation techniques such as progressive relaxation, autogenic training, biofeedback, hypnosis, meditation, Benson relaxation response, the Multimodal Relaxation Method, etc. Emotional outlets such as writing and talking about stressors can be helpful. Physical outlets include aerobic exercise, sports, walking, jogging, yoga, and strength and endurance training (Cox *et al.*, 1988).

At the tertiary level the focus is on helping the employee once they are suffering from the symptoms of stress. This is usually undertaken by receiving medical care and/or individual or group psychotherapy/counselling. Attendance at stress and anxiety management groups can also be beneficial. Specific treatment programmes for panic attacks, phobias or post-traumatic stress disorder may be necessary. Outplacement counselling and careers guidance is recommended for employees who are about to be made redundant.

According to Cox *et al.* (1990) organization-focused interventions can also be made at three different levels:

Level	*Intervention*
Primary	Remove hazard or reduce employees' exposure to it, or its impact on them.
Secondary	Improve the organization's ability to recognize and deal with stress-related problems as they occur.
Tertiary	Help employees cope with and recover from work-related problems.

At the primary level Elkin and Rosch (1990) recommend a range of strategies to reduce occupational stress: establish flexible work schedules; redesign the task and work environment; promote employee involvement in career development; encourage participative management; provide social support and feedback; analyse work roles and establish goals; share the rewards; establish fair employment policies; build cohesive teams. At the secondary level, methods are used to improve the ability of the organization to recognize and subsequently deal with stress-related problems as they arise (see Cox *et al.*, 1990). The use of annual stress audits and psychometric tests such as the Occupational Stress Indicator (OSI) can aid this process (see Cooper *et al.*, 1988; Cooper and Cartwright, 1996; Palmer, 1995b). Tertiary organizational-focused interventions are the same as in the previous section (Quick and Quick, 1984).

SUMMARY

This chapter has given a brief overview of the main issues involved in occupational and organizational stress. This will help the counsellor understand some of the problems involved. However, we recommend that counsellors working in organizational settings or those whose case load includes many clients suffering from occupational stress or burnout would benefit from reading further texts on this subject (see Carroll, 1996; Cooper and Payne, 1988; Palmer and Dryden, 1996; Ross and Altmaier, 1994). In the next chapter we focus on group stress counselling and stress-management workshops in clinical and work settings.

CHAPTER 9

Group Stress Management and Counselling

Group counselling . . . is a forum in which clients become helpers.

Egan (1998: 145)

In this chapter we cover three areas of group work: workplace stress management courses, group stress counselling, and family-based stress management interventions. As the problem-focused approach is psychoeducational, it very easily adapts to a variety of settings. We will also discuss pre-training material and suitable bibliotherapy.

Although it may be stating the obvious, we would strongly recommend that counsellors become experienced in using the problem-focused approach with clients in one-to-one counselling before attempting to run stress-management or counselling groups. If counsellors are inexperienced in working with groups we suggest that they may benefit from receiving specific training in group work and running a group with an experienced group facilitator, as the dynamics of interaction and communication patterns are more complex in groups than in one-to-one counselling. To help you assess whether you have some of the key skills required to run groups we have provided a checklist for your own self-assessment (see Box 9.1). Most of the skills have been described in the previous chapters; the others are self-explanatory. Refer back to Box 9.1 on a regular basis and re-assess your skills looking for those areas in which you need further training and supervision.

WORKPLACE STRESS MANAGEMENT COURSES AND WORKSHOPS

Counsellors who work in-house for organizations may recognize a need for staff to attend stress management courses or workshops. In other cases, counsellors or trainers may be asked to run courses for external companies. As suggested in the previous chapter, it is advisable to undertake a stress audit to ensure that a workshop is the most suitable intervention. However, in recent years the levels of stress at work have increased as modern financial management methods have led to

Box 9.1 *Skills checklist for counsellors running groups*

Instructions: circle the number that applies

Skills	Poor	Adequate			Good
Active listening	1	2	3	4	5
Empathizing	1	2	3	4	5
Reflecting feelings	1	2	3	4	5
Restating	1	2	3	4	5
Clarifying	1	2	3	4	5
Paraphrasing	1	2	3	4	5
Summarizing	1	2	3	4	5
Open/closed questioning	1	2	3	4	5
Confronting/challenging	1	2	3	4	5
Supportive and encouraging	1	2	3	4	5
Initiating group direction and participation	1	2	3	4	5
Giving feedback	1	2	3	4	5
Goal setting	1	2	3	4	5
Evaluating	1	2	3	4	5
Creativity	1	2	3	4	5
Modelling behaviour	1	2	3	4	5
Recognizing and minimizing the effect of harmful risks upon individual members	1	2	3	4	5
Blocking counterproductive behaviour	1	2	3	4	5
Self-disclosing	1	2	3	4	5
Closing/termination	1	2	3	4	5
Problem focused	1	2	3	4	5
Additional stress-management techniques and skills	1	2	3	4	5
Communication	1	2	3	4	5
Interpersonal and assertion	1	2	3	4	5
Lecturing	1	2	3	4	5

fewer staff doing more work. Although the most appropriate intervention would be to reduce the workload for some people, management are likely to be less accommodating of this idea while staff may be keen to receive any kind of help such as attending workshops. This does pose a dilemma for counsellors and other stress–management practitioners as the most obvious solution will often not be possible.

Assuming that a course or workshop is desirable its duration usually depends upon time and financial restraints. The workshop could last between a couple of hours to five days, or consist of ongoing weekly sessions lasting between one to four hours for between five to ten sessions. In our experience most organizations prefer one- or two-day courses as this is easier to organize than ongoing short sessions. Whenever possible, we recommend that a half-day follow-up is run a few months later to focus on any difficulties that the participants may have encountered applying the stress-management techniques at work or in social situations.

The majority of employees are used to attending training courses at work which have an educational format whereby the trainer teaches them relevant theory and then they may practise specific skills such as tele-sales techniques. As the problem-focused stress training approach also takes a similar format this avoids any similarity with therapy, which is generally less acceptable to employees in workplace settings.

Potential workshop participants can be asked to complete a brief questionnaire or be interviewed to discover what they would like to learn from the stress-management workshop prior to attending the course. This helps the counsellor or trainer to design a workshop and also set the participants relevant pre-course reading such as *Stress Management: A Quick Guide*, by Palmer and Strickland (1996) or workbooks to complete such as *How to Manage Stress* by Clarke and Palmer (1994a). Other useful forms of bibliotherapy include: *Think Rationally: A Brief Guide to Overcoming Your Emotional Problems* by Dryden and Gordon (1992); *Self Management: Strategies for Personal Success* by Ellis and DiMattia (1991); *Living with Stress* by Cary Cooper and associates (1988); *Think Your Way to Happiness* by Dryden and Gordon (1990); *Peak Performance: Become More Effective at Work* by Dryden and Gordon (1993); and *Dealing with People Problems at Work* by Palmer and Burton (1996). We have found it useful to ask participants to keep a 'Stress Diary' for one workday as it can provide much material for a workshop. The stress diary involves keeping a note of the day's events, in particular, situations that the participants become stressed about. They are asked to bring their diary to the workshop for later discussion.

To maximize the effective use of the time available in stress management workshops, apart from coffee breaks, all of the time available is focused on stress and its management. Typical workshop or course contents for a two-day 'stress management' or 'managing pressure to improve performance' programme are shown below (adapted from: Palmer, 1995b; Ellis *et al.*, 1997).

Day 1
1. Discussion of ground rules (including discussing the benefits of confidentiality, if unclear to the participants).
2. Ask what the participants are hoping to learn and achieve over the duration of the workshop. (This confirms the requirements they sent in prior to the course.)
3. Participants share their 'Stress Diaries' with the group if they so wish. The counsellor/trainer focuses on how different members of the group would have felt and dealt with the disclosed stress scenarios emphasizing the diverse cognitive, emotive, biological and behavioural dynamics. It is important to highlight how one participant's stressor can be another participant's challenge.

4. Discussion of a simple definition of stress; for example, stress occurs when pressure exceeds one's ability to cope – pressure can be internal or external, or a combination of both. (Include 'demands' versus 'coping resources' if helpful.)
5. Group discussion of the symptoms of stress (small group work if necessary).
6. Discuss the psychophysiology of stress. (If available, use suitable video that explains the physiology of stress in simple terms.)
7. Participants use biodots (i.e., biofeedback instruments), if available, to monitor skin temperature.
8. Trainer discusses thinking errors and thinking skills using examples.
9. Thinking skills practice, that is, in small group work, participants discuss a recent stress scenario and help each other to challenge thinking errors (in afternoon of first day of course).
10. Debrief.
11. Suitable homework assignment may be set, for example, re-read relevant section in pre-course reader.

Day 2
12. Deal with any queries raised from Day 1 or from homework assignment.
13. Participants can be shown how to use a problem facilitating form to aid practice of problem-thinking skills (see Appendix 2).
14. Small group work focusing on a current problem or a situation that is avoided by using the problem facilitating form (in morning of second day).
15. Debrief. Trouble shoot any problems that arose from the exercise.
16. Teach the multimodal relaxation method to the group (see Chapter 7).
17. Debrief. If available, the trainer demonstrates how to use a Galvanic Skin Response (GSR) biofeedback instrument to monitor the effectiveness of the relaxation exercise. Then the trainer shows the group how quickly a person can trigger the stress response just by thinking of a stressful situation. (This highlights how the situation itself does not cause stress but it is the individual's beliefs about it that triggers the stress response.) If sufficient GSR instruments are available, each participant can practise relaxing by using the GSR as a monitor.
18. Imagery techniques can be taught to the group, for example, rational–emotive imagery, coping and time-projection imagery (see Chapter 7).
19. Lifestyle interventions, such as nutrition, weight/alcohol control, exercise, stop smoking, time management, assertion, can be discussed depending upon the needs and interests of the group.
20. Group discussion on organizational/occupational stress. Possible workplace interventions discussed in small group work.
21. Type A behaviour, locus of control and workplace coping strategies discussed (Cooper et al., 1988).
22. OPTIONAL. Group OSI reports given to each participant (Cooper et al., 1988; Palmer, 1995b). The trainer explains each section of the report and leads discussion about the issues raised. (NB. Although useful, it is not essential to use an OSI in the workshop. This also applies to activity 23.)
23. OPTIONAL. Individual OSI reports given to each participant. Trainer answers general questions about the reports and highlights that the 'logical thinking'

section relates to how effectively the individual is using thinking skills. (Individual one-to-one feedback with each group member is necessary and needs to be inserted into the programme.)

24. Small group work focusing on each participant's workplace problems and also on how they can overcome these issues. For example, if appropriate, start to act assertively with a passive–aggressive manager, and only feel concerned instead of feeling anxious about this exercise.

25. Debrief activity 24. If appropriate, a group stress management plan is developed. For example, how the group can manage their manager's excessive demands upon them.

26. Individual stress management plans developed by each participant (see Box 9.2) and then discussion in small groups on how to ensure that they can keep to their plans and overcome any obstacles that may arise (see Appendix 12).

27. Discussion of 'where to go from here'.

28. Evaluation of course.

29. Possibility of follow-up day discussed if appropriate, and acceptable to the organization.

Box 9.2 *Stress management plan*

ACTION TO BE TAKEN BY: Jean	Date: 21/3/97
Thinking Skills:	Challenge my perfectionist beliefs. Remind myself that I can stand difficult situations and I don't have to like them.
Imagery:	Practise positive imagery daily to help me unwind and relax. Practise coping imagery before each difficult event.
Time Management:	Ensure that I keep to my priority list. Don't be distracted by red herrings.
Assertion:	Be assertive with my boss. Say 'No', when I need to.
Relaxation:	Do 10 minutes of self-hypnosis every day at lunchtime.
Nutrition:	Eat fresh fruit and vegetables daily. Eat fish at least three times per week. Drink herbal tea and reduce intake of coffee.
Exercise:	Walk to work and go swimming twice a week.

The main focus of a stress-management course or workshop is helping participants to understand the nature of stress and learning stress management skills and techniques. On Day 1 it is useful to allow the participants to discuss how frustrated they are about their organization. However, by Day 2 the trainer can show them that organizations are unlikely to change just because they demand that they 'should' change. This encourages the participants to spend energy attempting to change what can be changed, and not wasting any time attempting to change what cannot be changed. Interestingly, some research indicates that workshop participants can benefit from talking to each other about stress without necessarily being taught any stress management skills by a counsellor or trainer. This may be helped by the participants realizing that they are not unique or alone in suffering from stress and thereby normalizing the experience. This reinforces the concept of human fallibility and encourages self-acceptance (see Yalom, 1985). Also participants tend to share with the group how they deal with difficult situations thereby teaching each other new skills and strategies.

A follow-up one-day or half-day would focus on how the participants fared with the application of the stress management techniques. The trainer can focus on how the participants prevented themselves from regularly practising the techniques and skills that formed part of their individual stress-management action plans. A typical dialogue is as follows:

Trainer: John, what was the first goal on your stress management action plan?

John: I was going to start each day by writing a priority list of key tasks I needed to achieve.

Trainer: How did you get on?

John: One of the biggest problems I had was that I just didn't have enough time to do it.

Trainer: Hmm. How did you prevent yourself from making adequate time?

John: How did I prevent myself!!

Trainer: Yes. Was somebody literally abducting you and removing you from your office first thing every morning. (humorously) Or did you fail to put aside five minutes to write your priorities for the day?

John: Well, put like that, I suppose I allowed myself to be distracted.

Trainer: How?

John: My telephone never stops ringing.

Trainer: Ah. I understand now. Correct me if I'm wrong. As soon as you walk into your office the telephone rings and it grabs you by the throat and forces you at gun point to answer it! (humorously)

John: (laughing) Of course not. I just feel guilty when I don't answer the phone.

Trainer: Now that's different. If you remember at the last workshop you believed that you would become a more effective manager if you started to manage your time efficiently and commenced each day with a priority list. (Trainer reminding John of the benefits of change.)

John: Yeah.

Trainer: Do you think it would be beneficial to focus on how you are preventing yourself from doing this by examining your block to effective action: in this case the problem interfering thoughts that trigger your guilt?

John: Makes sense to me.

Trainer: (Talking to the group.) Are you all interested in looking at this particular issue?

Emma: Yep. I have the same problem too. (laughs)

The trainer then helped John to examine his problem-interfering and self-defeating beliefs which triggered his guilt. He encouraged the other participants to challenge John's beliefs and then formulate problem facilitating beliefs which would help John to cope with telephone calls on his return to work. It is important that the group joins in the discussion to avoid boredom and the exercise becoming an individual counselling session. In addition, their comments may also highlight issues that need further clarification by the trainer.

Other options

In the previous section we described a broad-spectrum approach to running stress-management groups. Depending upon the needs of the participants, the course could solely concentrate on the problem-focused approach by teaching the seven-step model and then the ABCDE approach of Ellis (1994). However, in our experience it is still generally worthwhile teaching additional stress management techniques such as coping/positive imagery and relaxation exercises. Typical course or workshop contents for the problem-focused stress management approach are as follows:

1. Discussion of ground rules (including benefits of confidentiality, if unclear to the participants).
2. Ask what the participants are hoping to learn and achieve over the duration of the course. (This confirms the requirements they sent in prior to the course.)
3. Participants share their 'Stress Diaries' in the group if they so wish. The trainer focuses on how different members of the group would have felt and dealt with the disclosed stress scenarios emphasizing the diverse cognitive, emotive, biological and behavioural dynamics.
4. Discussion of a simple definition of stress; for example, when pressures or problems exceed your ability to cope, then the result is stress.
5. Discuss symptoms of stress and the consequences of poor problem resolution.
6. Discuss the physiology of stress.
7. Brief overview of the problem-focused training model using diagram.
8. Teach the ABCDE paradigm. Illustrate how self-defeating beliefs and thinking errors exacerbate stress and reduce problem resolution.
9. Teach group how to use a problem facilitating form (see Appendix 2).
10. Thinking skills practice, that is, in small group work participants discuss a recent stress scenario and help each other to complete a problem facilitating form (see Figure 5.4).
11. Debrief.
12. Teach seven-step problem-focused model.
13. Seven-step skills practice, that is, in small groups participants discuss a recent problem and use the seven-step model to find an appropriate solution. Show the group how to use the seven-step problem-focused form (Appendix 3). Depending upon the skills of the group, this exercise may need breaking down into the different steps with group feedback at suitable times.,
14. Group debrief. Trainer shows the participants how to integrate the two models: for example, if a relatively simple problem, start with the seven-step model; if an emotional block such as anxiety arises, then switch to using the ABCDE model; return to the seven-step model as necessary.
15. In small groups practise both models using new problems.
16. Group debrief.
17. Teach additional skills that may be required such as relaxation, time management, assertion, etc.

18. Discussion of 'where to go from here'.
19. Possibility of follow-up day discussed if appropriate.
20. Evaluation of course.

With some adaptation, the course or workshop can be run over a one- or two-day period or split into smaller sessions. If time does not permit then only one of the models could be taught and practised in the workshop. It is important that the participants are given adequate time to practise the models otherwise they may experience difficulty in putting them into practice at work or in other situations. Once again, whenever possible, we recommend that a follow-up session is arranged to help troubleshoot any difficulties that may have arisen in the application of the problem-focused model.

D'Zurilla (1986: 95) describes a programme schedule for problem-solving training consisting of eight units. Although slightly different from our problem-focused model it has been adapted to individual, small group (six to eight members) and larger group settings such as a workshop or course. The following programme is suitable for a small group setting:

Unit 1. Initial structuring (one session)
Unit 2. Problem orientation (one session)
Unit 3. Use and control of emotions in problem solving (two sessions)
Unit 4. Problem definition and formulation (two sessions)
Unit 5. Generation of alternative solutions (two sessions)
Unit 6. Decision making (two sessions)
Unit 7. Solution implementation and verification (two sessions)
Unit 8. Maintenance and generalization (two to four sessions).

One of the most useful elements in D'Zurilla's suggested programme is a Rapid Problem-Solving Model, which is taught in the last session. This model helps to prevent lapse or total relapse once the course is finished and is detailed below (D'Zurilla, 1986: 140–1.)

Step 1
Make the following self-statements:
   a) 'Take a deep breath and calm down.'
   b) 'There is no immediate catastrophe.'
   c) 'Think of this problem as a challenge.'
   d) 'I can handle it.'
   e) 'Stop-and-think.'

Step 2
Ask yourself the following questions:
   a) 'What's the problem?' (State the discrepancy between 'what is' and 'what should be'.)
   b) 'What do I want to accomplish?' (State a goal.)
   c) 'Why do I want to achieve this goal?' (Broaden the goal, if appropriate.)

Step 3.
  a) Think of a solution.
  b) Now think of several other alternative solutions (at least two or three).

Step 4
  a) Think of the most important criteria for evaluating your solution ideas (at least two or three) (for example 'Will it achieve my goal?' 'What effect will it have on others?' 'How much time and effort will it take?' Some other important criterion?)
  b) Decide quickly on the solution alternative that seems best.
  c) Think of one or two quick ways to improve the solution.

Step 5
  a) Implement the solution.
  b) Are you satisfied with the outcome?
  c) If not, try out your second choice if you still have time to cope with the problem.

In this section we have covered a number of ways the problem-focused approach can be applied to group training settings. In the next section we look at group stress counselling.

GROUP STRESS COUNSELLING

The approach taken by the trainer running group stress-management courses or workshops tends to be educational whereas counsellors facilitating group stress counselling take a more psychotherapeutic approach. The latter is mainly used in clinical or counselling settings. However, problem-focused counsellors usually adopt a psychoeducational approach and will offer educational input in addition to using their counselling and therapeutic skills to facilitate group therapy. Clients attending stress counselling groups have normally been referred by other mental health professionals who have diagnosed stress and anxiety whereas participants joining training groups may only be interested in prevention and management of stress. There are no hard and fast rules about this as we have often found that at least 20 per cent of organizational course participants may be suffering from considerable stress. In some professions such as medicine, social work and nursing far higher rates of distress may be found.

Advantages and disadvantages

Group stress counselling has a number of advantages compared to individual counselling. Some of the main advantages are listed below:

- cost-effective
- members realize that stress is a normal reaction
- new stress management skills learnt from both peers and counsellor

- members can try out their new skills on each other
- peers may offer each other support in times of crisis
- social or interpersonal skills can be readily practised
- seeing peers improve acts as positive reinforcement for the approach
- relatively safe environment for risk-attacking exercises
- wide range of solutions may be available
- sharing of problems with the group may be therapeutic.

Obviously there are a number of disadvantages too. For example, scapegoating and collusion can occur; sometimes members offer each other poor advice and solutions to problems; members may suggest overwhelming homework assignments; members may reinforce self-defeating behaviour and thinking. The group integrative problem-focused stress counsellor needs to be aware of these possible problems and deal with them if they arise.

PRE-GROUP ISSUES

Gerald Corey (1990: 86–7) believes that counsellors who are setting up a group need to consider a number of issues:

- basic purposes of group
- the population to be served
- a clear rationale for the group, that is, the need for and justification of that particular group
- ways to announce the group and recruit members
- the screening and selection of members
- the size and duration of the group
- the frequency and time of meetings
- the group structure and format
- the methods of preparing members
- whether the group will be closed or open
- whether membership will be voluntary or involuntary
- the follow-up and evaluation procedures.

We recommend counsellors initially develop a written plan which attempts to answer all the above issues. This procedure will help the counsellor to troubleshoot potential problems before they even arise. The plan or proposal also provides other mental health professionals with information about the proposed group. In the early stages of development, other professionals will be in a position to provide useful feedback and comment on your ideas once they have sight of the plan.

Stress counselling groups also have a variety of formats. We will briefly consider the options.

1. Intensive one- or two-day groups which may or may not have a follow-up day.
2. Ongoing groups which meet weekly for between one-and-a-half to two-and-a-half

hours. These groups can be open-ended and participants can join when there is an available space.

3. Ongoing groups which meet weekly for between one-and-a-half to two-and-a-half hours. These groups can be closed, that is, no new members join once started. The group can be run for a fixed period of time. This is generally between six to twelve sessions, with a follow-up session a month or two later.
4. Group marathon sessions can be run for up to fourteen straight hours with from 10 to 16 participants.

For maximum effectiveness we would recommend option 3 as the members all join at the same level of understanding therefore avoiding repetition of the same material by the counsellor. If new members join when a place becomes available in an open-ended group then time is often spent returning to teaching the approach and the various stress-management techniques. In addition, the new member can feel 'left out' and the cohesion of the group may alter. In these situations the counsellor needs to devote time to helping the new member become integrated into the group. Unfortunately, this can lead to original group members feeling neglected although this depends upon the skills of the counsellor. This can sometimes be overcome by encouraging the experienced members to explain the problem-focused model to the new member. With closed groups (option 3) if too many members leave prematurely then this can affect the effectiveness of the group. As institutions and private health insurance companies become more interested in reducing costs, option 3 is likely to become a standard model for stress, anxiety and depression counselling groups. The optimum number of clients in such a group is normally between six and twelve although White and associates (1990, 1992) have demonstrated that many more members can be accommodated if a purely educational approach is used to deal with stress and anxiety.

The format adopted will depend upon the setting in which the counsellor is working. Counsellors working in general practice or out-patient clinics tend to run open-ended or closed groups on a weekly or twice weekly basis whereas counsellors working in private practice often find it easier to set-up one- or two-day events. Marathon sessions can be emotionally and physically tiring for the participants and the counsellors alike (see Ellis *et al.*, 1997).

We recommend that groups are composed of members who wish to attend. In some institutions counsellors may be expected to lead groups with involuntary clientele. In these cases the counsellor needs to explain the possible benefits of attendance and attempt to overcome any resistance. One of the main criteria for screening out potential group members is whether the person can participate in an appropriate manner. Even disturbed people may still be able to learn how to cope with stress without participating too much in group counselling. However, if a member becomes highly disruptive once on a programme then the counsellor would need to refer the person to individual counselling and exclude them from the group (Wessler and Wessler, 1980). Homogeneous groups consisting of members with a particular problem such as anxiety, phobias, hypertension, or alcohol dependence normally benefit from attending groups with a similar problem. This allows the group counsellor to focus on the specific issue to maximize the time available. In our experience it is important to ensure that the presenting problems are suitably matched to the group. Thus a person suffering from severe depression or chronic obsessive compulsive disorder would be an unsuitable candidate for a stress counselling group, although they may still benefit from attending a group focusing on the particular disorder in question.

Prospective members should be given clear details about the stress counselling group. A written statement or brochure could include the following points (adapted Corey, 1990):

- the type of group
- the purpose of the group
- the procedure for joining
- the time and place of meetings
- fees being charged (if any)
- a statement of what the members can expect from the counsellor(s)
- a statement of the counsellor's qualifications and background
- code of ethics to which the counsellor (or agency) abides
- guidelines for determining who is suitable for the group.

However, even clearly written details can be misinterpreted by potential group members. It is advisable to discuss such issues at the interview stage.

Initial sessions

Problem-focused stress counselling groups tend to be run on similar lines whether they are open or closed. At the first meeting, an explanation of the role of the counsellor is given; that is, the group leader who will be taking an active-directive approach, will be helping members to improve their problem solving skills, will help members to modify their problem interfering and self-defeating beliefs, and will teach a variety of stress-management techniques such as imagery, time management, assertion and relaxation exercises. The counsellor negotiates suitable ground rules such as confidentiality of personal information and time-keeping; explores with members their expectations, goals, fears, and misconceptions; the values and limitations of groups; the basics of group process; getting the most out of group counselling; and the psychological risks associated with group counselling and how to limit them (see Corey, 1990).

In the first session it is helpful to describe a simple model of stress and encourage members to discuss their symptoms. The counsellor may decide to ask the members to develop a CABB assessment of their own problems. This can act as a guide to their stress counselling programme. If there is time available then the counsellor can provide an overview to the seven-step model and discuss with the members the type of problems they would like to deal with during the course of group counselling. The counsellor should explain that by dealing with problems, symptoms of stress are likely to be alleviated or completely disappear. In other cases they may need to use specific techniques to overcome phobias and panic attacks. These techniques will be covered in later sessions. Suitable bibliotherapy or self-monitoring of symptoms can be set as homework assignments. How the members progressed with the assignments is always discussed at the beginning of the next session. This ensures that members realize that these exercises are considered extremely important in the problem-focused approach; otherwise they are less likely to undertake them if reinforcement does not regularly occur. We would normally recommend that either in the first or second session the counsellor spends a few minutes discussing the relevance and importance of assignments to the group. I have described how I (SP) usually discuss this issue (adapted Ellis *et al.*, 1997: 159):

Counsellor: In problem-focused stress counselling we believe that the other 166 hours outside of the therapeutic two hours in every week are just as important. This is one of the main reasons why we always recommend that group members undertake assignments in between sessions. I would like to give you an analogy. How many of you drive a car?

Paul: I've been driving for years.

Mitch: I passed only recently.

Sue: I've now failed two times.

Sara: I'm taking my test next month.

Counsellor: Good. So you all have some idea about driving cars. Think back to your first driving lesson. For most people it wasn't easy.

Sue: You're not joking! I must have stalled it at least five times.

Sara: It still isn't easy!

Counsellor: Good. I'm glad you can recall it so well. Now just imagine that a good friend taught you how to drive. After many driving lessons you finally take your driving test and unfortunately fail it. Then you decide to have professional driving classes and the instructor tells you that you are driving incorrectly, for example, not checking the mirror in the correct manner at the right time. Now imagine the difficulty you would experience having to relearn how to drive correctly.

Sue: This actually happened to me. It's been impossible! I should have taken professional lessons after I failed the first time.

Counsellor: (laughs) This is quite a common problem. Now let's relate this to homework assignments. Just imagine how many hours and years of your lives you have been thinking and behaving in a self-defeating manner, 20 years, 30 years, 40 years, and 50 years for some of you. Up to 50 years thinking and behaving in ways that exacerbate stress. Think of all the daily practice you've all had thinking and behaving in a way that causes you all so much distress. Do you honestly believe that just attending a stress counselling group once a week for two hours is going to make much impact on your thinking and behaving skills deficits?

Paul: Put that way, no. I just hadn't thought of it like that before. I've actually spent 45 years practising how to escalate my stress levels!

Counsellor: Can you see why we believe that the other 166 hours of a week when you are not here are so important?

Mitch: I can now.

Counsellor: Incidentally Mitch, can you imagine what would have happened if you turned up on the day of your driving test having had NO lessons at all? What would have happened?

Mitch: I definitely would have failed.

Counsellor: Absolutely right! And this also applies to problem-focused therapy. If you don't regularly practise your new thinking, feeling and behaving skills you are more likely to experience stress when the next difficulty arises. Today, when you are driving home from here, because of all your previous practice, hopefully, you will automatically slam your brakes on if a pedestrian walks out in front of you. Eventually these new thinking, feeling and behaving skills will also start to occur more instinctively. But it takes hard work and practice.

We have found that using a good analogy is far more persuasive than just asking members to undertake assignments.

Over the next couple of sessions the counsellor can teach the members the seven-step model and they can be shown how to complete a Seven-Step Problem Focused Form (Appendix 3). In small groups they can work with each other dealing with one person's problem at a time. As these early sessions can set a precedent, it is important for the counsellor to encourage the group members to participate and not just expect the counsellor to do the majority of the work.

In later sessions, the counsellor can give a presentation on the ABCDEs. By this stage it is likely that a number of the members would have raised problems that they are too anxious to face or situations in which they have panic attacks. It is useful to demonstrate to the group how holding demanding beliefs, that is, musts, shoulds, have to's, ought to's, can elevate stress levels in a specific situation in contrast to holding preferential beliefs, that is, wants, desires, wishes. If this is not undertaken at an early stage of therapy members may not see the point of disputing demanding, self-defeating beliefs.

In Ellis and associates (1997), I (SP) described how I usually explain the ABC model to groups. Although a problem from a group member could be used to illustrate the model it is usually more satisfactory to use an example of an ABC chain that most people can relate to such as the emotional consequences of arriving somewhere late. This can be illustrated on a flip chart, whiteboard or on a handout as below:

A . . . Arriving late for an important meeting

B . . . I must not arrive late but if I do
      it would be awful
      I could not stand it and
      it would prove that I'm a failure

C . . .

A typical dialogue the stress counsellor uses to explain the ABC model is given below (adapted Ellis *et al.*, 1997: 157–8):

Counsellor: I would like you all to imagine arriving late for an important meeting. (Counsellor points to the flip chart.) Is anybody having any difficulty?
John: That's easy. It only happened last week to me!
Sue: It only happened today to me. I thought I was going to turn up here late. (laughs)
Sara: No problem! I get so worked up about being late.
Counsellor: OK. We call this situation the activating event or 'A' for short.
      Now imagine that you hold the following beliefs about turning up late, 'I MUST not arrive late but if I do it would be AWFUL, I could not STAND IT, and it would

	prove that I'm a FAILURE. (Counsellor points to the beliefs on the flip chart.) How would you emotionally feel?
Jayne:	I do hold those beliefs! I would feel really anxious. (The counsellor writes anxiety alongside the 'C' on the flip chart.)
Counsellor:	What does everybody else think they would feel? (The counsellor is ensuring that everybody understands the model and can imagine the situation.)
Sara:	When I turn up late I feel guilty.
Paul:	I'd feel nothing. I don't care if I turn up late anywhere.
Counsellor:	That's an interesting point Paul. We may come back to that later. However, just for the purpose of this exercise can you really have a go at imagining that you do hold these beliefs which we call 'B'. (Counsellor then goes around the group to ensure that the other members can relate to this exercise.) If I held on to these beliefs and I arrived late I would probably appear very nervous and act in a clumsy manner. Can anybody relate to this additional consequence of 'C' as we call it?
Mitch:	I remember being late for an important presentation I had to give. I was so nervous that I dropped all of the acetates onto the floor. I felt so stupid. I really was a failure.
Counsellor:	That was a good example Mitch of how becoming anxious in a situation tends to reduce performance and a person becomes less problem-focused. This is a behavioural 'C'. Most unhelpful emotions such as anxiety have behavioural components.

Now, can you all imagine the same situation but this time you are telling yourself something different. (Counsellor turns over to another pre-prepared ABC sheet.) This time you are telling yourself, 'It's strongly PREFERABLE to arrive on time but if I don't, it's BAD but not awful, it's certainly not the end of my world, I CAN STAND IT and although I may have failed, I'm NOT a failure.' How do you feel this time? |
Mitch:	If I really could believe it, which I don't, I would feel less anxious.
Sue:	I would probably just feel concerned. (The counsellor writes concern next to the 'C' on the second sheet.)
Counsellor:	Now can you see how it is not the 'A', in this case arriving late, that causes 'C', but what you think about 'A' that largely contributes to the 'C'?
Mitch:	Yeah.
Sara:	But are you saying that I shouldn't care whether I turn up late?
Counsellor:	Sara, I'm glad you've raised this important point. What would a person have to say at 'B' not to care about arriving late? (Counsellor points to the 'B' on the flip chart.)
Paul:	What I normally say. (laughs) 'I don't care if I turn up late.'
Counsellor:	Paul's correct. In the second example I gave with more flexible and less catastrophic beliefs, Sue, like the average person would still be CONCERNED about arriving late and would remain problem-focused. Whereas Paul does not care about arriving late and would feel nothing, neither anxious nor concerned. Who is more likely to turn up late with these different attitudes, Sue or Paul?
Sara:	Paul. Does that explain why you've turned up late for each meeting so far? (pointing to Paul)
Paul:	I suppose so.

> *Counsellor:* So not only do the attitudes and beliefs at 'B' lead to emotions at 'C' they also lead to behaviours at 'C' too. I just want to ensure I've explained the model reasonably well. Who would like to tell the group how the ABC model works? You can use the two flip chart examples if you wish.

It is important to ensure that the members have understood this model. If the counsellor just asks, 'Do you all understand the ABC model', it is likely that there will be a furious nod of heads supposedly indicating in–depth appreciation of the model. In our experience, often the nods of the heads are in direct proportion to group members NOT understanding a concept! Receiving ongoing feedback and correcting misconceptions in individual counselling and in group counselling is an essential part of most psychoeducational approaches to counselling, psychotherapy and training. Sometimes feedback may not be forthcoming especially in a new group. In the previous example the lack of response or silence can become another ABC for the counsellor to demonstrate as below:

> *Counsellor:* Hmm. You all seem very quiet. Perhaps it would be worth examining this situation in ABC terms. (Counsellor writes 'A = Explaining model to the group' on the flipchart.)
> Now, in my experience the 'C' in this case would be anxiety and/or shame. The behavioural component would be avoidance (Counsellor writes 'C = anxiety/shame/avoidance' on the flipchart.) Now, I wonder what you are telling yourselves at 'B' this very moment. Perhaps something like, 'I must not make a mistake otherwise they will think I'm stupid'.
> Does anybody recognize these kind of thoughts at this moment? (Counsellor writes the hypothesized beliefs on the flipchart.)
> *Group:* (Another nod of heads.)
> *Counsellor:* Let's be realistic. Nobody here is going to bite your head off if you make a mistake, especially me. (humorously) I'm only interested in the attempt.
> (Counsellor encouraging members to explain the model.)
> Now who wants to have a go at explaining the model to the group? If you do you will be undertaking one of Albert Ellis's famous shame-attacking exercises too.
> *Paul:* Okay. I've got nothing to lose and all to gain. I'll give it a go. (laughs)

For an easy life counsellors may collude with clients. However, in the long term their acquiescent behaviour may set a poor role model for clients and group members who could benefit from observing the counsellor using challenging skills.

If we now return to the previous exercise, the counsellor ensures that the group understands that the demanding self-defeating and problem-interfering beliefs mainly contribute to the distressing emotional disturbance at 'C'. Whereas preferential self-helping beliefs at 'B' lead to a more helpful, problem-focused response at 'C'. The counsellor answers any queries the group has and then describes the relevance of the 'D' and 'E' of the ABCDE model. As this approach may be new to many group members it is important to put aside adequate time for this activity. Then if there is still sufficient time left in the session, the counsellor can demonstrate the complete ABCDE process with an example from a group member. Suitable bibliotherapy (e.g. Dryden and Gordon, 1990 or 1992) to read prior to the session can save time and increase understanding of the ABCDE model (e.g. Dryden and Gordon, 1990; 1992).

Later sessions

In subsequent sessions the members are given the opportunity to discuss current problems and stress scenarios. Also they are encouraged to focus on anything that they would normally avoid; for example, giving presentations, if there is a long-term benefit such as improved job prospects.

The counsellor encourages the members to dispute each other's problem-interfering and self-defeating beliefs. Unlike many other forms of group counselling or therapy, members will often work in pairs or triads attempting to help each other overcome their problems by using the seven-step problem-solving and five-star models. The counsellor recommends that they can start applying the ABCDE model to challenge their problem-interfering beliefs if their anxiety becomes too great to undertake step 6, the agreeing action stage, of the seven-step model. In some cases the counsellor will need to demonstrate to the group additional techniques such as coping imagery or relaxation exercises to help a member deal with a specific problem or disorder (see Chapter 7). The explanation of the theory underpinning a behavioural or imaginal exposure programme may also need to be taught depending upon the problems the group members are suffering from (see Chapter 7). In later sessions the counsellor acts as a guide to keep the group on track and avoid any unnecessary departures from the basic seven-step problem-solving and five-star models. At the start of a session the counsellor can negotiate a group agenda which will help this process and also allow the group to 'touch base'. However, it is always useful to start the session by asking the members how they have been since the last session otherwise the counsellor may discover rather late in the session that a member is feeling suicidal. It is essential to keep this as brief as possible or valuable therapeutic time may be lost (see Palmer and Dryden, 1995). If difficulties have arisen, then the counsellor can ask the member whether he or she wishes to put it on the agenda.

Counsellor: Good evening everybody. How are you? (Counsellor wants to ensure that distressed members have the opportunity at the beginning of the session to share how they feel with the group. If a group member is very disturbed or suicidal his allows the counsellor to devote sufficient time to dealing with this problem.)

Paul: Fine.

Counsellor: Glad to see you've arrived on time Paul.

Sara: (laughs) I'm feeling a lot better too.

Mitch: I'm still anxious about the presentation at work.

Sue: I'm becoming really stressed about my driving test.

Emma: I've managed to travel on the train today so I'm feeling really good with myself.

Margaret: I'm getting really fed up and depressed about my son's bad behaviour. The school have put him on report too. My husband is no help either. He is actually encouraging Tom's violent behaviour.

Counsellor: I'm sorry to hear that. It may be an idea to look at this problem this evening.

Margaret: I would like to, thanks.

Counsellor: Tracy, how are you?

Tracy: My manager has given me too much work to do again. I'm stressed.

The counsellor is now aware of how stressed the members are and has realized that Margaret's problem may need to take priority. Group agenda setting starts at this point in the proceedings.

Counsellor: Okay. Let's keep to the usual format. We can start by reviewing how you all got on with your homework assignments. Then we can look at problems you wish to discuss this evening. We can start with Margaret as she sounds really fed up about her son's behaviour and her husband's lack of support. As we deal with each problem we can set relevant homework assignments. As usual we can finish with troubleshooting and discuss what you thought and how you felt about this evening's session. Would anybody like to add anything else?

Tracy: No. Sounds fine to me.

Sara: I'm not sure whether I totally understand how to use coping imagery. You discussed it last time. Can we go over it again?

Counsellor: Okay. We can review it when it's your turn to discuss your target problem. (Counsellor allocates this to the time allotted to Sara.)

Paul: I'm keen to get on. (Nods of agreement from the others to this comment.)

Counsellor: (Going around the group for convenience in a clockwise manner.)

Right. If everybody is in agreement we can now review how you got on with your homework assignments.

Sara, how did you get on with reaching your deadline?

An alternative is to ascertain at the agenda setting stage the specific target problem each member wants to deal with during the session. However, the counsellor should ensure that time is not lost at this stage allowing members to talk about the problem in-depth, because this will be repeated later in the session. Thoughts and feelings about the last session can be put onto the session agenda. 'Trouble shooting' refers to ensuring that the homework assignments or exercises devised during the session will actually be undertaken. We would always recommend that assignments and exercises should be challenging but not overwhelming. The following dialogue illustrates the counsellor trouble shooting:

Counsellor: Let's debrief. You've all worked in small groups and devised action plans for your particular problems. Who would like to share with the group their plan.

Sue: Well, my driving test is in two weeks. I am going to have four more driving lessons before the test; read my highway code; and use coping imagery every day to help reduce my anxiety. I really don't want to fail my driving test again.

Counsellor: Sounds good. Shall we just examine your strategy in a little more depth and do some troubleshooting. What is going to prevent you from having four driving lessons before the test?

Sue: I've already thought of that problem. My instructor has spare time during the day so I'm going to take a couple of half-days off work. I'm owed them so there will not be any difficulty arranging it with my boss.

Counsellor: Good. Let's be very specific. When are you going to read your highway code?

Sue: Every evening after my dinner.

Counsellor: What time?

Sue: Immediately after I've finished the washing-up.

Counsellor: What will prevent you from reading it.

Sue: My partner may want to watch the television. The telephone might ring.

Counsellor: What could you do about your partner watching the television?

Sue: The quietest place in the flat is probably the bedroom. I could either go to bed early or ask him to turn the TV off.

Counsellor: What's most likely to work?

Sue: Going to bed early!

Counsellor: What can you do about the telephone ringing?

Sue: I suppose I could take it off the hook.

Counsellor: You don't sound very sure about this idea.

Sara: You've got an answerphone. Why don't you just leave it on?

Counsellor: Now that sounds like a good idea.

Sue: But I always feel obliged to answer it.

Counsellor: Okay. What could you do about feeling less obliged and less guilty.

Sue: I suppose I could write a coping statement again.

Counsellor: What would the statement be?

Sue: Perhaps something like, 'Just because I would like to answer the telephone I don't have to. I can always ring them back later or tomorrow.'

Counsellor: Sounds good. How can you ensure you use the coping imagery daily.

Sue: This is easy. Every morning I have a fifteen minute bath. I can practise my coping imagery of me doing the driving test when I have my bath.

Counsellor: We'll see how you get on next week.

In counselling, sufficient time should be set aside to troubleshoot whereby possible blocks to action can be investigated and subsequently overcome or bypassed.

Occasionally a group member does not bring problems to counselling or stays silent. Assuming that the client is not highly disturbed, the counsellor will usually bring the person into the conversation using a variety of methods, for example, 'Emma, can you relate to Sue's problem?' or 'Emma, have you ever experienced a similar problem?' or 'You've been rather quiet today. What's going through your mind at this very instant?' If the member is avoiding discussing his or her own problems or talking in the group, then this can be examined in ABCDE terms using the five-star model (see Ellis *et al.*, 1997; Wessler and Wessler, 1980).

Final stage

It is usually a good idea to review the learning and therapeutic experience in the last session. Future blocks to change, lapse and relapse prevention should be high on the agenda. D'Zurilla's (1986) Rapid Problem-Solving Model described earlier in this chapter is a useful method to teach in the penultimate or last session. Corey (1990: 136) described eight key functions of a counsellor or trainer during the final stage of group counselling. These are worth noting:

- assisting members in dealing with any feelings they may have about termination
- giving members an opportunity to express and deal with any unfinished business within the group
- reinforcing changes that members have made and ensuring that members have information about resources to enable them to make further changes
- assisting members in determining how they will apply specific skills in a variety of situations in daily life
- working with members to develop specific contracts and homework assignments as practical ways of making changes
- assisting participants to develop a conceptual framework that will help them understand, integrate, consolidate, and remember what they have learned in the group
- providing opportunities for members to give one another constructive feedback
- re-emphasizing the importance of maintaining confidentiality after the group is over.

Follow-up

In our experience a follow-up session a couple of months later can be very useful in preventing lapse or relapse as members can discuss the achievements and difficulties they have encountered applying the problem-focused approach without professional assistance. Action plans can be reviewed and blocks to change can be examined. This will help to maximize the chances of long-lasting benefits from the group stress counselling or therapy experience. A follow-up session also gives the counsellor the opportunity to obtain valuable feedback about the programme and undertake an evaluation of the overall effectiveness. If tests were used at the screening stage to assess levels of stress anxiety, somatic symptoms, phobias and depression, they can also be used post-counselling to assess whether the programme has been beneficial. At this stage it may become apparent that some group members may require further professional assistance. The counsellor can discuss these issues and suggest appropriate assistance elsewhere such as counsellors or suitable agencies.

In the next section we conclude by briefly examining how problem-focused approaches are applied to family settings.

STRESS MANAGEMENT PROGRAMMES FOR THE FAMILY

Sometimes family-orientated interventions may be more effective than individual counselling or stress management for a member of a family. Family-based interventions have tended to concentrate on improving communication, thereby increasing the number of discussions and reducing the incidence of rows or 'expressed emotion'. However, this approach has been less effective when the underlying causes of conflicts were mainly due to a family member suffering from severe mental or physical disorder. In recent years, this has led to the inclusion of additional problem-focused strategies into the approach (see Falloon et al., 1993).

The problems most likely to benefit family therapy strategies (Falloon *et al.*, 1993: 11) are: adolescent behavioural disturbance, anxiety disorders, bipolar disorders, learning disabilities and autism, children's conduct disorders, chronic physical health problems, criminal offending problems, dementias, depression, drug and alcohol misuse, eating disorders, family violence and child abuse, marital and family conflict, sexual dysfunction, divorce mediation, premarital counselling, prevention of stress-related disorders in high-risk groups, relapse prevention, suicide prevention, residential care, schizophrenia.

Falloon and associates have found that few families in Western societies structure their problem solving. They suggest that 'Ideally, a family or household can sit down together, without major distractions, discuss openly and clearly a particular issue of concern to one or more of its members, and at the end of the discussion devise a plan of action that can be readily implemented' (Falloon *et al.*, 1993: 112). We wonder how many counsellors structure their problem solving too!

Falloon and associates described the main steps of a time-limited family-based stress-management intervention as follows (1993: 22):

- assessment of current ways of dealing with stress, and current personal goals
- education about specific disorders
- enhancing communication about problems and goals
- specific strategies for dealing with difficult problems.

A stress-management programme is developed after undertaking a thorough assessment to ascertain the individual and group needs and skills deficits. To ensure that family members know how to communicate and listen actively to each other they are given communication skills training. This is crucial if the family or household members are going to use a problem-focused approach. One of the long-term goals is to train the family to be able to cope with stressful problems without the constant aid of a therapist. Falloon and associates collapsed the model down to six steps as follows:

- identify the problem (or goal)
- list all possible solutions
- highlight probable consequences
- agree on the 'best' strategy
- plan and implement
- review results.

Usually the counsellor adopts the role of coach or teacher assisting the family or household to achieve greater efficiency in their problem-solving discussions. Treatment sessions are considered to be training sessions and seldom therapy sessions. Occasionally the counsellor may model one or more of the steps of the problem-focused model to the household. This is of particular importance when group members have limited verbal skills. Group members are encouraged to complete forms similar to Appendix 2 at their family meetings. These forms are retained to provide a record of the plans agreed and are discussed at the subsequent session when the results are being reviewed and revised. With time families start to incorporate efficient problem solving and goal achievement into everyday discussions without any external help from mental health professionals. Controlled studies have demonstrated the effectiveness of the problem-solving approach in a variety of different settings (see Falloon, 1991). We recommend that counsellors wishing to apply this approach in family and other settings refer to Falloon's publications on this subject.

CHAPTER 10

Personality Factors You May Wish to Consider

We cannot safely assume that other people's minds work on the same principles as our own . . . others do not reason as we reason, or do not value the things we value, or are not interested in what interests us.

Isabel Briggs Myers and Peter Myers (1995) *Gifts Differing*

Experience leads us to include some concluding thoughts on the ways in which people's gifts and stresses may be said to differ. People are complex and individual, but certain common, as well as differing, characteristics are discernible. A stress counselling programme which suits people of one personality type may not be as fitting nor as helpful for those with a different personality. We suggest that our personality type plays a major role in determining not only our stress tolerance level, but also the particular thoughts and experiences which are likely to stress us. It also may indicate some ways of managing stress which are likely to be most individually helpful to us. Stressed people introduced to an incompatible stress-relieving model, particularly if that is the only model readily available, may become discouraged and perhaps give up all attempts at developing responsibility for managing their own stress. The same could be said about incompatible clients and counsellors, for another suggestion is that the personality types of client and counsellor are a determining factor in establishing whether clients are effectively helped to manage their stress. This is not to imply that for example, counsellors with extravert personalities cannot work well with stressed clients with introvert personalities, or vice versa, but rather that it is important for the counsellor to be adaptable in such a working alliance.

The concept of personality types can be taken as 'an insult and a threat to individuality' or as '[profound] differences in kind . . . which fit actual people to varying degrees and are intended to help in self-understanding, not to be definitive' (Bayne, 1995: 12).

DIFFERENT TYPES OF PEOPLE

Throughout history there have been attempts to create some order out of what has sometimes appeared to be the chaos of human differences. To name but a few, Sheldon and associates (1940) based their theory of human types on physical constitution: endomorphic or basically short, jolly, friendly person who is inclined to fatness; mesomorphic or basically competitive, aggressive person who is strong and athletic; ectomorphic or sensitive, imaginative, intellectual person who is thin and unathletic.

This information at first glance seems of limited value in terms of stress counselling. It can be viewed as a very broad brush stroke approach having little to say about the inner dynamics of women and men and therefore contributing little to any deep understanding of their personality. However, size and shape have a profound influence upon the individual who dwells within the body. A boy who is short or lightly muscled may have lost status among his friends because he did not measure up to their popular notions of masculinity. His compensation may have been to work grindingly hard, or to decline to work at all, or become a class comedian, or a recluse, or to play truant or to become verbally aggressive or to develop other habits and behaviour patterns which he may not have chosen if given a different physical constitution.

A tall girl may become retiring, or go in for athletics, or politics or a career in modelling and in common with some tall boys have physical and psychological difficulties of adjustment. Chairs, desks, beds, driving seats of cars are still often too small for tall people. Whenever tall people are on their feet they are constantly being reminded of their height by enquiries about the condition of the atmosphere 'up there', or other such high-flown pleasantries!

It is in this way that our physical genetic inheritance can contain the beginnings of patterns of living which may stress us in adolescence and adult life. We may have 'forgotten' these, or put them to the back of our mind but they can nevertheless exercise a powerful, sometimes insidious, influence on our lives. Physical constitution is often our initial, non-verbal communication and can be one of our most powerful ones.

Other attempts to define personality included Kurt Lewin's 'field theory' (Hall and Lindsey, 1970) with its proposal that we develop our personality within a 'life space' of personal perceptions of reality from our psychological and non-psychological environment. The ways in which these influences are integrated, accepted or rejected constitute the fluid, yet unique organization which is that particular individual. The emphasis on the potential for creativity and the multi-dimensional nature of a person give an exciting vitality to such an approach, even though it may be possible to question its objectivity.

Maslow (1969) proposed that the structure of human personality evolves from the hierarchical pattern of needs, which emerge as an individual develops in response to life situations. There is great variation in the relative importance of these needs and the degree to which the person is able to fulfil them, or reach self-realization. Different cultures place more or less emphasis on certain of the needs and the individual may not even be aware of some of them, as such, while instinctively or even unconsciously acting because of them.

Many of the theories concerning the structure of personality have developed round a series of relatively effective therapies, including Freud's psychoanalysis, Jung's analytical psychology and Carl Rogers' self-actualizing person-centred therapy.

Mowrer (1960) thought that the personality is developed through confrontation with problems and people and that avoidance of these prevented the 'normal' process of adjustment, leading him to advocate group therapy and the self-disclosing relationship between therapist and client. Mowrer may be seen as one of the fathers of the current cognitive therapies, assuming as he did that phobias and the avoidance reactions which accompany them are learned by the individual; phobias do not occur as a result of innate factors; and phobias are not the result of an underlying psychic or psychological disturbance.

An attempt to reduce the enormously complex phenomenon of personality to 'manageable' dimensions was made by Dollard and Miller (1950) with their controversial perception of personality as springing from a limited number of innate drives, which are later expanded by a learning process based upon reinforcement arising from specific experiences. They assumed that the first level of response is automatic, but that there is a second level of response which takes account of images and ideas which in turn provide clues for subsequent responses. They also described the manner in which overt language might play an important role in creating emotional response. They reasoned that our emotional state frequently resulted from the way in which we evaluated or labelled an event or experience (a stimulus) and not necessarily from the objective characteristics of the situation itself, so that if a personal labelled a situation as 'dangerous', the upset they experienced would be in direct response to the label 'dangerous'. To the extent that the situation was appropriately labelled – for example, if you were sitting in a car which had stalled on a level crossing in the path of an on-coming train – then the emotion aroused by the label 'dangerous' would be appropriate and might even save your life. However, if you are a person who is anxious and uncomfortable, even among friends, the label dangerous may be describing an inappropriate and perhaps unhelpful reaction.

This basic assumption that emotional arousal and maladaptive behaviour are mediated by the interpretations that we put on situations laid the groundwork for Albert Ellis's (1962) rational–emotive therapy.

Existentialist psychologists understand individuals as unique and emergent identities, who are self-responsible, self-developed and self-conscious. We are each our own creator and a constantly evolving organism, free to make choices and therefore responsible for them. An important part of our self-creativity is our development of meaningful relationships. Since our own experiences are seen as our full 'frame of reference', the only reality that our unique individuality can know is our own. This important focus upon the individual self that we create from our experiences has been very influential in the work of Rollo May (1961) in the USA, and also that of Carl Rogers.

SIMILARITIES AND DIFFERENCES IN THEORIES

The various personality theorists all differ at least in some respects from each other. Probably none would disregard the presence of some inherited features in the pattern of personality, and presumably none disregards environmental influences altogether. The differences between the theories consist partly in the relative weight given to the various possible components, partly in the extent to which the patterns are seen to result mainly from internal growth or external pressures, and partly in the degree of purposefulness which is assumed to be inherent in the developing personality. What one theorist stresses most another may ignore – a diversity which surely has some origin in the differences and life experiences of the theorists themselves. A social scientist does not see the same things in human conduct as a counsellor sees and neither sees things that would be obvious to a statistician.

Currently the five-factor theory espoused by McCrae and Costa (1995) is dominant. This comprehensive major trait theory of personality describing five independent factors – emotional stability, extraversion, culture, agreeableness and conscientiousness – has been well researched. Although it is a little early to be able to see its influence on counselling, Bayne (1995) makes some comparisons and links which have relevance for counsellors between the Big Five and the Myers–Briggs Type Indicator (MBTI) that are based on Jung's theory of personality.

INTERNAL AND EXTERNAL

The experience of our internal reality of thoughts, feelings, images and memory and our external reality of people and the world around us are described by Rowe (1995: 54) in a straightforward way:

> If your ultimate reason is concerned with the development and achievement of you as an individual, you will consistently turn toward your internal reality.
>
> If your ultimate reason is concerned with relationships with other people, you consistently turn toward your external reality because other people are in your external reality.

Thus it is that we arrive at two broad personality groups the introverts and the extraverts.

Ninety years ago William James, in a series of popular lectures on philosophy, proposed that there are basically two types of people, the tender-minded and the tough-minded. He suggested that the two types are dichotomous: the tender-minded characterized by idealism, optimism, dogmatism and rationalism (following prin-ciples); while the tough-minded are irreligious, pluralistic, sceptical and empirical (following facts). According to James (1906) the two types think badly of each other: tender minds often find tough minds callous, brutal or unrefined; tough minds think of the tender as soft-headed sentimentalists.

One of the most imaginative and influential therapeutic practitioners who also supported the bi-polar separation of personality into the fundamental groups of introvert and extravert was Carl Jung, the founder of analytical psychotherapy. For Jung (1976), the extravert turns with a ready welcome to the world outside, while the introvert prefers the world within themselves.

Descriptions of personality characteristics are a potential minefield. What follows is offered as differences in kind which fit people in varying degrees and are not definitive. They may be considered by some counsellors and not by others. They are drawn from Jung, 1976; Bryant, 1983; Fowke, 1992; Myers, 1995.

Extraverts

If I have an extravert world view people, things and happenings around me are likely to be supremely important and I need to be on good terms with them to have peace of mind and minimize stress.

It is also likely that I will tend to:

- go out to interact with others and be active in the world around me and only when I have done this will I have enough energy to tackle the tasks of life and minimize stress
- create my own reality by talking and formulate my thoughts and ideas by the very process of speaking them aloud. My maxim may well be 'How do I know what I think until I hear what I say?'
- need the support of others to engage in the discipline of developing my inner life without becoming over-stressed because I prefer the activity and companionship of a life that is outwardly directed
- generally talk easily and am able to share freely what is most precious to me because that way I can savour it the more.
- make my decisions on the basis of creating and maintaining relationships and be fearful of being rejected or abandoned. This fear can make me anxious and I will work actively to avoid this happening
- be a shy person when I think that people will reject me if I try to do something and make a mess of things. I will sometimes avoid doing things in a group for this reason
- flow with things as they happen rather than have too many timetables and predetermined plans and have a lifestyle characterized by a spontaneous and flexible approach. I think there is a lot to discover about everything and I put off making definitive decisions as long as I can so as not to miss the next bit of information, which might make all the difference to my choice!
- find introverts difficult to work with because they seem so impractical

My characteristics may be overvalued and over-esteemed in an activist society.

Clients who prefer extraversion tend to:

- want a more active counsellor
- be less comfortable with reflection
- be optimistic and energetic (Bayne 1995: 112).

The strengths of an extravert counsellor are likely to be:

- helping the client to explore a range of issues
- making an easy initial contact
- able to think 'on feet' (Bayne 1995: 115).

Introverts

If I have an introvert world view I tend to preserve my inner integrity at all costs and to be on the defensive against the world outside me and somewhat uncomfortable in it. Being true to my own self, to my own ideas and feelings and to my own vision is usually what brings me peace of mind and minimizes stress.

It is also likely that I will tend to:

- be de-energized by continuous activity with others and with the world outside me and need time apart from others to restore my energy level in order to be able to engage with people once more and minimize stress
- often find it difficult to express myself until I have had sufficient time to formulate within my mind what I want to say. My maxim may well be 'How can I speak until I have had time to think out what I want to say?'
- not like being asked to speak on the spur of the moment but be able to do so if given time to write or prepare my contribution beforehand
- be by nature a private person, seldom disclosing what is most precious to me and only sharing my inner world with people I know well and trust greatly
- make my decisions on the basis of organizing, clarifying, developing and achieving, disliking mess or disorder and being somewhat fearful of chaos. This fear makes me anxious and I will work actively to avoid this happening
- not necessarily be a shy person and if I develop and use my social skills, I can be very personable and can really enjoy being sociable
- like to be decisive and cultivate a lifestyle characterized by a love of precision, neatness and predictability. I prefer things to be done properly and on time
- not always know how to address the needs of extraverts because they seem so superficial.

Clients who prefer introversion tend to:

- feel easy with silence
- be less comfortable with action
- be less enthusiastic about counselling (Bayne 1995: 112).

The strengths of an introvert counsellor are likely to be:

- helping the client to explore a few issues deeply
- using silence
- reflecting on strategies, etc. (Bayne 1995: 115).

These thumbnail sketches of the two broad personality groupings give an indication of those aspects of living which may generate stress for each of them. They also give an inkling of the ways in which people from the two groups can stress each other in family or work situations, particularly if they are unaware of the fundamental differences in their ways of perceiving the world.

In reality, rather than in theory we all have both introvert and extravert tendencies. Eysenck (1967) suggested that (in theory) each of us could be placed on a continuum, one end of which is extreme extraversion and the other end extreme introversion and that we would find ourselves grouped with a majority of other people somewhere in the middle.

The psychologist Dorothy Rowe (1995) has written consistently, wisely and refreshingly about the meanings, consequences and life aspects of introverts, whom she calls 'What I have achieved today people', and extraverts, whom she terms 'People Persons'. In terms of the purpose of life she believes that

- introverts say that life is about personal achievement
- extraverts say that life is about people
- 'Thus the reasons why we do the things we do come to the different ways we experience our sense of existence' (Rowe 1988: 91).

Counsellors working with stressed clients may find the distinction of introvert and extravert sufficiently definitive to support differential ways of working with people from each broadly defined group among their clients. There is certainly a great deal of material in these groupings to enable counsellors to integrate their working processes with the introvert or extravert person's differently perceived stresses.

'What I have achieved today persons' doubt their external reality more than their internal reality. Under stress they may find their external reality has become less real, or even unreal, but internal reality remains as real as ever.

'People Persons' doubt their internal reality more than their external reality, under stress they may find that internal reality has become less real, even unreal, but their external reality remains as real as ever.

'Very sensibly we turn to and prefer the reality which seems the more real.' Rowe (1995: 53–4).

WHO ELSE ARE WE?

Those counsellors, extravert or introvert, who prefer a fuller view of the differences between the personalities of clients, either from personal interest or from a wish to make the counselling process more individually relevant, both to themselves and their clients, may find themselves drawn to Jung's further division of introverts and extraverts according to four principal ways of dealing with life and its problems.

The four ways are:

- through the senses (seeing, hearing, touching)
- through intuition
- through thought
- through feeling.

While we all exercise each of these functions to some degree, Jung (1976) classified us according to whichever one we exercise predominently.

In addition the four functions are paired: sensation with intuition and thinking with feeling. Sensation and intuition are paired as perceptive functions because they are concerned with grasping facts. Thinking and feeling are paired as judging functions because they try to evaluate facts: thinking judges statements and opinions as true or false; feeling judges people and things as good or bad, attractive or unattractive.

In part innately and in part influenced by our training and early experience we tend to rely more on one of these four ways of coping with our tasks and problems than we do the other three. In life, as in bridge, we prefer to play our strong suit, and use this as our dominant function.

Sensation

Those of us who rely more on our senses to help us may be seen as the practical realists of life, who tend to:

- be precise people who observe detail, enjoy dealing with facts and live very much in the present
- be broadly life's doers liking simple, uncomplicated action in orderly sequence, yet, that simplicity may be expressing great depth
- be reliant on our physiological senses – sight, hearing, touch, taste and smell – to tell us about the physical world which surrounds us, and in counselling perhaps to need the tangible to lead us to the intangible and the visible to show us what is not so apparent. We are after all, realists
- like to hear or make music and use visible pictures as well as the written word to inform us, if we are sensitive to beauty
- take things literally and may struggle to see abstract things, or patterns and connections between the facts we observe
- be so normally and naturally rooted in the present that our stronghold on reality may make it difficult to acknowledge that anything else is possible and we can have a problem in imagining anything else
- consequently find change and seeing alternative ways of managing our stress problems problematic unless we can be helped to root the concepts in our current actuality. If something is not happening for us now, it is difficult for us to comprehend its ever happening in the future or its having happened in the past
- be introvert or extravert.

IMPLICATIONS FOR STRESS COUNSELLING

If we are introverts we have imagination, but we possibly need help to locate it in the present in order to be able to use it to solve our problems.

A sensing person who is also an extravert is more likely to be drawn to an active counselling process, which gives them not only frequent opportunities to talk themselves, but also active ways of working on problems. Such a person can also respond to a talking and active counsellor, because this will allow the counselling process to engage their senses and bring them into an active relationship.

Realists who prefer a perceptive life style (one that is open to experiences) regardless of whether they are extravert or introvert, may find it more congenial to work on their problems while going about their daily lives, rather than by sitting quietly working things out, which is largely foreign to their nature and interests.

When introducing realists to counselling it is important to consider their personality traits. They will probably find a brief and factually simple approach more helpful than a complex and ambiguous one. Initially they may need their counselling in small doses if they are to come back for more.

Clients who prefer sensing tend to:

- be detailed and concrete
- proceed step by step
- like a 'practical' approach
- not see many options
- find novelty uncomfortable (Bayne 1995: 112).

The strengths of a sensing counsellor are likely to be in:

- being realistic
- noticing details
- helping client to work out practical action plans (Bayne 1995: 115).

Intuition

Jung (1976) defined the second function of the perceiving pair as perception by way of the unconscious, that storeroom of past experience which we have apparently forgotten, but which lives an unseen life within us and includes quickly forgotten fleeting impressions, or telepathic impressions which may never have been conscious. The sea of the unconscious washes things up on the shore of life for the intuitive person to beachcomb into awareness, for the benefit of themselves and others (Bryant 1983). If we are intuitive then we may:

- see with the eye of the mind, rather than the bodily senses and are likely to be more imaginative than observant, and to rely more on inspiration than perspiration
- be interested not so much in facts and figures as in their possibilities – the facts behind the facts fascinate us
- tend to be concerned with the possibility of what might be, rather than what actually is and to be focused on the future rather than the present
- miss the experience of the present because of our absorption with the possibilities of the future; sometimes we do something 'in our head' and then omit to carry it through in reality because we can confuse thinking about it and doing it
- have wide horizons, notice patterns and trends rather than specific details and readily respond to symbolism
- have expectations, whether optimistic or pessimistic. We are good guessers and rely on flair and hunch, so may be considered 'lucky' people

- often 'know' without being able to say how we know and though sometimes we are mistaken, we are often right!
- be introvert or extravert.

IMPLICATIONS FOR STRESS COUNSELLING

An intuitive person who is also an extravert is interested in people and events in the world around and may be drawn to politics or become a successful business person, thriving on variety, sometimes to the extreme!

> Both extravert and introvert intuitive people take in so much, have such wide horizons and make so many connections between all that impinges on them that they need time for reflection. (Fowke, 1992)

People with intuitive personality traits can be likened to the Oliver Twists of the experiential life who are always wanting more. Because they have such a wide ranging curiosity they may need to guard against expecting everyone else to have a similarly extensive appetite for life. They are inclined to want everyone to wade into the sea with them in their beachcombing and this may mean that a counsellor of a differing personality needs to recognize that they may be taken too far out of their depth for comfort.

Fowke (1992) suggests that intuitive people tend to be different from those of all other personality types because even those who are extravert need plenty of quiet and personal space, while those who are introvert often have the need to talk about their experiences in order to lead themselves to further insight. Intuitive people who make their decisions on an analysis of a situation need to structure their stress counselling within a well thought-out framework based on reason and logical order. Other intuitive people who make decisions on the basis of their value judgements about their total situation require a counselling process which is more holistic and involves their entire being. Intuitive people could be especially drawn to a counselling process which gives limitless possibilities and is full of symbolism. They need to be able to make their own interpretations however because they are able to dream up endless possibilities and applications for themselves. Their capacity to 'do things in their head' without carrying them out in reality may account for their apparent inability to achieve some of the tasks they set themselves in counselling. For them, thinking is doing. Intuitive people may generally be more attracted to long-term counselling.

Clients who prefer intuition tend to:

- present broad pictures
- hop around from topic to topic
- see options which are unrealistic
- see many options
- overlook facts
- like approaches which are novel and imaginative. (Bayne, 1995: 112)

The strengths of an intuitive counsellor are likely to be:

- ability to see an overall picture
- brainstorming
- able to use hunches (Bayne, 1995: 112).

Thinking-type people

Those of us for whom thinking is the dominant function prefer to direct our lives through logic and principle rather than through the senses or intuition.

It is likely that:

- we can be personally detached from the judgements we make because we have an analytical, objective approach to life
- we make decisions on the basis of facts and all the information we have gathered; our personal likes and dislikes are less likely to come into the equation
- we also make decisions on the basis of what we see as right or wrong without mitigating circumstances and do not easily understand others who do not make black and white decisions, but whose nature compels them to take into account the many shades of grey involved in their decision-making process
- we have a deep concern for truth and justice and if we are convinced that what we are doing is right, we do not have to like doing it in order to carry it out
- we can appear cold and uncaring people looking on at the flow of life rather than being active participants
- we take a long overview of life from the outside, rather than a close personal inside look
- we have a very real need to know the reason behind anything we are asked to do or refrain from doing
- we may be introvert or extravert.

IMPLICATIONS FOR STRESS COUNSELLING

Because analytical thinkers need to know the reasons for things, they will endeavour to understand and may need to understand what is going on in the counselling process in order to commit themselves to it. Because they spontaneously react by spotting the flaws in any proposal and then offer blunt and uncompromising criticism of it, they can behave implacably in counselling by urgently and pungently debating the contents of plans of action with little expression of emotion. They may have difficulty in seeing all their life activities as being grist for the counselling mill, but if they do commit themselves to work on their stress, they are likely to attend counselling regularly. Their major dilemma and a possible source of stress for them is that, because they can be so 'all or nothing' in their thinking and so uncompromising in their presentation, their valuable contributions may not be heard by others, unless they can learn how and when to communicate their insights to people of differing personalities. Until and unless they can do this their valid and objective criticism may well be disregarded by those people who probably need it most, those who are paired with them in the judging functions, the 'feelers', who are ruled by people values.

The capacity to think, analyse, harmonize facts with other facts, to make a system and (if an introvert) to think out and rationalize their own personal reactions to the problems and tasks of life as they find them, means that thinkers usually respond well to logical counselling approaches. Intelligibility and thought are often so important that thinkers will find feelings-based counsellors baffling and possibly incompetent. Yet thinkers need to resist the temptation to despise emotion and the irrational, for this is an equally important part of our capacity to think, which needs to find expression in our counselling if it is to find expression in our lives.

Clients who prefer thinking tend to:

- be wary of or even avoid feelings and values in early sessions
- be more at home with rationales and logic
- be critical and sceptical
- need and want to be admired
- be competitors (Bayne 1995: 112).

The strengths of a thinking counsellor are likely to be:

- capacity to be objective
- strong on challenging (Bayne, 1995: 112).

Feeling-type people

Like the thinker those of us of the feeling type are generally concerned with evaluating facts, but judge them not as true or false, but as good or bad, pleasant or unpleasant. We are still somewhat more likely to be women rather than men, but it is questionable how much this is the influence of genes, gender or of environmental and social factors on our psychology. The current moves among young people towards psychological androgyny may well have an effect on the balance of thinkers and feeling people.

It is probable that:

- we are usually much more competent in human relations than are thinkers, because we tend to relate to people on the basis of feeling which is a kinder relationship mode
- we can be indifferent to truth and impervious to logic and easily change our ground without any sense of inconsistency, because feeling has its own logic
- we feed on goodness and judge value, rather than seeking truth and we are closely related to the springs of action
- we can be convinced by our reason that a course of action is right, but we may refrain from acting on that conviction until we feel strongly enough about it
- we are not necessarily illogical or particularly emotional people, but feeling values are the determining factor in our lives
- we are very people-oriented and make decisions on the basis of the effect they are likely to have on those people concerned rather than on a more abstract principle
- we may be introvert or extravert.

IMPLICATIONS FOR STRESS COUNSELLING

Feeling people, being holistic, need to be enveloped by their counselling, to experience and draw meaning from it. Introverted feeling people usually need to experience the affective element of the counselling process, for if it is absent they may be discouraged and feel, and therefore think, that a counselling session has not been helpful at all.

Extraverted feeling clients may have no difficulty in expressing themselves in counselling, but may find it particularly confusing or even irritating that an intuitive counsellor says something that they themselves were just about to say!

Because this group of people value good interpersonal relationships and harmony between people, they may find their concentration is disturbed by any discord around them, even when they are not personally involved in it. This is likely to be a source of stress for them because just as they want to bring about harmony between people, they also want to resolve any inner discord within themselves. They may therefore need the counsellor's encouragement to stay in the difficult places long enough to learn from them and learn through them. Also their awareness of the sensibilities of people of other personalities may lead them to restrict themselves for the sake of others, and counsellors can help by being alert to this self-denying ordinance. Feeling people are inclined to learn best through the study of people rather than the study of abstract concepts.

Clients who prefer feeling tend to:

- keep a focus on values and their networks
- have a need to care about an ideal or value
- make 'too good' clients
- need and want to be appreciated (Bayne 1995: 112).

The strength of counsellors who are feeling people is likely to be:

- that they are warm and caring
- that they are good at empathy (Bayne 1995: 115).

DEVELOPING DIFFERING STYLES OF COUNSELLING FOR DIFFERENT CLIENTS

We have looked at some of the main differences that often characterize the personality style, and therefore to some extent the counselling style, that is, the style of the client in counselling, and the style or the approach used by the counsellor. In practice it is likely that the counselling style of any individual client will contain elements of more than one of these personality styles in varying proportions, according to circumstances. Nevertheless the one particularly used most of the time will be recognizably that of the sensing realist, the experiencing intuitive, the thinking analyst or the feeling person.

There will be occasions upon which clients may, to their own and the counsellor's surprise, show in counselling a personality style which is opposite to their normal one. A sensing realist may use intuition, which is an opposite way of getting information and the information they gather in this way will be different in character. A thinking analyst may occasionally make a decision on the basis of feeling and a feeling person on the basis of analysing the information which arises from the counselling process. A realist who does not normally have a facility with words, who does not like writing and displays little imagination may find themselves moved to write a poem in response to one of life's circumstances. Alternatively, a feeling person may find themselves writing entries in their counselling journal which concentrate on principle rather than people and are brief and analytical.

The aspects that are coming into use in these situations will tend to be their weaker, inferior or less dominant functions of personality; it is as if because these least developed psychological functions are the ones over which they themselves have least control, they give the unconscious or their creative aspect more chance of being heard when under particular stress. It is wise to limit the conscious adoption of those personality styles which differ from our natural patterns. Moving into an alternative way of being or behaving which is out of character for a long period of time is likely to drain the person's energy, instead of being an enabling activity which increases energy.

An intuitive person who undergoes a sensing experience or an analytic thinking person who encounters a feeling one, may need to move out of that and back into their natural function in order to reflect upon or think analytically about that situation. This will help them to integrate it within their psychological framework. Having done that successfully, with hard work, a thinker will then be freer to move again into an expressive feeling mode from time to time to enhance their main personality function.

Finally some wise words for those counsellors who are interested in adapting their approach and interpersonal style to suit their client's personality type, following the style of the authentic chameleon.

If you are an extravert counsellor with an introvert client you might deliberately talk less than usual, or less than you would with an extravert client, or you might discuss the differences between you with your client. Similarly, the counsellor might be more concrete and pragmatic with clients who prefer sensing (but also be aware of their tendency to miss options); more experimental with intuitives (but perhaps also helping them to focus); aware of the tendency of clients with a feeling preference to like to please and therefore to be too good a client, and ready to challenge it gently, because feeling types also tend to be more sensitive to criticism; ready not to press thinking types on their emotions, especially early in counselling; more formal with judging types (but also ready to challenge them to plan some 'play'); and more informal with perceiving types (but also ready to challenge them to plan a little more).

(Bayne, 1995: 113)

Afterword

Although this book may have provided the reader with a useful insight into how we have applied the integrative problem-focused approach to the field of stress counselling and stress management, we believe that both trainee and experienced professionals benefit from ongoing continual professional development which includes further training. Specific training in problem-focused counselling is available at the Centre for Problem Focused Training and Therapy in London. The Centre is run in association with the Centre for Stress Management and the services include a modular training programme for members of the helping professions, counselling services, consulting and training services for organizations, and a mail order service supplying books, questionnaires and audiovisual materials for educational, self-help and professional use.

For further information about training courses held in England on problem-focused counselling and training, rational emotive behaviour therapy, stress counselling and stress management contact:

Centre for Problem Focused Training and Therapy
156 Westcombe Hill
Blackheath
London, SE3 7DH England
Tel: 44 (0) 181 293 4114
Fax: 44 (0) 181 293 1441

In the US, the principle centre for training in REBT is the Albert Ellis Institute in New York. For further information please contact:

Albert Ellis Institute for Rational Emotive Behaviour Therapy
45 East 65th Street
New York
NY 10021–6593
USA
Tel: (001) 212 535 0893

In the appendices of this book we have included a range of forms that you may find useful in your practice of stress counselling and stress management.

We suggest that counsellors and human resources personnel who are interested in the problem-focused approach to work settings also consult *Dealing with People Problems at Work*, S. Palmer and T. Burton, McGraw-Hill, 1996.

The authors would be interested to hear your views and experience of the integrative problem-focused approach. Please write to:

Pat Milner and Stephen Palmer at the Centre for Problem Focused Training and Therapy, London. (Address above.)

References

Abrams, M. and Ellis, A. (1996) Rational emotive behaviour therapy in the treatment of stress. In S. Palmer and W. Dryden (eds), *Stress Management and Counselling: Theory, Practice, Research and Methodology*. London: Cassell.

Allison, T., Cooper, C.L. and Reynolds, P. (1989) Stress counselling in the workplace. *The Psychologist*, 384–8.

Bandura, A. (1986) *Social Foundations of Thought and Action: A Social Cognitive Theory*. Englewood Cliffs: Prentice-Hall.

Bayne, R. (1995) *The Myers-Briggs Type Indicator: A Critical Review and Practical Guide*. London: Chapman and Hall.

Beck, A. T., Rush, A. J., Shaw, B. F. and Emery, G. (1979) *Cognitive Therapy of Depression*. New York: Guilford.

Benson, H. (1976) *The Relaxation Response*. London: Collins.

Bond, M. (1986) *Stress and Self Awareness: a Guide for Nurses*. Oxford: Heinemann.

Bowers, K.S. (1973) Situationism in psychology: an analysis and critique. *Psychology Review*, **80**, 307–35.

Bryant, C. (1983) *Jung and the Christian Way*. London: Darton, Longman and Todd.

Carkhuff, R.R. (1969a) *Helping and Human Relations*, Vol. 1. New York: Holt, Rinehart and Winston.

Carkhuff, R.R. (1969b) *Helping and Human Relations*, Vol. 2. New York: Holt, Rinehart and Winston.

Carkhuff, R.R. (1987) *The Art of Helping* (6th edn). Amherst, MA: Human Resource and Development Press.

Carkhuff, R.R. and Berenson, B.G. (1967) *Beyond Counselling and Therapy*. New York: Holt, Rhinehart and Winston.

Carrington, P. (1993) Modern forms of meditation. In P.M. Lehrer and R.L. Woolfolk (eds), *Principles and Practice of Stress Management* (2nd edn). New York: Emilford Press.

Carroll, M. (1996) *Workplace Counselling*. London: Sage.

Cautela, J.R. (1967) Covert Sensitization. *Psychological Reports*, **20**, 459–68.

Clarke, D. and Palmer, S. (1994a) *Stress Management: Trainer Notes*. Cambridge: National Extension College.

Clarke, D. and Palmer, S. (1994b) *How to Manage Stress*. Cambridge: National Extension College.

Clarke, P. (1996) A person-centred approach to stress management. In S. Palmer and W. Dryden (eds), *Stress Management and Counselling: Theory, Practice, Research and Methodology*. London: Cassell.

Connor, M. (1994) *Training the Counsellor: An Integrative Model*. London: Routledge.

Cooper, C.L. and Cartwright, S. (1996) Stress-management interventions in the workplace: stress counselling and stress audits. In S. Palmer and W. Dryden (eds), *Stress Management and Counselling: Theory, Practice, Research and Methodology*. London: Cassell.

Cooper, C. and Payne, R. (eds) (1988) *Causes, Coping and Consequences of Stress at Work*. Chichester: John Wiley.

Cooper, C.L., Cooper, R. and Eaker, L. (1988) *Living with Stress*. Harmondsworth: Penguin Books.

Cooper, C.L., Sloan S. and Williams, S. (1988) *Occupational Stress Indicator: Management Guide*. Windsor: NFER-Nelson.

Corey, G. (1990) *Theory and Practice of Group Counseling*. Pacific Grove: Brooks Cole Publishing.

Cowen, E.L. (1982) Help is where you find it. *American Psychologist*, **37**, 385–95.

Cox, T. (1993) *Stress Research and Stress Management: Putting Theory to Work*. London: Health and Safety Executive.

Cox, T. and Mackay, C.J. (1976) A psychological model of occupational stress. A paper presented to Medical Research Council meeting Mental Health in Industry. London, November.

Cox, T., Leather, P. and Cox, S. (1990) Stress, health and organisations. *Occupational Health Review*, **23**, 13–18.

Cox, T., Gotts, G., Boot N. and Kerr, J. (1988) Physical exercise, employee fitness and the management of health at work. *Work and Stress*, **2** (1), 71–6.

Culley, S. (1991) *Integrative Counselling Skills in Action*. London: Sage.

Culley, S. (1992) Counselling skills: an integrative framework. In W. Dryden (ed.), *Integrative and Eclectic Therapy: A Handbook*. Milton Keynes: Open University Press.

D'Zurilla, T.J. (1986) *Problem-Solving Therapy: A Social Competence Approach to Clinical Intervention*. New York: Springer Publishing.

Daly, M.J. and Burton, R.L. (1983) Self-esteem and irrational beliefs: an exploratory investigation with implications for counseling. *Journal of Counseling Psychology*, **30**, 361–6.

Dickson, A. (1982) *A Woman In Your Own Right: Assertiveness and You*. London. Quartet.

Dollard, J. and Miller, N.E. (1950) *Personality and Psychotherapy An Analysis in Terms of Learning Thinking and Culture*. New York: McGraw-Hill.

Dryden, W. (1987) *Counselling Individuals: The Rational-Emotive Approach*. London: Sage.

Dryden, W. (ed.) (1989) *Key Issues for Counselling in Action*. London: Sage.

Dryden, W. (1990) *Rational Emotive Counselling in Action*. London: Sage.

Dryden, W. (1994) *Progress in Rational Emotive Behaviour Therapy*. London: Whurr.

Dryden, W. (1995) *Preparing for Client Change in Rational Emotive Behaviour Therapy*. London: Whurr.

Dryden, W. and Gordon, J. (1990) *Think Your Way to Happiness*. London: Sheldon.

Dryden, W. and Gordon, J. (1992) *Think Rationally: A Brief Guide to Overcoming Your Emotional Problems*. London: Centre for Rational Emotive Behaviour Therapy.

Dryden, W. and Gordon, J. (1993) *Peak Performance: Become More Effective at Work*. Didcot: Mercury Business Books.

Dryden, W. and Norcross, J. (eds) (1990) *Eclecticism and Integration in Counselling and Psychotherapy*. London: Gale Centre Publications.

D'Zurilla, T. J. and Nezu, A. (1982). Social problem solving in adults. In P. C. Kendall (ed.), *Advances in Cognitive-behavioural Research and Therapy* (vol. 1). New York: Academic Press.

Egan, G. (1975, 1982, 1986, 1990, 1994) *The Skilled Helper: A Problem Management Approach to Helping*. Pacific Grove, CA: Brooks/Cole.

Egan, G. and Cowan, M. (1979) *People in Systems: A Model for Development in the Human Service Professions and Education*. Pacific Grove, CA: Brooks/Cole.

Elkin, A.J. and Rosch, P.J. (1990) Promoting mental health at work. *Occupational Medicine State of the Art Review*, **5**, 739–54.

Ellingham, I. (1995) Quest for a paradigm: person-centred counselling vs. psychodynamic counselling. *Counselling: Journal of the British Association for Counselling*, **6** (4), 288–90. Also in S. Palmer, S. Dainow and P. Milner (eds, 1996), *Counselling: The BAC Counselling Reader*. London; Sage.

Ellis, A. (1962) *Reason and Emotion in Psychotherapy*. Secaucus, NJ: Citadel.

Ellis, A. (1976) The biological basis of human irrationality. *Journal of Individual Psychology*, **32** (145), 68. (Reprinted, Institute for Rational Emotive Therapy, New York, 1976.)

Ellis, A. (1979) The practice of rational-emotive therapy. In A. Ellis and J.M. Whiteley (eds), *Theoretical and Empirical Foundations of Rational-Emotive Therapy*. Monterey, CA: Brooks/Cole.

Ellis, A. (1983) How to deal with your most difficult client, you. *Journal of Rational-Emotive Therapy*, **1**, 3–8.

Ellis, A. (1994) *Reason and Emotion in Psychotherapy: Revised and expanded edition*. New York: Birch Lane Press.

Ellis, A. (1996) *Better, Deeper and More Enduring Brief Therapy*. New York: Brunner-Mazel.

Ellis, A. and DiMattia, D. (1991) *Self Management: Strategies for Personal Success*. New York: Institute for Rational-Emotive Therapy.

Ellis, A. and Dryden, W. (1987) *The Practice of Rational Emotive Therapy*. New York: Springer.

Ellis, A., Gordon, J., Neenan, M. and Palmer, S. (1997) *Stress Counselling: A Rational Emotive Behaviour Approach*. London: Cassell.

Ellis, A. and Harper, R.A. (1997) *A Guide to Rational Living*. North Hollywood, CA: Wilshire.

Eysenck, H.J. (1967) *The Biological Basis of Personality*. Springfield, IL: C.C. Thomas.

Falloon, I.R.H. (1991) Behavioral family therapy. In A.S. Gurman and D. Kniskern (eds), *Handbook of Family Therapy*. New York: Brunner/Mazel.

Falloon, I.R.H., Laporta, M., Fadden, G. and Graham-Hole, V. (1993) *Managing Stress in Families*. London: Routledge.

Feller, R. (1984) *Job Search Agreements*. Monograph: Colorado State University.

Feltham, C. and Dryden, W. (1993) *Dictionary of Counselling*. London: Whurr.

Fennell, M.J.V. (1989) Depression. In K. Hawton, P. Salkovskis, J. Kirk and D. Clark (eds), *Cognitive Behaviour Therapy for Psychiatric Problems: A Practical Guide*. Oxford: Oxford University Press.

Fowke, R. (1992) Personality and prayer. Clinical Theology Association Newsletter, No. 60. July 1992.

Frank, J.D. (1982) Therapeutic components shared by all psychotherapies. In J.H. Harvey and M.M. Parks (eds), *Psychotherapy Research and Behavior Change: 1981 Master Lecture Series*. Washington DC: American Psychological Association.

Frankl, V.E. (1960) Paradoxical intention: a logotherapeutic technique. *American Journal of Psychotherapy*, **14**, 520–35.

Friedman, M. and Ulmer, D. (1985) *Treating Type A Behaviour and Your Heart*. London: Michael Joseph.

Gale, D. (1990) *What is Psychodrama?* Loughton: Gale Centre Publications.

Ganster, D. and Victor, B. (1988) The impact of social support on mental and physical health. *British Journal of Medical Psychology*, **61**, (1), 17–36.

Garfield, S.L. (1980) *Psychotherapy: An Eclectic Approach*. New York: Wiley.

Gendlin, E. (1981) *Focusing*. New York: Everest House.

Goddard, K. (1993) In defence of the past: a response to Ron Wilgosh. *Counselling: Journal of the British Association for Counselling*, **4**, 205–6. Also in S. Palmer, S. Dainow and P. Milner (eds, 1996). *Counselling: The BAC Counselling Reader*. London: Sage

Goldstein, A.P. (1975) Relationship enhancement methods. In F.H. Kanfer and A.P. Goldstein (eds), *Helping People Change*. New York: Pergamon.

Gore, S. (1978) The effect of social support in moderating the health consequences of unemployment. *Journal of Health and Social Behaviour*, **19**, 157–65.

Hall, C.S. and Lindsey, G. (1970) *Theories of Personality* (2nd edn). New York: Wiley.

Hartland, J. (1987) *Medical and Dental Hypnosis and Its Clinical Applications*. London: Bailliere Tindall.

Hawton, K. and Catalan, J. (1987) *Attempted Suicide: A Practical Guide to its Nature and Management* (2nd edn). Oxford: Oxford University Press.

Hawton, K. and Kirk, J. (1989) Problem solving. In K. Hawton, P. Salkovskis, J. Kirk and D. Clark (eds), *Cognitive Behaviour Therapy for Psychiatric Problems: A Practical Guide*. Oxford: Oxford University Press.

Henry, J.P. (1980) Present concept of stress theory. In E. Usdin, R. Kvetnansky and I.J. Kopin (eds), *Catecholamines and Stress: Recent Advances*. New York: Elsevier/North-Holland.

Henry, J.P., Kross, M.E., Stephens, P.M. and Watson, F.M.C. (1976) Evidence that differing psychological stimuli lead to adrenal cortical stimulation by autonomic pathways. In E. Usdin, R. Kvetnansky and I.J. Kopin (eds), *Catecholamines and Stress*, Oxford: Pergamon Press.

Inskipp, F. (1996) *Skills Training for Counselling*. London: Cassell.

Ivey, A.E. (1983) *Intentional Interviewing and Counselling*. Monterey, CA: Brooks/Cole.

Ivey, A.E. (1995) *Intentional Interviewing and Counselling: Facilitating Client Development in a Multicultural Society*. Pacific Grove, CA: Brooks/Cole.

Jacobson, E. (1938) *Progressive Relaxation*. Chicago: University of Chicago Press.

James, W. (1975 [1906]) *Pragmatism and the Meaning of Truth*. Cambridge, MA and London: Harvard University Press.

Jung, C.G. (1976) Psychological Types. In *Collected Works*, Vol. 6. London: Routledge and Kegan

Karasek, R.A. (1981) Job socialisation and job strain: the implications of two psychosocial mechanisms for job design. In B. Gardell and G. Johansson (eds), *Working Life: A Social Science Contribution to Work Reform*. Chichester: Wiley.

Karasu, T.B. (1977) Psychotherapies: an overview. *American Journal of Psychiatry*, **134**, 851–63.

Karasu, T.B. (1986) The specificity versus non-specificity dilemma: toward identifying therapeutic change agents. *American Journal of Psychiatry*, **143**, 687–95.

Kelly, G.A. (1955) *The Psychology of Personal Constructs*. New York: Norton.

Kirchner, J.H. and Hogan, R.A. (1966) The therapist variable in the implosion of phobias. *Psychotherapy: Theory, Research and Practice*, **3**, 102–4.

Kramer, D. (1992) *Personality and Psychotherapy: Theory, Practice and Research*. Milton Keynes: Open University Press.

Landreth, G.L. (1984) Encountering Carl Rogers: his views on facilitating groups. *American Personnel and Guidance Journal*, **62**, 323–26.

Laungani, P. (1995) Can psychotherapies seriously damage your health? *Counselling: Journal of British Association for Counselling*, **6**, (2), 110–15.

Lazarus, A.A. (1973) 'Hypnosis' as a facilitator in behavior therapy. *International Journal of Nervous and Mental Disease*, **156**, 404–11.

Lazarus, A.A. (1977) Toward an egoless state of being. In A. Ellis and R. Grieger (eds), *Handbook of Rational-Emotive Therapy*. New York: Springer.

Lazarus, A.A. (1981) *The Practice of Multimodal Therapy*. New York: McGraw-Hill.

Lazarus, A.A. (1984) *In the Mind's Eye*. New York: Guilford Press.

Lazarus, A.A. (1987) The multimodal approach with adult outpatients. In N.S. Jacobson (ed.), *Psychotherapists in Clinical Practice*. New York: Guilford Press.

Lazarus, A.A. (1989) *The Practice of Multimodal Therapy*. Baltimore, MD: Johns Hopkins University Press.

Lazarus, A.A. (1993) Tailoring the therapeutic relationship, or being an authentic chameleon. *Psychotherapy*, 3, 404–7.

Lazarus, R.S. and Folkman, R. (1984) *Stress, Appraisal and Coping*. New York: Springer.

Lazarus, A.A. and Lazarus, C.N. (1991) *Multimodal Life History Inventory*. Champaign, IL: Research Press.

Lazarus, A.A., Lazarus, C.N. and Fay, A. (1993) *Don't Believe it for a Minute: Forty Toxic Ideas that are Driving You Crazy*. San Luis Obispo, CA: Impact.

Levine, M. (1986) *The Principles of Effective Problem Solving*. Englewood Cliffs, NJ: Prentice Hall.

McCrae, R.R. and Costa, P.T. (1995) Toward a new generation of personality theories: theoretical contexts for the five factor model. In J Wiggins (ed), *The Five Factor Model of Personality: Theoretical Perspectives*. New York: Plenum.

McGuigan, F.J. (1993) Progressive relaxation: origins, principles, and clinical applications. In P.M. Lehrer and R.L. Woolfolk (eds), *Principles and Practice of Stress Management* (2nd edn). New York: Guilford Press.

McLeod, J. and Wheeler, S. (1995) Person-centred and psychodynamic counselling: a dialogue. *Counselling: Journal of British Association for Counselling* 6, (4), 283–7. Also in S. Palmer, S. Dainow and P. Milner (eds, 1996), *Counselling: The BAC Counselling Reader*. London: Sage.

McMullin, R.E. (1986) *Handbook of Cognitive Therapy*. New York: Norton.

Marks, I.M. (1986) *Living with Fear*. New York: McGraw-Hill.

Marks, I.M. (1987) Nightmares. *Integr. Psychiatry*, 5, 71–81.

Maslow, A.H. (1969) *Motivation and Personality* (2nd edn). New York: Harper and Row.

Maultsby, M.C. Jr (1975) *Rational Behavior Therapy*. Englewood Cliffs, NJ: Prentice-Hall.

May, R. (ed.) (1961) *Existential Psychology*. New York: Random House.

Mearns D. and McLeod, J. (1984) A person-centred approach to Research. In R.F. Levant and J.M. Schlien (eds), *Client-Centred Therapy and The Person-Centred Approach: New Directions in Theory, Research and Practice* (pp. 370–89). New York: Praeger.

Mearns D. and Thorne, B. (1988) *Person-Centred Counselling in Action*. London: Sage.

Mehrabian, A. (1971) *Silent Messages*. Belmont, CA.: Wadsworth.

Milner, P. (1974) *Counselling in Education*. London. Dent.

Milner, P. (1980) *Counselling in Education*. London: Milner.

Morris, D. (1994) *Body Talk*. London: Jonathan Cape.

Mowrer, O. (1960) *Learning Theory and Behaviour*. New York: Wiley.

Muss, D. (1991) *The Trauma Trap*. London: Doubleday.

Myers, I.B. and Myers, P. (1995) *Gifts Differing: Understanding Personality Type*. Paolo Alto, CA: Davies Black.

Naylor-Smith, A. (1994) Counselling and psychotherapy: is there a difference? *Counselling: Journal of the British Association for Counselling*, 5 (4), 284–6. Also in S. Palmer, S. Dainow and P. Milner (eds, 1996), *Counselling: The BAC Counselling Reader*. London: Sage.

Neenan, M. and Palmer, S. (1996) Stress counselling: a cognitive-behavioural perspective. *Stress News*, 8 (4), 5–8.

Nelson-Jones, R. (1988) *Practical Counselling and Helping Skills*. London: Cassell.

Nelson-Jones, R. (1989) *Effective Thinking Skills: Preventing and Managing Personal Problems*. London: Cassell.

Nelson-Jones, R. (1994) Hello DASIE! Introducing the lifeskills helping model. *Counselling: Journal of British Association for Counselling*, 5 (2), 109–12. Also in S. Palmer, S. Dainow and P. Milner (eds, 1996), *Counselling: The BAC Counselling Reader*. London: Sage.

Nelson-Jones, R. (1995) Lifeskills counselling. In R. Nelson-Jones (ed.) *Counselling and Personality: Theory and Practice*. Sydney. Allen and Unwin

Nelson-Jones, R. (1996a) The STC of lifeskills counselling. *Counselling: Journal of British Association for Counselling*, **7** (1), 46–9.

Nelson-Jones, R. (1996b) *Relating Skills: A Practical Guide to Effective Personal Relationships*. London: Cassell.

Norcross, J.C. (ed.) (1986) *Handbook of Eclectic Psychotherapy*. New York: Brunner-Mazel.

Palmer, S. (1988) *Personal Stress Management Programme Manual*. London: Centre for Stress Management.

Palmer, S. (1989) The use of stability zones, rituals and routines to reduce or prevent stress. *Stress News*, **1** (3), 3–5.

Palmer, S. (1990a) Stress mapping: a visual technique to aid counselling or training. *Employee Counselling Today*, **2**, 9–12.

Palmer, S. (1990b) *Assertion, Journal for Women in the GMB, Northern Region*. Newcastle: GMB.

Palmer, S. (1991a) Behaviour therapy and its application to stress management. *Health and Hygiene*, **12**, 29–34.

Palmer, S. (1991b) Holiday stress: fact or fiction. *Counselling News*, September, 14–15.

Palmer, S. (1992) Guidelines and contra-indications for teaching relaxation as a stress management technique. *Journal of the Institute of Health Education*, **30** (1), 25–30.

Palmer, S. (1993a) The 'Deserted Island Technique': a method of demonstrating how preferential and musturbatory beliefs can lead to different emotions. *Rational-Emotive Therapist*, **1** (1), 12–14.

Palmer, S. (1993b) *Multimodal Techniques: Relaxation and Hypnosis*. London: Centre for Stress Management and Centre for Multimodal Therapy.

Palmer, S. (1993c) Occupational stress: its causes and alleviation. In W. Dekker (ed.), *Chief Executive International*. London: Sterling Publications.

Palmer, S. (1995) A comprehensive approach to industrial rational emotive behaviour stress management workshops. *Rational Emotive Behaviour Therapist*, **3** (1), 45–55.

Palmer, S. (1995a) The stresses of running a stress management centre. In W. Dryden (ed.), *The Stresses of Counselling in Action*. London: Sage.

Palmer, S. (1996a) Developing stress management programmes. In R. Woolfe and W. Dryden (eds), *Handbook of Counselling Psychology*. London: Sage.

Palmer, S. (1996b) The multimodal approach: theory, assessment, techniques and interventions. In S. Palmer and W. Dryden (eds), *Stress Management and Counselling: Theory, Practice, Research and Methodology*. London: Cassell.

Palmer, S. (1997a) Modality assessment. In S. Palmer and G. McMahon (eds), *Client Assessment*. London: Sage.

Palmer, S. (1997b) Multimodal Therapy. In C. Feltham (ed.), *Which Psychotherapy?* London: Sage.

Palmer, S. (1997c) Problem focused stress counselling and stress management training: an intrinsically brief integrative approach, Part 1. *Stress News*, **9** (1), 7–12.

Palmer, S. (1997b) Problem focused stress counselling and stress management training: an intrinsically brief integrative approach. *Stress News*, **9** (2), 6–10.

Palmer, S. (1997e) Self-acceptance: concept, techniques and interventions. *Rational-Emotive Behaviour Therapist*, **5** (1), 4–30.

Palmer, S. and Burton, T. (1996) *Dealing with People Problems at Work*. Maidenhead: McGraw-Hill.

Palmer, S., Dainow, S. and Milner, P. (eds) (1996) *Counselling: The BAC Counselling Reader*. London: Sage.

Palmer, S. and Dryden, W. (1995) *Counselling for Stress Problems*. London: Sage.

Palmer, S. and Dryden, W. (1996) *Stress Management and Counselling: Theory, Practice, Research and Methodology*. London: Cassell.

Palmer, S. and Stickland, L. (1996) *Stress Management: A Quick Guide*. Dunstable: Folens Publishing.

Palmer, S. and Szymanska, K. (1994) Referral guidance for participants attending stress management training courses. *Stress News*, **5** (4), 11.

Perlman, H.H. (1957) *Social Casework: A Problem Solving Process*. Chicago: University of Chicago Press.

Perlman, H.H. (1970) The problem-solving model in social casework. In R.W. Roberts and R.H. Nee (eds) *Theories of Social Casework* Chicago: University of Chicago Press.

Quick, J.C. and Quick J.D. (1984) *Organisational Stress and Preventive Management*. New York: McGraw Hill.

Rogers, C.R. (1957) The necessary and sufficient conditions of therapeutic personality change. *Journal of Consulting Psychology*, **21**, 95–103.

Rogers, C. R. (1961) *On Becoming a Person*. Boston: Houghton Mifflin.

Rogers, C. R. (1980) *A Way of Being*. Boston: Houghton Mifflin.

Rogers, C.R., Gendlin, E., Kiesler, T.D. and Trua, C.B. (eds) (1967) *The Therapeutic Relationship and its Impact: A Study of Psychotherapy with Schizophrenics*. Madison: University of Wisconsin Press.

Ross, R.R. and Altmaier, E.M. (1994) *Intervention in Occupational Stress*. London: Sage.

Rowe, D. (1988) *The Successful Self*. London: HarperCollins.

Rowe, D. (1995) *Guide to Life*. London: HarperCollins.

Rozenzweig, S. (1936) Some implicit common factors in diverse methods of psychotherapy. *American Journal of Orthopsychiatry*, **6**, 412–15.

Salkovskis, P. and Kirk, J. (1989) Obsessional disorders. In K. Hawton, P. Salkovskis, J. Kirk and D. Clarke (eds), *Cognitive-Behavioural Therapy for Psychiatric Problems: A Practical Guide*. Oxford: Oxford University Press.

Selye, H. (1956) *Stress of Life*. New York: McGraw-Hill.

Sheldon, W. H., Stevens, S. S. and Tucker, W. B. (1940) *The Varieties of Human Physique*. New York: Harper and Row.

Sloan, S., and Cooper, C. (1986) *Pilots Under Stress*. London: Routledge and Kegan Paul.

Thorne B. (1997) Counselling and psychotherapy: the sickness and the prognosis. In S. Palmer and V. Varma (eds), *The Future of Counselling and Psychotherapy*. London: Sage.

Trower, P., Casey, A. and Dryden, W. (1988) *Cognitive-Behavioural Counselling in Action*. London: Sage.

Tyler, L. E. (1969) *The Work of the Counsellor*. New York: Appleton Century Crofts.

Wasik, B. (1984) Teaching parents effective problem solving: a handbook for professionals. Unpublished manuscript. Chapel Hill: University of North Carolina.

Wessler, R.A. and Wessler, R.L. (1980) *The Principles and Practice of Rational-Emotive Therapy*. San Francisco: Jossey-Bass.

White, J. and Keenan, M. (1990) Stress control: a pilot study of large group therapy for generalised anxiety disorder. *Behavioural Psychotherapy*, **18**, 143–6.

White, J., Keenan, M. and Brookes, N. (1992) Stress control: a controlled comparative investigation of large group therapy for generalised anxiety disorder, *Behavioural Psychotherapy*, **20**, 97–114.

Wilgosh, R. (1993) How can we see where we're going if we're always looking backwards? *Counselling: Journal of British Association for Counselling*, **4** (2), 98–101. Also in S. Palmer, S. Dainow and P. Milner (eds, 1996), *Counselling: The BAC Counselling Reader*. London: Sage.

Wolpe, J. and Lazarus, A.A. (1966) *Behavior Therapy Techniques*. New York: Pergamon.

Yalom, I. (1985) *The Theory and Practice of Group Psychotherapy* (3rd edn). New York: Basic Books.

Issues for the Client to Consider in Counselling or Psychotherapy

1. Here is a list of topics or questions you may wish to raise when attending your first counselling (assessment) session:

a. Check that your counsellor has relevant qualifications and experience in the field of counselling/psychotherapy.

b. Ask about the type of approach the counsellor uses, and how it relates to your problem.

c. Ask if the counsellor is in supervision (most professional bodies consider supervision to be mandatory; see footnote).

d. Ask whether the counsellor or the counselling agency is a member of a professional body and abides by a code of ethics. If possible obtain a copy of the code.

e. Discuss your goals/expectations of counselling.

f. Ask about the fees if any (if your income is low, check if the counsellor operates on a sliding scale) and discuss the frequency and estimated duration of counselling.

g. Arrange regular review sessions with your counsellor to evaluate your progress.

h. Do not enter into a long term counselling contract unless you are satisfied that this is necessary and beneficial to you.

If you do not have a chance to discuss the above points during your first session discuss them at the next possible opportunity.

GENERAL ISSUES

2. Counsellor self-disclosure can sometimes be therapeutically useful. However, if the sessions are dominated by the counsellor discussing his/her own problems at length, raise this issue in the counselling session.

3. If at any time you feel discounted, undermined or manipulated within the session, discuss this with the counsellor. It is easier to resolve issues as and when they arise.

4. Do not accept significant gifts from your counsellor. This does not apply to relevant therapeutic material.

5. Do not accept social invitations from your counsellor. For example dining

in a restaurant or going for a drink. However, this does not apply to relevant therapeutic assignments such as being accompanied by your counsellor into a situation to help you overcome a phobia.

6. If your counsellor proposes a change in venue for the counselling sessions without good reason do not agree. For example, from a centre to the counsellor's own home.

7. Research has shown that it is not beneficial for clients to have sexual contact with their counsellor. Professional bodies in the field of counselling and psychotherapy consider that it is unethical for counsellors or therapists to engage in sexual activity with current clients.

8. If you have any doubts about the counselling you are receiving then discuss them with your counsellor. If you are still uncertain, seek advice, perhaps from a friend, your doctor, your local Citizens Advice Bureau, the professional body your counsellor belongs to or the counselling agency that may employ your counsellor.

9. You have the right to terminate counselling whenever you choose.

Footnote: Counselling supervision is a formal arrangement where counsellors discuss their counselling in a confidential setting on a regular basis with one or more professional counsellors.

APPENDIX 2
Problem Facilitating Form

Workplace/other Problem A	Thinking Interfering With Problem-Solving B	Emotional/Behavioural/ Physical Reaction (C)	Thinking Facilitating Problem-Solving (D)	New & Effective Approach to Problem (E)

Seven-Step Problem-Focused Form

STEP 1: IDENTIFY THE PROBLEM
What is the problem.

_____

_____

_____

STEP 2: SELECT GOALS
Select specific, realistic, substantial and verfiable goal(s).

_____

_____

_____

_____

STEP 3: EXPLORE OPTIONS
Write down possible ways of reaching your goals.

_____

_____

_____

_____

_____

_____

STEP 4: CONSIDER THE CONSEQUENCES
Weigh up the pros and cons of the different options/solutions.

_____

_____

_____

_____

_____

_____

_____

STEP 5: TAKE DECISIONS
Choose the most feasible solution.

_____

_____

_____

_____

STEP 6: AGREE ACTIONS
Develop a step by step action plan.

_____

_____

_____

_____

STEP 7: EVALUATE THE STRATEGY
Focus on achievement. Review and revise plan as necessary.

_____

_____

_____

Source: Palmer (1997c, d)

APPENDIX 4

Action Plan

Action Plan for .... (Name) Made on .... (date)

Action to be taken: _____

_____

Resources needed: _____

_____

Start date: _____ Date for review _____

_____

Action to be taken: _____

_____

Resources needed: _____

_____

Start date: _____ Date for review _____

_____

Action to be taken: _____

_____

Resources needed: _____

_____

Start date: _____ Date for review _____

APPENDIX 5
Individual Assignment Record

Name .... Date .... Negotiated with ....

Agreed assignment:

The purpose(s) of the assignment:

What obstacles, if any, stand in the way of your completing this assignment and how can you

overcome them?

Obstacle   To be overcome by

1

2

3

4

Signed ....

Irrational Belief: Cost Benefit Form

Irrational Belief: ....

....

....

Advantages	Disadvantages

N.B. An irrational belief consists of a rigid and unqualified must, should, have to, got to, ought and a derivative which is usually awfulizing, I-can't-stand-it-itis (LFT) or damnation of self and/or others.

Rational Belief: Cost Benefit Form

Rational Belief: ....

....

....

Advantages	Disadvantages

N.B. A rational belief consists of a flexible preference, wish, want, desire and a derivative which is usually de-awfulizing, I can stand it (HFT) or acceptance of self and/or others.

APPENDIX 8

Relaxation Diary

RELAXATION DIARY

Name:

Date	Session		Time in minutes	Relaxation Technique used	Tension Levels Relaxed - 0 Tense - 10		Feelings		Comments
	began	ended			before	after	during	after	

Instructions: Note the date, time, duration and type of relaxation exercise used. On a scale of 0–10, where 0 represents a relaxed state and 10 represents a tense state, write down scores before and after a training exercise. Monitor emotions and bodily feelings in the appropriate column. Record any variations to the technique used and any other comments.

Source: Palmer, 1993b

Homework Diary

Name ....

Week commencing: ....

Goals for the week

1.
2.
3.
4.

Anxiety scale:

0	2	4	6	8
no anxiety	slight anxiety	moderate anxiety	marked anxiety	panic/high anxiety

| Session | | Goal no. | Task performed | Anxiety | | | Comments incl. coping tactics |
Date	Began	Ended			Before	During	After	

Source: Palmer, 1991a

APPENDIX 10

Assertiveness Problem Hierarchy Form

Name

Date

1

2

3

4

5

6

7

8

9

10

Continue if necessary

Source: Palmer and Dryden (1995: 244)

APPENDIX 11
Assertiveness Behaviour Diary

Name:

Date	Describe Situation	Person/people involved	Assertiveness skills used	Evaluation of skills	Areas for improvement

Source: Palmer and Dryden (1995: 245)

APPENDIX 12

Stress Management Plan

Stress management plan

Date _____

Action to be taken _____

_____

_____

_____

_____

_____

_____

_____

_____

_____

_____

_____

_____

_____

_____

_____

_____

_____

_____

_____

_____

_____

_____

Source: Palmer, 1988

Index

BRITISH ASSOCIATION for COUNSELLING

Code of Ethics and Practice for Counsellors
(*January 1998*)

1. Status of this Code

In response to the experience of members of BAC, this code is a revision of the (1992) 1993 code, amended by the Management Committee (May 1996).

2. Introduction

2.1 The purpose of this code is to establish and maintain standards for counsellors who are members of BAC, and to inform and protect people who seek or use their services.

2.2 All members of this Association are required to abide by the current codes appropriate to them. Implicit in these codes is a common frame of references within which members manage their responsibilities to clients, colleagues, members of BAC and the wider community. No code can resolve all issues relating to ethics and practice. In this code we aim to provide a framework for addressing ethical issues and encouraging best possible levels of practice. Members must determine which parts apply to particular settings, taking account of any conflicting responsibilities.

2.3 The Association has a Complaints Procedure which can lead to the expulsion of members for breaches of its Codes of Ethics and Practice.

3. The Nature of Counselling

3.1 The overall aim of counselling is to provide an opportunity for the client to work towards living in a way he or she experiences as more satisfying and resourceful. The term 'counselling' includes work with individuals, pairs or groups of people often, but not always, referred to as 'clients'. The objectives of particular counselling relationships will vary according to the client's needs. Counselling may be concerned with developmental issues, addressing and resolving specific problems, making decisions, coping with crisis, developing personal insight and knowledge, working through feelings of inner conflict or improving relationships with others. The counsellor's role is to facilitate the client's work in ways which respect the client's values, personal resources and capacity for choice within his or her cultural context.

3.2 Counselling involves a deliberately undertaken contract with clearly agreed boundaries and commitment to privacy and confidentiality. It requires explicit and informed agreement. The use of counselling skills in other contexts, paid or voluntary, is subject to the Code of Ethics and Practice for Counselling Skills.

3.3 There is no generally accepted distinction between counselling and psychotherapy. There are well founded traditions which use the terms interchangeably and others which distinguish between them. Regardless of the theoretical approaches preferred by individual counsellors, there are ethical issues which are common to all counselling situations.

4. **Equal Opportunities Policy Statement**
All BAC members abide by its Equal Opportunities Policy statement. The full statement can be found at the end of this Code.

5. **The Structure of this Code**
This code has been divided into two parts. The Code of Ethics outlines the fundamental values of counselling and a number of general principles arising from these. The Code of Practice applies these principles to the counselling situation.

A. **CODE OF ETHICS**
Values
Counsellors' basic values are integrity, impartiality and respect.

A.1 **Responsibility**
All reasonable steps should be taken to ensure the client's safety during counselling sessions. Counselling is a non-exploitative activity. Counsellors must take the same degree of care to work ethically whatever the setting or the financial basis of the counselling contract.

A.2 **Anti-discriminatory Practice**
Counsellors must consider and address their own prejudices and stereotyping and ensure that an anti-discriminatory approach is integral to their counselling practice.

A.3 **Confidentiality**
Counsellors offer the highest possible levels of confidentiality in order to respect the client's privacy and create the trust necessary for counselling.

A.4 **Contracts**
The terms and conditions on which counselling is offered shall be made clear to clients before counselling begins. Subsequent revision of these terms should be agreed in advance of any changes.

A.5 **Boundaries**
Counsellors must establish and maintain appropriate boundaries around the counselling relationship. Counsellors must take into account the effects of any overlapping or pre-existing relationships.

A.6   **Competence**
        Counsellors shall take all reasonable steps to monitor and develop their own
        competence and to work within the limits of that competence. Counsellors
        must have appropriate, regular and ongoing counselling supervision.

B.   **CODE OF PRACTICE**
        Introduction
        This code applies these values and ethical principles outlined above to more
        specific situations which may arise in the practice of counselling. The
        sections and clauses are arranged in the order of the ethics section and
        under the same headings. No clause or section should be read in isolation
        from the rest of the Code.

B.1   **Issues of Responsibility**
B.1.1   The counsellor–client relationship is the foremost ethical concern. However,
        counselling does not exist in social isolation. Counsellors may need to
        consider other sources of ethical responsibility. The headings in this section
        are intended to draw attention to some of these.

B.1.2   Counsellors take responsibility for clinical/therapeutic decisions in their
        work with clients.

B.1.3   Responsibility to the Client

        Client Safety
B.1.3.1 Counsellors must take all reasonable steps to ensure that the client suffers
        neither physical nor psychological harm during counselling sessions.

B.1.3.2 Counsellors must not exploit their clients financially, sexually, emotionally,
        or in any other way. Suggesting or engaging in sexual activity with a client
        is unethical.

B.1.3.3. Counsellors must provide privacy for counselling sessions. The sessions
        should not be overheard, recorded or observed by anyone other than the
        counsellor without informed consent from the client. Normally any record-
        ing would be discussed as part of the contract. Care must be taken that
        sessions are not interrupted.

        Client Self-determination
B.1.3.4 In counselling the balance of power is unequal and counsellors must take
        care not to abuse their power.

B.1.3.5 Counsellors do not normally act on behalf of their clients. If they do, it will
        be only at the express request of the client, or else in exceptional
        circumstances.

B.1.3.6 Counsellors do not normally give advice.

B.1.3.7 Counsellors have a responsibility to establish with clients, at the outset of
        counselling, the existence of any other therapeutic or helping relationships
        in which the client is involved and to consider whether counselling is
        appropriate. Counsellors should gain the client's permission before confer-
        ring in any way with other professional workers.

Breaks and Endings
B.1.3.8 Counsellors work with clients to reach a recognised ending when clients have received the help they sought or when it is apparent that counselling is no longer helping or when clients wish to end.

B.1.3.9 External circumstances may lead to endings for other reasons which are not therapeutic. Counsellors must make arrangements for care to be taken of the immediate needs of clients in the event of any sudden and unforeseen endings by the counsellor or breaks to the counselling relationship.

B.1.2.10 Counsellors should take care to prepare their clients appropriately for any planned breaks from counselling. They should take any necessary steps to ensure the well-being of their clients during such breaks.

B.1.4 Responsibility to other Counsellors
B.1.4.1 Counsellors must not conduct themselves in their counselling-related activities in ways which undermine public confidence either in their role as a counsellor or in the work of other counsellors.

B.1.4.2 A counsellor who suspects misconduct by another counsellor, which cannot be resolved or remedied after discussion with the counsellor concerned, should implement the Complaints Procedure, doing so without breaches of confidentiality other than those necessary for investigating the complaint.

B.1.5 Responsibility to Colleagues and Others
B.1.5.1 Counsellors are accountable for their services to colleagues, employers and funding bodies as appropriate. At the same time they must respect the privacy, needs and autonomy of the client as well as the contract of confidentiality agreed with the client.

B.1.5.2 No one should be led to believe that a service is being offered by the counsellor which is not in fact being offered as this may deprive the client of the offer of such a service from elsewhere.

B.1.5.3 Counsellors must play a demonstrable part in exploring and resolving conflicts of interest between themselves and their employers or agencies, especially where this affects the ethical delivery of counselling to clients.

B.1.6 Responsibility to the Wider Community
Law
B.1.6.1 Counsellors must take all reasonable steps to be aware of current law as it applies to their counselling practice. (See BAC Information Guide 1 'Counselling, Confidentiality and the Law').

Research
B.1.6.2 Counsellors must conduct any research in accordance with BAC guidelines (see BAC Information Guide 4 'Ethical Guidelines for Monitoring, Evaluation and Research in Counselling').

Resolving Conflicts between Ethical Priorities
B.1.6.3 Counsellors may find themselves caught between conflicting ethical principles, which could involve issues of public interest. In these circumstances, they are urged to consider the particular situation in which they find themselves and to discuss the situation with their counselling supervisor

and/or other experienced counsellors. Even after conscientious consideration of the salient issues, some ethical dilemmas cannot be resolved easily or wholly satisfactorily.

B.2   **Anti-discriminatory Practice**
       Client Respect
B.2.1 Counsellors work with clients in ways that affirm both the common humanity and the uniqueness of each individual.

       They must be sensitive to the cultural context and world view of the client, for instance whether the individual, family or the community is taken as central.

       Client Autonomy
B.2.2. Counsellors are responsible for working in ways which respect and promote the client's ability to make decisions in the light of his/her own beliefs, values and context.

       Counsellor Awareness
B.2.3 Counsellors are responsible for ensuring that any problems with mutual comprehension due to language, cultural differences or for any other reason are addressed at an early stage. The use of an interpreter needs to be carefully considered at the outset of counselling.

B.2.4 Counsellors have a responsibility to consider and address their own prejudices and stereotyping attitudes and behaviour and particularly to consider ways in which these may be affecting the counselling relationship and influencing their responses.

B.3   Confidentiality
B.3.1 Confidentiality is a means of providing the client with safety and privacy and thus protects client autonomy. For this reason any limitation on the degree of confidentiality is likely to diminish the effectiveness of counselling.

B.3.2. The counselling contract will include an agreement about the level and limits of confidentiality offered. This agreement can be reviewed and changed by negotiation between counsellor and client. Agreements about confidentiality continue after the client's death unless there are overriding legal or ethical considerations.

B.3.3 Settings
B.3.3.1 Counsellors must ensure that they have taken all reasonable steps to inform the client of any limitations to confidentiality that arise within the setting of the counselling work, e.g updating doctors in primary care, team case discussion in agencies. These are made explicit through clear contracting.

B.3.3.2 Many settings place additional specific limitations on confidentiality. Counsellors considering working in these settings must think about the impact of such limitations on their practice and decide whether or not to work in such settings.

B.3.4 Exceptional Circumstances
B.3.4.1 Exceptional circumstances may arise which give the counsellor good grounds for believing that serious harm may occur to the client or to other people.

In such circumstances the client's consent to a change in the agreement about confidentiality should be sought whenever possible unless there are also good grounds for believing the client is no longer willing or able to take responsibility for his/her actions. Normally, the decision to break confidentiality should be discussed with the client and should be made only after consultation with the counselling supervisor or if he/she is not available, an experienced counsellor.

B.3.4.2 Any disclosure of confidential information should be restricted to relevant information, conveyed only to appropriate people and for appropriate reasons likely to alleviate the exceptional circumstances. The ethical considerations include achieving a balance between acting in the best interests of the client and the counsellor's responsibilities to the wider community.

B.3.4.3 Counsellors hold different views about the grounds for breaking confidentiality, such as potential self-harm, suicide, and harm to others. Counsellors must consider their own views, as they will affect their practice and communicate them to clients and significant others, e.g supervisor, agency.

B.3.5 Management of Confidentiality
B.3.5.1 Counsellors should ensure that records of the client's identity are kept separately from any case notes.

B.3.5.2 Arrangements must be made for the safe disposal of client records, especially in the event of the counsellor's incapacity or death.

B.3.5.3 Care must be taken to ensure that personally identifiable information is not transmitted through overlapping networks of confidential relationships.

B.3.5.4 When case material is used for case studies, reports or publications the client's informed consent must be obtained wherever possible and their identity must be effectively disguised.

B.3.5.5 Any discussion about their counselling work between the counsellor and others should be purposeful and not trivialising.

B.3.5.6 Counsellors must pay particular attention to protecting the identity of clients. This includes discussion of cases in counselling supervision.

B4 Contracts
B.4.1 Advertising & Public Statements
B.4.1.1 Membership of BAC is not a qualification and it must not be used as if it were. In press advertisements and telephone directories, on business cards, letterheads, brass plates and plaques, etc. counsellors should limit the information to name, relevant qualifications, address, telephone number, hours available, a list of the services offered and fees charged. They should not mention membership of BAC.

B.4.1.2 In oral statements, letters and pre-counselling leaflets to the public and potential clients, BAC membership may not be mentioned without a statement that it means that the individual, and where appropriate the organisation, abides by the Codes of Ethics and Practice and is subject to the Complaints Procedure of the British Association for Counselling. Copies of these Codes and the Complaints Procedure are available from BAC.

B.4.1.3 Counsellors who are accredited and/or registered are encouraged to mention this.

B.4.1.4 All advertising and public statements should be accurate in every particular.

B.4.1.5 Counsellors should not display an affiliation with an organisation in a manner which falsely implies sponsorship or validation by that organisation

B.4.2   Pre-counselling information

B.4.2.1 Any publicity material and all written and oral information should reflect accurately the nature of the service on offer, and the relevant counselling training, qualifications and experience of the counsellor.

B.4.2.2. Counsellors should take all reasonable steps to honour undertakings made in their pre-counselling information

B.4.3   Contracting with Clients

B.4.3.1 Counsellors are responsible for reaching agreement with their clients about the terms on which counselling is being offered, including availability, the degree of confidentiality offered, arrangements for the payment of any fees, cancelled appointments and other significant matters. The communication of essential terms and any negotiations should be concluded by having reached a clear agreement before the client incurs any commitment or liability of any kind.

B.4.3.2 The counsellor has a responsibility to ensure that the client is given a free choice whether or not to participate in counselling. Reasonable steps should be taken in the course of the counselling relationship to ensure that the client is given an opportunity to review the counselling.

B.4.3.3 Counsellors must avoid conflicts of interest wherever possible. Any conflicts of interest that do occur must be discussed in counselling supervision and where appropriate with the client.

B.4.3.4 Records of appointments should be kept and clients should be made aware of this. If records of counselling sessions are kept, clients should also be made aware of this. At the client's request information should be given about access to these records, their availability to other people, and the degree of security with which they are kept.

B.4.3.5 Counsellors must be aware that computer-based records are subject to statutory regulations. It is the counsellor's responsibility to be aware of any changes the government may introduce in the regulations concerning the client's right of access to his/her records

B.4.3.6 Counsellors are responsible for addressing any client dissatisfaction with the counselling.

**B.5   Boundaries
With Clients**

B.5.1   Counsellors are responsible for setting and monitoring boundaries through-out the counselling sessions and will make explicit to clients that counselling is a formal and contracted relationship and nothing else.

B.5.2   The counselling relationship must not be concurrent with a supervisory or training relationship.

With Former Clients

B.5.3 Counsellors remain accountable for relationships with former clients and must exercise caution over entering into friendships, business relationships, sexual relationships, training, supervising and other relationships. Any changes in relationship must be discussed in counselling supervision. The decision about any change(s) in relationship with former clients should take into account whether the issues and power dynamics present during the counselling relationship have been resolved.

B.5.4 Counsellors who belong to organisations which prohibit sexual activity with all former clients are bound by that commitment.

B.6 Competence

B.6.1 Counsellor Competence

B.6.1.1 Counsellors must have achieved a level of competence before commencing counselling and must maintain continuing professional development as well as regular and ongoing supervision.

B.6.1.2 Counsellors must actively monitor their own competence through counselling supervision and be willing to consider any views expressed by their clients and by other counsellors.

B.6.1.3 Counsellors will monitor their functioning and will not counsel when their functioning is impaired by alcohol or drugs. In situations of personal or emotional difficulty, or illness, counsellors will monitor the point at which they are no longer competent to practise and take action accordingly.

B.6.1.4 Competence includes being able to recognise when it is appropriate to refer a client elsewhere.

B.6.1.5 Counsellors are responsible for ensuring that their relationships with clients are not unduly influenced by their own emotional needs.

B.6.1.6 Counsellors must consider the need for professional indemnity insurance and when appropriate take out and maintain adequate cover.

B.6.1.7 When uncertain as to whether a particular situation or course of action may be in violation of the Code of Ethics and Practice, counsellors must consult with their counselling supervisor and/or other experienced practitioners.

B.6.2 Counsellor Safety

B.6.2.1 Counsellors should take all reasonable steps to ensure their own physical safety.

B.6.3 Counselling Supervision

B.6.3.1 Counselling supervision refers to a formal arrangement which enables counsellors to discuss their counselling regularly with one or more people who are normally experienced as counselling practitioners and have an understanding of counselling supervision. Its purpose is to ensure the efficacy of the counsellor–client relationship. It is a confidential relationship.

B.6.3.2 The counselling supervisor role should wherever possible be independent of the line manager role. However, where the counselling supervisor is also the line manager, the counsellor must have additional regular access to independent counselling supervision.

B.6.3.3 Counselling supervision must be regular, consistent and appropriate to the counselling. The volume should reflect the volume of counselling work undertaken and the experience of the counsellor.

B.6.4 Awareness of Other Codes

Counsellors must take account of the following Codes and Procedures adopted by the Annual General Meetings of the British Association for Counselling:

Code of Ethics & Practice for Counselling Skills (1988) *applies to members who would not regard themselves as counsellors, but who use counselling skills to support other roles.*

Code of Ethics & Practice for Supervisors of Counsellors (1996) *applies to members offering supervision to counsellors and also helps counsellors seeking supervision.*

Code of Ethics & Practice for Trainers (1997) *applies to members offering training to counsellors and also helps members of the public seeking counselling training.*

Complaints Procedure (1997) *applies to members of BAC in the event of complaints about breaches of the Codes of Ethics & Practice.*

Copies and other guidelines and information sheets relevant to maintaining ethical standards of practice can be obtained from the BAC office, 1 Regent Place, Rugby CV21 2PJ.

EQUAL OPPORTUNITIES POLICY STATEMENT

The British Association for Counselling (BAC) is committed to promoting Equality of Opportunity of access and participation for all its members in all of its structures and their workings. BAC has due regard for those groups of people with identifiable characteristics which can lead to visible and invisible barriers thus inhibiting their joining and full participation in BAC. Barriers can include age, colour, creed, culture, disability, education, 'ethnicity', gender, information, knowledge, mobility, money, nationality, race, religion, sexual orientation, social class and status.

The work of BAC aims to reflect this commitment in all areas including services to members, employer responsibilities, the recruitment of and working with volunteers, setting, assessing, monitoring and evaluating standards and the implementation of the complaints procedures. This is particularly important as BAC is the 'Voice of Counselling' in the wider world.

BAC will promote and encourage commitment to Equality of Opportinity by its members.

© BAC 1997

BAC Codes are up-dated on a regular basis. Please check with BAC for most recent versions.

The Periglacial Environment

Third Edition

Hugh M. French
The University of Ottawa

John Wiley & Sons, Ltd

Other Wiley Editorial Offices

John Wiley & Sons Inc., 111 River Street, Hoboken, NJ 07030, USA

Jossey-Bass, 989 Market Street, San Francisco, CA 94103-1741, USA

Wiley-VCH Verlag GmbH, Boschstr. 12, D-69469 Weinheim, Germany

John Wiley & Sons Australia Ltd, 33 Park Road, Milton, Queensland 4064, Australia

John Wiley & Sons (Asia) Pte Ltd, 2 Clementi Loop #02-01, Jin Xing Distripark, Singapore 129809

John Wiley & Sons Canada Ltd, 6045 Freemont Blvd, Mississauga, Ontario, L5R 4J3, Cananda

Wiley also publishes its books in a variety of electronic formats. Some content that appears in print
may not be available in electronic books.

Library of Congress Cataloging-in-Publication Data

French, Hugh M.
  The periglacial environment / Hugh French. – 3rd ed.
    p. cm.
  Includes bibliographical references.
  ISBN-13: 978-0-470-86588-0
  ISBN-13: 978-0-470-86589-7
  1. Frozen ground. 2. Glacial landforms. 3. Cold regions. I. Title.
  GB641.F73 2007
  551.3'84–dc22
                                                    2006022730

Anniversary Logo Design: Richard J. Pacifico

British Library Cataloguing in Publication Data

A catalogue record for this book is available from the British Library

ISBN 978-0-470-86588-0 (HB)
ISBN 978-0-470-86589-7 (PB)

Typeset in 9.5/11.5 pt Times by SNP Best-set Typesetter Ltd., Hong Kong

This book is printed on acid-free paper responsibly manufactured from sustainable forestry in which at
least two trees are planted for each one used for paper production.

Contents